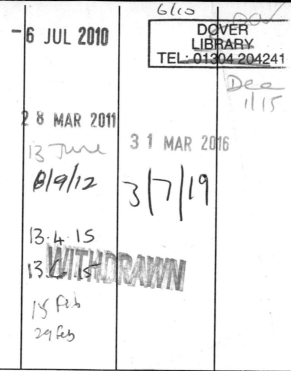

FootprintFrance

- 6 JUL 2010

6/10

Dec
1/15

2 8 MAR 2011

13 June

0/9/12

3 1 MAR 2016

3/7/19

13·4·15

13...WITHDRAWN

15 Feb

29 Feb

Please return on or before the latest date above.
You can renew online at www.kent.gov.uk/libs
or by phone 08458 247 200

CHARTER MARK

CUSTOMER SERVICE EXCELLENCE

Libraries & Archives

Kent
County
Council

Rutherford
Kathryn Tomasetti

Introducing
the region

About the region

The Riviera

Hyères to
St-Tropez

Haute-Provence

Marseille & the Calanques

Aix-en-Provence & the Lubéron

Arles, Avignon & Western Province

Practicalities

Tristan Rutherford's first travel writing assignment took him to Nice and he's been based there ever since. His favourite things to do in Provence are eating, drinking wine and pastis, snorkelling around Cap d'Ail and the Iles de Lérins, and walking along its coastal paths. He has visited over 60 countries and written about 20 of them for the likes of *The Independent*, the *Sunday Times Travel Magazine* and *Condé Nast Traveller*. Tristan also lectures in travel journalism at Central St Martin's and Kingston University in London.

Kathryn Tomasetti formed a teenage crush on the South of France during an Interail trip in the early 1990s. It wasn't until 2005 that she made a permanent move to Provence, by way of an anthropology degree at the University of Manchester and a career as a modern art curator across Europe and the Far East. Kathryn provides features and photographs for several travel and food magazines including *The Guardian* and *Time Out*. A self-confessed foodie, she rates her favourite restaurants as Pizzeria Chez Etienne in Marseille, L'Atelier de Jean-Luc Rabanel in Arles and La Merenda in Nice.

Acknowledgements

The authors would like to thank their families, in particular Nancy 'Lucky Charm' DiMauro, Elizabeth 'Stardust' Tomasetti, Susan and Paul Rutherford for the cosy week in Pin Dore, and Harvey Rutherford for the photographs. Thanks also to Cynthia, the flamboyant seed, who drew the world to the South of France.

Thanks also go to Antonia Spanos and James Shanks for the Lubéron off-road vehicle and massage machine, and to Ornella Bortolato for her continued support. A shout out to Michael Furniss for the sub-aqua tour of the Côte d'Azur and to Matt and Gayle for the apartment. Hi to Inga, Alvin, Adrian, Mehmet and Constantine. Alan Murphy and the staff at Footprint were a vision of patience and trust.

A special mention also goes to William and Myles Howorth for their driving skills in Juan-les-Pins.

Sleeping price codes
€€€€ over €200 per night for a double room in high season.
€€€ €100-200
€€ €60-100
€ under €60

Eating & drinking price codes
€€€€ over €40 per person for a 2-course meal with a drink, including service and cover charge
€€€ €30-40
€€ €20-30
€ €20

About the book

The guide is divided into four sections: Introducing the region; About the region; Around the region and Practicalities.

Introducing the region comprises: **At a glance**, which explains how the region fits together by giving the reader a snapshot of what to look out for and what makes this region distinct from other parts of the country; **Best of Provence & Côte d'Azur** (top 20 highlights); **A year in Provence & Côte d'Azur**, which is a month-by-month guide to pros and cons of visiting at certain times of year; and **Screen & page**, which is a list of suggested books and films.

About the region comprises: **History**; **Art & architecture**; **Provence & Côte d'Azur today**, which present different aspects of life in the region today; **Nature & environment**, an overview of the landscape and wildlife); **Festivals & events**; **Sleeping**, an overview of accommodation options; **Eating & drinking**, an overview of the region's cuisine, as well as advice on eating out; **Entertainment**, an overview of the region's cultural credentials, explaining what entertainment is on offer); **Shopping**, what are the region's specialities and recommendations for the best buys; and **Activities & tours**.

Around the region is broken down into six areas, each with its own chapter. Here you'll find all the main sights and at the end of each chapter is a listings section with all the best sleeping, eating & drinking, entertainment, shopping and activities & tours options plus a brief overview of public transport.

Picture credits

Contents

Introducing the region

Racing on Juan-les-Pins' beach.

Introduction

Provence and the Côte d'Azur conjure up a volley of sun-kissed images. From lavender fields (the Lubéron), Picasso paintings (the Cap d'Antibes) and *French Connection* chase scenes (Marseille) to panoramas of *pétanque* players, hilltop villages and pavement cafés (all three just about anywhere in the region), this is France at its most beautiful.

And for every celebrated shot, there's another cover-shoot portrait waiting to be discovered. Try Provence's sub-tropical islands (Port-Cros and Ste-Marguerite), the Haute Provence mountain express (Train des Pignes) or the rollercoaster route D41 (Massif des Maures) and you'll see what we mean.

Waves of invaders have claimed a piece of the above for over two millennia, and who can blame them? They may have soaked up more than their share of Provence's sun and drunk vats of its wine, but in return they left one of the most vibrant cultural legacies in Europe. From the Rhône to the snow-capped Alps and the Italian border, there are more castles, museums, forts, amphitheatres and rococo mansions than most countries possess in their entirety. And with a public transport system that's second to none, a fair share of these can be seen in a single week. Visit once and you'll discover that a year in Provence is a very tempting proposal indeed.

At a glance

A whistle-stop tour of Provence & Côte d'Azur

Diversity is the watchword of Provence and the Côte d'Azur, a vast area of lakes, mountains, rivers and coast. Covering six distinct areas larger than many countries, it's lapped by the Mediterranean to the south and covered in year-round snow to the north. But delve deeper into each region and differences are even more disparate: in Marseille one can dine on a century-old *bouillabaisse* recipe or pop round the corner for a bowl of Vietnamese pho. Thanks to its all-encompassing history, Provence is littered with Roman ruins, papal strongholds, Saracen hilltowns, art galleries, untouched beaches and casinos of the belle époque. And best of all, you can flit between all of them in a single afternoon.

The Riviera

A region blessed with a sub-tropical microclimate, it's no surprise that Europe's most beautiful bit of coast has been so squabbled over. Saracen invasions pushed locals inland, dodgy politics hacked Nice away from France, and the Grimaldi family robbed Monaco for the Genoese (and have been robbing visitors ever since). The result is an architectural legacy of fairy-tale perched villages,

Italianate piazzas and chichi summer playgrounds, all of which are a joy to wander round. The 20th-century arrival of Picasso and pals, coupled with a vast array of writers, royals and *bons vivants*, has gifted the region more museums, art galleries and fine dining establishments than almost anywhere else in the world. But if the sights and smells get too much, it's easy to emulate St Honoratus: escape to the monastic silence of the Iles de Lérins, the Côte d'Azur's tropical islands. Or seek out any of the secret beaches, rooftop bars or botanical gardens listed in this chapter.

Belles Rives Plage at dawn, Juan-les-Pins.

The Lowdown

Money matters Provence is not expensive. A simple *café* or baguette costs around €1, while a good lunch with wine costs approximately €15 wherever you travel. Hotel prices vary greatly depending on the season, but every town in this book has great accommodation options ranging from €60 up to €300. Allow €50 per person per day for a bargain basement holiday, or double that amount for exciting excursions and delicious dinners. Visitors can save by renting an apartment to use as a base and making picnics from the region's many markets.

Opening hours and holidays Banks, shops and post offices close for two or more hours at lunch, even if there's a queue of potential customers outside. Restaurant hours are strict: try to arrive between 1200 and 1330 for lunch and after 1900 for dinner. In summer everything is open, with some tourist-orientated resorts along the coast shutting up from November to March. Many businesses in Provence take a month's annual holiday in November or January.

Discounts Over-60s and under-18s (and often adults under 25) receive discounts of up to 50% on public transport and museum entrance fees. Don't forget to ask or the reduction may be 'forgotten'. Children under 10 years old can often visit sights, plus travel, for free.

Tourist information Incredibly informative tourist offices lie in every town and village and are the best sources for local events, sights and rural accommodation options. Visit the local office websites listed in each chapter. Also, try voyages-sncf.com for trains, viamichelin. co.uk for restaurants and france.angloinfo.com for local news and events.

Chalkboard menus in Vence.

Collection Lambert, Avignon.

Hyères to St-Tropez

This unhurried region is 80% coast, 20% countryside. The former is a delight, covered with deserted beaches and cute, little-known resorts, such as Giens, Rayol-Canadel and Bormes-les-Mimosas. Conversely, St-Tropez is the one place that everyone *has* heard of. Although few would credit it, Europe's capital of fun is simply an overgrown fishing village with a great modern art museum and nightly urban street performances where everyone's invited. On its vine-covered peninsula are some of the most chilled hilltop towns and beaches in Provence, plus more than 50 km of coastal walks. Inland things get rugged, and quickly. The Massif des Maures is one vast forest filled with lonely monasteries and villages that time forgot, with two hair-raising roads corkscrewing through.

Plage Gigaro, St-Tropez peninsula.

Haute Provence

Wild and under-populated, you're more likely to see an eagle or a stag than a human being in many parts of Haute Provence. The prehistoric rock carvings in the Vallée des Merveilles attest to the region's status as the cradle of Provençal civilisation. But mountain ranges have carved the region into distinct valleys each with its own diverse culture, from the Italianate flavour of the Roya River to the ridge of medieval settlements that stretch from Aups to Bargemon. Sprinkled throughout are waterfalls, forests and lakes that serve the kayaking, hiking and rafting excursions detailed later in this guide. Top these outdoor activities with the ultimate theatrical backdrop by hitting the Gorges du Verdon, Europe's very own Grand Canyon.

Marseille & the Calanques

A hip urban and appealing rural mix creates this most unique area of Provence. Bookending the region are Marseille and Toulon, two working centres, a blend of ethnic diversity and counter culture. The former is gearing up to become Europe's Capital of Culture in 2013 and has one of France's best music, theatre and 21st-century art scenes. The first part of Provence to be colonised by Greek traders in around 600 BC, Marseille has since welcomed Romans, Jews, Spaniards, North Africans, South Americans and Vietnamese. Between Marseille and Toulon is a region so attractively dated that painter Paul Signac or author Virginia Woolf would probably still recognise it if passing through today. Of the scores of villages in the area, perhaps Cassis and Bandol are the most lovely: wines from these two resorts are the shining stars of the coastal wine industry.

Aix-en-Provence & the Lubéron

The Romans discovered a thermal source in Aix and quickly laid a beautiful settlement on top of it. Locals have been taking care of themselves, and their city, ever since. A former capital of Provence, it's still a staunchly middle-class location, with wide tree-lined boulevards and fountain-filled squares,

a far cry from its louche coastal cousins: Marseille, Toulon and Nice. The artist Paul Cézanne was born to a merchant family here in 1839. He's now synonymous with the town, taking inspiration from nearby Mont Ste-Victoire which features in dozens of his landscapes. The clean, green Lubéron countryside surrounds this regional capital, its only harsh edge the yearly *mistral* gales. It would take a year in Provence to fully explore the myriad villages around Gordes and Roussillon. For visitors with just a few days, head to the lavender fields that have made the area famous, starting with those around Abbaye Notre-Dame de Sénanque, where monks still press the purple blossom into oil, soap and liqueurs.

Avignon, Arles & Western Provence

In this region of great contrasts, Avignon stands out as the largest and most orderly city. It owes these attributes to the popes, who relocated here from Rome in 1309, bringing the papacy and all its wealth to Provence. The popes lived in style, as showcased in the must-see Palais des Papes; they also laid out summer châteaux and encouraged vineyards at Châteauneuf-du-Pape. Running southwards, the Rhône forms the western border of Provence, passing through Arles, a gorgeous gastronomic capital that owes its allegiance to a much older Rome. Its amphitheatres and 2000-year-old baths are as renowned as the city's most famous resident, Vincent Van Gogh. From Arles, the Rhône splits and disperses into the Camargue, a salt marsh cowboy country filled with horses, bulls, and flocks of pink flamingos.

Best of Provence & Côte d'Azur

Top 20 things to see & do

❶ Juan-les-Pins Jazz Festival

Jazz à Juan is an awesome event and one of the best music festivals in France. The open-air stage – backed by palm trees and the moonlit Mediterranean – has welcomed some of history's all-time finest jazz musicians, from Dizzy Gillespie to BB King. The star-studded 2009 programme hosted Joss Stone, Jamie Callum, Jeff Beck and MC Solaar. Page 48.

❷ The Camargue

This 1000 sq km triangle of shallow lakes, salt marshes and reed beds supports an exotic array of indigenous wildlife, including the white Camargue horse and pink flamingos. Try riding, kayaking or mountain biking through the vast National Park. Page 260.

❸ Provence's coastal path

A *maquis*-scented coastal path runs almost continuously from the Camargue to the Italian border. Known locally as the *sentier des douaniers* (or custom officers' trail), it passes deserted beaches, fishing villages, dive sites and picnic spots, as well as some of Europe's most over-the-top villas. Best of all, it's completely free. Page 106.

2 Flamingos at the Camargue's Parc Ornithologique de Pont de Gau.

3 Trail between St-Paul and Vence.

4 Driving the Monaco Formula One circuit.

5 Lac de Ste Croix.

❹ Driving the Monaco Formula One circuit
Trace the Grand Prix circuit on YouTube or grab a map from the tourist office. By car, scooter or on foot the route takes in statues of F1's greats and legions of million-Euro cars. Can you beat Felipe Massa's 75-second fastest lap? Page 125.

❺ Gorges du Verdon & Lac de Ste-Croix
Little will prepare you for the vertiginous embrace of the Gorges du Verdon. Europe's largest canyon, it's now a haven for hikers, rock-climbers and bungee-jumpers, who dive 180 m off the Pont d'Artuby, one of the highest falls in the world. The Verdon seeps into Lac de Ste-Croix, a serene emerald green lake, perfect for kayaking, trekking around and birdwatching. Page 162.

❻ Dining in Marseille
Home to the world-famous *bouillabaisse* fish stew, Marseille's ethnic mix lets you eat your way around the world any evening: try Japanese, Moroccan, Italian, Vietnamese or Portuguese. Page 204.

❼ St-Tropez's Musée l'Annonciade
A perfect palette of Provence's modern art scene. The changing nature of European painting from realistic representation to colour-filled excess is caught on canvas by the likes of Matisse, Marquet and Signac. Their paintings of lavender fields, fishing villages and passing sailboats document dreamy scenes from across the region. Page 132.

❽ Nice's Musée Masséna
This neoclassical seaside mansion is the perfect setting for a local history lesson. The Musée Masséna highlights the artists, heiresses and celebrities that made the Riviera great, by way of paintings, period jewellery and photos from the belle époque. Barring Paris, Nice has more museums than any of other city in France. Most of them, like this one, are completely free. Page 78.

❾ Provence's trains
Clean, efficient and comprehensive, Provence's rail system is world-class. Three lines in particular – the Train des Pignes, the Roya Valley and the Cannes-Italy coastal train – are achingly beautiful. And that's before you've even stepped off the train. Pages 165, 167 and 125.

❿ Ski slopes
Daily ski buses hit Auron, Isola 2000 and Valberg each winter morning. The price? From Nice, just €1 each way. Resorts boast hundreds of kilometres of runs, with an emphasis on beginners and snowboarders. Book a moderate ski-in ski-out hotel for a night, or bus it back to the coast for dinner. Page 168.

Introducing the region

⑪ The Promenade des Anglais

Take a seafront stroll next to Nice's 4-km-long public beach. The *plage* is bursting with bathers, volleyball players, bodybuilders and yoga gurus, while the esplanade hums with bikers and rollerbladers. All too much? Hit one of the beach clubs for a sunset cocktail instead. Page 75.

⑫ Rosé

Once dismissed as a rough locals-only drink, Provence's famed tipple is back in vogue. Removing the tannin-rich skins during the winemaking process leaves a soft blush-coloured wine, a perfect accompaniment to the area's cuisine. Visitors are welcome at most of the beautiful vineyards that line the way. Page 199.

⑬ Provence's coastal islands

A sprinkling of verdant islands bobs off the Provence shoreline. One is home to a monastery and boasts some of the best snorkelling on the

coast, while another hosts a colony of nudists, seabirds and rare exotic fauna. All are laced with waymarked nature trails and offer tranquil respite, away from the crowds on the coast. Page 94.

⑭ Cassis & the Calanques

Cassis, a pastel-blue fishing village little changed from the 1950s, sits among the Calanques, a series of spectacular limestone cliffs and clear turquoise bays. Try seaside dining, rock-climbing, cliff-diving and touring the local vineyards on foot. Provence at its most picturesque. Page 192.

⑮ Arles market

The capital of the Camargue hosts the region's finest food market every Wednesday and Saturday morning. Stalls selling bull salami, French cheese and the famed local olive oil flank the colourful Old Town. Then step through the city walls to discover Arles's Roman amphitheatre and a volley of amazing restaurants. Page 259.

11 Nice's Promenade des Anglais and city beach.

⑯ Château des Baux
Balanced on a rocky tip above a medieval village, Château des Baux was a fortified medieval hill town, commanding the countryside and vineyards all the way down to the sea. Expect jaw-dropping panoramas, cliff-edge walks and a collection of larger-than-life siege weaponry. Page 253.

⑰ Palais des Papes
For half a century Avignon was the capital of the Holy Roman Empire. Its legacy is a massive Gothic edifice, now a UNESCO World Heritage site, which dominates the medieval walled city. Floor-to-ceiling frescoes, preserved under 500 years of paint and now on display, give an inkling of the pampered papal lifestyle. Page 243.

17 The Palais des Papes, Avignon.

20 Lavender field, Plateua de Valensole.

⑱ The coast between Hyères & St-Tropez
Some of the best beaches in France lie along this stretch of coast. Several are little-visited coves or nudist spots, others are family-friendly stretches packed with activities or sandy patches where you can catch *le jet-set* at play. Tiny Le Lavandou boasts 12 beaches alone. Page 144.

⑲ Cézanne's Aix-en-Provence
Step into a Cézanne painting and see where the father of modern art lived and worked. Visit the Jas de Bouffan, where he decorated the walls of the family mansion with a dozen masterpieces, or his final atelier. Then carry on to Mont Ste-Victoire, the landscape that inspired countless Cézanne creations. Page 222.

⑳ Lavender
The purple lavender-cloaked hills are one of Provence's most enduring symbols. Enthusiasts can hit the Musée de la Lavande, a shrine to the fragrant purple blossom. Or drive deep into the Lubéron to Abbaye Notre-Dame de Sénanque, a 12th-century Cistercian abbey where visitors can buy the monks' home-made lavender oil, soap and honey. Page 226.

Month by month

A year in Provence & Côte d'Azur

January & February

After New Year's Eve's celebrations comes the hangover. Much of Provence settles down in early January, paying a penance for seasonal excesses with Epiphany (6 January) services in churches all over the region. Transport links over a sombre sleepy countryside remain sketchy. But it's hard to keep a Provençal local quiet: the *carnaval* season begins in earnest with two weeks of street parties in Nice and a lemon festival in Menton. In Marseille, locals flood to the St-Victor Abbey on 2 February, where the statue of the Black Virgin is taken out of its crypt and blessed. Shoppers hit the city sales – the dates of which are strictly regulated by each *département* – and skiers hit the slopes. Combined with an utter dearth of tourists, all this action leaves Provence's amazing museums almost empty.

Whether walking in the hauntingly beautiful countryside, or hiking on the sunny coast, it's necessary to bring a heavy jacket. Leave the umbrella at home: it's rarely damp and the icy *mistral* wind that drives up through Marseille, Aix and the Lubéron will turn it inside out anyway.

March & April

With warmth in the sun and an extra hour of daylight, the region is poised to spring back into life. Hardy swimmers return to the sea and tourists brave al fresco dinners, willing on the arrival of summer. Skiers use the snow until mid-April, when it melts and gushes down the Roya, Vésubie, Rhône and a score of other valleys to the sea. Street markets see the arrival of the first asparagus and sweet broad beans around Easter, which signals the return of the season.

Early visitors take advantage of the deserted coast for long walks and trips to the islands. Head into the hills for country jaunts and hearty rural cooking, but bring a scarf. Avignon and Marseille celebrate the season with processions through the streets. As the airline schedules return to capacity and rural hotels reopen, it's an inexpensive time to visit. Although it can rain heavily, the first sunny weekend of spring signals a sixth-sense reflex in café owners across Provence: their tables and chairs spill on to the pavements and are left outside until October.

May & June

The region comes into its full, festive stride. Along the coast in early May, locals wake up to one extraordinarily hot and sunny day. It will suddenly jump to 25°C, rather than hovering around winter's 15°C, and five months of summer will be here to stay. Inland, the earth is carpeted with wild flowers, already basking in the long daylight hours. This is the best time for hiking, biking, kayaking and camping from the Gorges du Verdon to the Camargue. Visitors can tour any of Provence's still quiet towns on foot with a cheap bag of strawberries, or laze by the sea in front of a freshly opened beach bar. And getting around is a cinch: buses, trains and boats are geared up for the season. The only thing still missing is the crowds.

Culturally, the region is at its wildest. Europe's gypsies converge on Stes-Maries-de-la-Mer to

Top: Jujube dates and Herbes de Provence, Vieux Port, Marseille.
Above: The stunning Gorges du Verdon.
Opposite page: The Citrus Parade, Menton.

Introducing the region

Harbour on Étang de Berre, Martigues.

parade the statue of Black Sara, their patron saint, down to the sea. Wine festivals cover Châteauneuf-du-Pape, photography festivals Hyères and flower festivals Grasse. The region's two biggies, the Cannes Film Festival and Monaco Grand Prix, coincide for a week of glitzy debauchery in late May. The season culminates in the pan-French Fête de la Musique on 21 June, the longest day of the year. Started by the government in 1982, this all-night free music festival takes place in almost every town, street corners throbbing with jazz, ska, classical, hip hop, techno, metal and soul.

July & August

A heap of amazing attractions draw visitors from around the world during high summer. Every day is hot and sunny. Bring shorts, a hat, sunscreen and water bottle, and plan the day efficiently. Provence's beaches are blessed with sea breezes

and azure waters, both offering a flop-down follow-on from a day spent museum-hopping, market shopping or driving. Some sandy stretches throng with picnic blankets, volleyball tournaments and lifeguards; others offer Robinson Crusoe-style desolation, if you know where to look. The season is celebrated with firework displays along the entire coast.

In terms of cultural events, summer is the time to visit, particularly in the west. There's opera in Seillans, Lacoste and Orange, street theatre in Avignon and Arles, and floating festivals in Martigues and L'Isle-sur-la-Sorgue. Back east are hopping jazz festivals in Nice and Juan-les-Pins. With so much going on, an advance hotel reservation is a necessity. If inland, try and pick a place that has a pool, as many do. Believe us, it's a huge bonus.

Roads become very busy in summer, but fear not. Provence's world-class public transport system comes into its own, with boats departing from Le

Lavandou, St-Tropez, Cannes, Menton and most places in between, plus trains running in air-conditioned serenity throughout the region. Unlike the rest of the region, much of Marseille empties on to the surrounding coast or over to North Africa, as the city's ethnically diverse population summers in the old country. It's the one city you can have to yourself in summer.

September & October

The crowds suddenly depart in the first week of September. For many, this is a golden time of balmy sun and warm seas combined with spare seats in restaurants and discounted hotel rooms. St-Tropez tries to keep *la saison* going a little longer with the prestigious Voile d'Or sailing regatta. Otherwise larger festivals pack up until Christmas, leaving celebrations more localised, with neighbourhood party nights for Halloween and countryside *vendanges*, where the back-breaking work of harvesting and pressing the grapes precedes much drinking and eating. As the beautiful countryside slowly turns red in October, the markets are ever colourful, with chestnuts,

apples and pumpkin the flavours of the month. Public transport, especially to tourist hotspots like Les Baux and Cassis, tails off well before the autumn rains arrive in mid-October.

November & December

Many seasonal businesses take their annual holiday and Europe is in full work mode: November is the best time of year if you're hankering after a quiet getaway. A touch of rain induces truffle and mushroom growth, making these months also a unique feasting time for foodies. The third Thursday of November marks the annual release of the latest Beaujolais Nouveau; wine shops offer free tastings and supermarkets discount deals. Working cities like Toulon and Marseille are at their most vibrant. The crisp sun of December brings a new excitement. It's still warm enough to sip morning *café* and eat lunch outside, as Christmas markets set up in many town and city squares. Hotels reopen for the festive period, and restaurants and bars become raucous. Renting a countryside *mas* or an apartment in Arles has never been so inviting.

Autumn mushrooms, Port Cros, Iles de Hyeres.

An abandoned windmill at the Château Les Baux.

Screen & page

Provence & Côte d'Azur in film & literature

J ust as the region pulled painters, sculptors and many other artists, Provence has long attracted writers with its weather, wine and liberal mores. The backdrop of mountains, sea and forests has been impressed on countless novels, while the region's glamour, sunshine and criminal elements form the setting for more recent works, many by local writers; even more await to be translated from French into English.

With several thousand years of history and possibly the world's best cuisine, there is no shortage of non-fiction titles to whet an appetite. In most cases listed here, each author has written several more historical, autobiographical or culinary tomes about the region. All of the following are widely available in UK bookshops, on Amazon or in the local bookshops listed in the shopping sections of each chapter.

Books

Fiction
The Count of Monte Cristo
Alexandre Dumas, 1844
Adventure around Provence and Marseille's Château d'If during Napoleon's downfall.

Tender is the Night
F Scott Fitzgerald, 1934
Wealth, lust and dust-ups on the Cap d'Antibes. Based on the real-life romance of socialites Gerald and Sara Murphy.

The Man Who Planted Trees
Jean Giono, 1953
Heart-warming tale of a shepherd who single-handedly re-forests the wild oak woods of Provence.

Traditional wooden fishing boat, Cap d'Antibes.

Jean de Florette
Marcel Pagnol, 1963
Fear and loathing on the farm. From Pagnol's series of superb novels, which include *Manon des Sources*.

Super-Cannes
J G Ballard, 2000
Ballard's sex, drugs and sand thriller. The backdrop is a thinly disguised Sophia Antipolis, the technology park behind Antibes.

Total Chaos
Jean-Claude Izzo, 2005
Part of excellent immigrant cop trilogy on Marseille's mean streets.

Jacquot and the Waterman
Martin O'Brien, 2005
Cavaillon's Chief Inspector Daniel Jacquot chases crime all over Provence. Fun beach-reading series.

Non-fiction
Travels through France and Italy
Tobias Smollett, 1766
Endearing account of very miserable Scottish author's sojourn in Provence.

J'accuse: the darker side of Nice
Graham Greene, 1982
Riviera resident Greene dishes the dirt on the corrupt Jacques Médecin years.

A Year in Provence
Peter Mayle, 1989
Hilarious must-read account of life near Ménerbes. Spawned a trilogy, and the southward exodus of half a million Brits.

Inventing the French Riviera
Mary Blume, 1992
Lucid summation of the arrival of foreigners on the Côte d'Azur. Brilliant.

At Home in Provence / The Provence Cookbook
Patricia Wells, 1996/2004
Acclaimed American cookbook author absorbs the flavours of Provence. Wonderful.

The Olive Farm
Carol Drinkwater, 2001
Ex-TV vet gets romantically involved with a Frenchman and a farmhouse in Provence. A lovely tour of the entire region.

High Season in Nice
Robert Kanigel, 2001
Riveting and amusing account of how the tourism capital of the Riviera came of age.

Chasing Matisse
James Morgan, 2005
American author obsessively chases Matisse's memory around Vence, St-Tropez and into the hills.

Secret Provence / Secret French Riviera
Jean-Pierre Cassely, 2006/2007
Non-guidebook guide to fascinating offbeat spots in Provence and the Côte d'Azur.

Plages Vues du Ciel
Giletta/Nice-Matin, 2007
Amazing photos of every beach in Provence from the air, available from most local newsagents. A favourite.

Pig in Provence
Georgeanne Brennan, 2007
Gourmet adventures and local colour in deepest Provence.

Provence A-Z: A Francophile's Essential Handbook
Peter Mayle, 2008
A subtle lifting of the lid on Provençal culture.

Films

The corkscrewing roads, wild mountains and fleshpot coastal towns of Provence are one long movie set. The sight of film crews shooting village scenes, car chases and actors coming out of knackered buildings is a common one. These dozen classics are widely available and sum up the region's loaded atmosphere with aplomb.

La Femme du Boulanger
Marcel Pagnol, 1938
Enchanting Provençal tale of village baker, Aimable, who marries a beautiful young bride, Aurélie. The latter makes off with a shepherd leaving the former heartbroken, and the village without any bread. Love and hilarity ensue.

To Catch a Thief
Alfred Hitchcock, 1955
Ex-cat burglar Cary Grant retires to the Riviera. While trying to keep his nose clean, another thief is lapping up the jewels of several prominent figures, forcing an innocent Grant into the fragrant arms of Grace Kelly, who aids and abets escape. Will they unmask the real thief and fall in love? You bet.

Et Dieu... créa la femme
Roger Vadim, 1957
Very saucy love story on the streets and beaches of St-Tropez. Spawned the Brigitte Bardot legend that continues half a century later.

French Connection
John Frankenheimer, 1975
Gene Hackman takes on the locals in a rainy, crime-ridden Marseille. Ace.

Jean de Florette / Manon des Sources
Claude Berri, 1986
Two awesome films set in pre-war Provence. Shot back to back in the Vaucluse, at the time they were the most expensive French films ever made. Gérard

Depardieu stars as Jean in the story about rural inheritance, while Manon's cast tell a tale of love, rabbits and jealousy.

Dirty Rotten Scoundrels
Frank Oz, 1988
Steve Martin and Michael Caine as con men, against the villa backdrop of Beaumont-sur-Mer, a cross between Beaulieu and Villefranche. Silly fun.

French Kiss
Lawrence Kasdan, 1995
Rom-com featuring prissy American (Meg Ryan) who becomes entwined with dodgy French jewel thief (Kevin Kline). The landscapes of Kline's 'home' in Provence, and early 1990s Cannes, are a delight.

Ronin
John Frankenheimer, 1998
Underrated classic in which Robert De Niro and Jean Reno chase an IRA gang around Nice, Eze, Villefranche and Arles. Thrilling.

Taxi
Gérard Pirès, 1998
Marseille road movie written by Luc Besson. Young pizza guy Daniel upgrades from a scooter to a taxi, but must help a police inspector – who naturally can't drive – to catch some robbers. Brilliant.

The Good Thief
Neil Jordan, 2002
Nick Nolte joins the Riviera's Russian, Arabian and local mafia, and breaks the bank at Monaco.

A Good Year
Ridley Scott, 2006
Fun Year in Provence-style romantic romp in which a British banker inherits a vineyard in the Lubéron. Smell the love story amid the beautifully shot backdrop a mile away.

Spot the scenery

The Riviera stars in several Bond movies, including *Goldeneye* (where Pierce Brosnan helicopters out of Monaco port), *Diamonds are Forever* (Cap d'Antibes) and *Never Say Never Again* (Monaco casino and Cap Martin). In *Dirty Rotten Scoundrels*, the Cosmo Bar in Villefranche and several of the Riviera's finest villas lend a sun-kissed backdrop to the movie.

It's generally easier to get up close to the locations that feature in less expensive sets. The café used by Russell Crowe in *A Good Year* is the Renaissance in Gordes. In *Ronin*, the hectic car chase through the Old Town of Nice (the production company had to buy new chairs and tables for several restaurants in place Rossetti) is followed by meetings in Hôtel Le Méridien on the promenade and outside La Mère Germaine restaurant in Villefranche. Les Distilleries bar in Nice Old Town, and Plage Larvotto in Monaco, are the backdrops for *A Good Thief*.

Further west in deepest Provence, the entire villages of Castellet, Mirabeau and Vaugines became movie sets for *La Femme du Boulanger*, *Manon des Sources* and *Jean de Florette* respectively. In *French Kiss*, Ryan and Kline dine, make out and fall out in Cannes' Hotel Carlton, before making up in the port of Juan-les-Pins. JLP also stands in for Long Island In the 1974 remake of *The Great Gatsby* starring Robert Redford, scenes of which were made inside the now defunct Le Provençal hotel (see page 93).

The Carlton Hotel was seen in the movie *French Kiss*.

Contents

About the region

Fort Royale, Ile Ste-Marguerite.

History

Above: A section of the amphitheatre at Arles.
Opposite page: The Theatre Antique, Orange.

Pre-Christian Provence

Given the Eden-like climatic conditions that prevailed over the area, it's no surprise that the first signs of life started early. The region's fertile valleys were watered by annual snowmelt, warmed by up to 300 days of sun a year and remained relatively sheltered from natural disasters: no Krakatoa or Pompeii-style explosions here. The first human traces were found in the Calanques: cave paintings of hands, bison and horses, which date from up to 27,000 years ago (see page 192). More settled communities sprang up around 4000 BC, both in the Gorges du Verdon and in the Vallée des Merveilles, where rock art depicts both man and beast.

Marseille's almost perfect harbour came to the attention of Greek traders in around 600 BC; they had stopped here to found the trading post of Massalia. More commercially savvy than their local counterparts, they shipped in vines, nuts and olive trees, all of which would come to thrive in the region. Trade with a nascent Rome grew, especially in wine, encouraging Marseille to ally itself with the expanding might of its partner to the south. Other natural harbours to the east were colonized with Roman commerce in mind, not least Antibes and Nice, founded as 'Nikaia' to commemorate Greek victory over neighbouring Ligurian tribes. In the west, the home port of Marseille backed a winner,

supporting Rome's battles with the Carthaginians of Spain, which concluded with the Third Punic war in 146 BC.

Post-victory, the Romans needed a secure route to their new Iberian empire. The Via Domitia was constructed in 118 BC and ran through Gap, Apt, Cavaillon and St-Rémy-de-Provence towards Spain, with feeding and rest stations a day's journey apart. The Germanic tribes of the Teutones and Ambrones were finally mopped up in 102 BC at the Battle of Aquae Sextiae, where the Romans stayed put and founded Aix-en-Provence. It became a constituent part of the Roman Empire, known as Provincia, with surrounding city-states paying tribute or collaborating with the settlers.

But wealthy Marseille blew the peace, favouring Pompey's claim to the Roman Empire over that of Julius Caesar. No prizes for guessing what happened next. Besieged and humiliated, Marseille's assets were given to various Roman colonies including Arles, which was linked directly to Rome with the Via Aurelia. The Via Agrippa, constructed in the decades before Christ, connected Arles to Orange and Avignon.

Under the protection of Pax Romana, Provence was left to build the amphitheatres and baths that scatter the region today.

Provence divided & rebuilt

Christianity arrived in Provence around the fourth century AD. St Honoratus disembarked on the Iles de Lérins to create his monastery in AD 410, while the Abbey of St Victor in Marseille was founded five years later. But when Rome and its Christian state religion fell in the late fifth century, an alien crowd of Goths, Visigoths, Burgundians and Franks poured into Provence. As in much of Europe, both the authority and aqueducts of the Roman Empire collapsed, and famine and pestilence were widespread. Muslim Saracens controlled the sea.

As the ports of coastal Provence fell into decline, the region looked inland for its wealth. The Carolingian dynasty brought in a period of continuity and peace, not least under the wonderfully named Pepin the Short, who drove the Saracens out of Gaul. Agriculture developed further

Top: **Abbaye Notre-Dame de Senanque, Lubéron.**
Above: **Cloitre Saint-Trophime, Arles.**

under his son, Charlemagne, who reunited the Western Roman Empire. But squabbles broke out over his inheritance and the empire disintegrated a generation later, leaving the interior open to Norman invasion and the coast to renewed Saracen attack, the latter occupying Ramatuelle, St-Tropez and other strategic towns in the Massif des Maures.

After a century of pillaging, locals tired of their Muslim guests and united under Count William of Arles (see box, page 33). Following a series of skirmishes, the local forces finally beat the Saracens at the Battle of Tourtour near La Garde-Freinet in AD 973, setting in stone the victor's reign as William 1st of Provence.

William's death heralded dynastic disagreements, which once again plagued the region. Provence was subsumed into the Holy Roman Empire in 1032, with the westernmost part governed by the Catalans. But this loose Christian overlordship brought more harmony to the area than was usual, and a great programme of building was embarked upon: Aix Cathedral and the St-Trophime church in Arles date from this time, as do the Sénanque abbey near Gordes, Le Thoronet abbey near Draguignan and Chartreuse de la Verne near Collobrières. The Provençal language spread, carried throughout the region by travelling Troubadour poets. The daughter of the last Count of Provence Raymond Bérenger IV (see box, page 33) tied the knot with Charles d'Anjou, brother of the French king Louis IX, ushering in 250 years of Angevin rule.

Meanwhile, as the maritime trading powers of Pisa and Genoa grew, so did their influence along the Provence coast. Monaco was seized on behalf of Genoa in 1297 by Francesco Grimaldi, also known as *Il Malizia* ('the Cunning'), who disguised himself as a Franciscan monk and opened the gates to his supporters. The Grimaldi family staged a management buyout of the rock in 1308 and have ruled there ever since. The relocation of the Papacy to Avignon for a 60-year sojourn in 1309 brought further cultural and trade links. In 1388, the Commune of Nice placed itself under the protection of the House of Savoy.

French takeover

Having lost the Kingdom of Naples in 1441, Angevin control of Provence was on its last legs when its ruler, 'Good King' René of Anjou, died in Aix in 1480. Governorship passed to his nephew, Charles, who died childless the following year. The inheritance then passed to Charles' cousin, Louis XI of France, whose nickname 'the Universal Spider' more than gently hints at his scheming, manipulative ways.

Louis took a sledgehammer to the subtle knot of local government. Toulon was razed and Provençal governors were forcibly replaced with French ones. The 'Act of Union' with France in 1486 was little more than a hostile incorporation of the southern province. The Ordinance of Villers-Cotterêts in 1539 decreed that all baptisms, deaths and marriages must be notarised, and that all must be done so in French, sealing the fate of Latin, Provençal and many other minority tongues. The country became even more united in the face of a common enemy during the 16th century wars with Italy, which led to the fortification of Marseille and Toulon.

But once again, Provence's enemy came from within. The spread of Calvinism throughout the region in the 1550s, most notably in Orange and the Lubéron, put these 'Huguenots' on a collision course with the staunchly Catholic former Papal lands around Avignon. The Wars of Religion slowed with Henry IV's Edict of Nantes in 1598, which guaranteed freedom of worship for both Protestants and Catholics, but not before decades of terrible atrocities from both sides. The rule of Louis XIII, aided by the crafty Cardinal Richelieu from 1624, ushered in a more peaceful balance together with a fortification programme along the Provence coast. Louis's childless wife of 23 years, Anne of Austria, visited Contignac in 1638 to pray for a son. Sadly, the new arrival may not have been what she wished for. That September, the over-confident fop Louis XIV, aka The Sun King, was unleashed on to the world.

In 72 years of eccentric reign, Louis cared little for Provence. Nevertheless, he still managed to send it into turmoil by repealing the Edict of Nantes, turning Marseille's guns on itself and converting the Chateau d'If into an Alcatraz-style prison for reactionaries. The Black Death paid a visit to Marseille in 1720, killing up to 100,000 people in the area. Back in Versailles, Louis XV fared little better than his great-grandfather. One feels sorry for poor Louis XVI, who was landed with the inheritance of a poverty-ridden powder keg in 1775; he ended up marrying Marie Antoinette then losing his head in 1793.

As revolution swept France, the dockyards of Marseille were up in arms and religious buildings all over the region were requisitioned. Churches in La Garde-Freinet even took to hiding their bells lest they be trashed by revolutionaries. Toulon was occupied by a pro-Royalist British fleet in 1793, and only the dogged determination of a young artillery officer, Napoleon Bonaparte, saw them on their way. An older, but no less confident, Napoleon returned from his exile on Elba to the beaches of Golfe-Juan in 1815 to begin his march to Paris via Grasse, Entrevaux and Digne. The restoration of the Bourbons after French disaster at Waterloo (personified by the originally-named Louis XVIII) did little to soothe the anti-royalist passions of the south.

With revolutions and coups in 1848 and 1851, it wasn't until the mid-1800s that Provence finally calmed down. As trade with France's new colonies in Algeria and the Far East expanded, so again did the southern ports and their hinterland. A rail link to Marseille and the upgrading of its harbour for steamships saw the city boom. French ruler Napoleon III helped the reunifying Italians defeat France's traditional enemy, the Austrians, during the Austro-Sardinian wars in 1859. The Duchy of Nice was added to Provence in the bargain. The entire region was finally safe enough for consumptive Brits and ladies of leisure to sojourn in the South of France. The Train Bleu to Nice arrived in 1864, and to Monaco in 1867. From Lord Brougham (see box, page 33) to Queen Victoria, wealthy wintering aristocrats brought a touch of class to the Côte d'Azur.

About the region

A thousand minor nobles imitated the major royals. Spending the winter in Hyères or Cimiez became the thing to do. Fabulous hotels sprang up along the eastern half of Provence's coast: the Carlton was constructed in Cannes in 1912, the Negresco in Nice in 1913. Local English-language newspapers printed details of which Russian count or American industrialist was currently in town. Further west, there was an artistic exodus to St-Tropez, Cassis and L'Estaque by the likes of Cézanne, Signac, Matisse, Bonnard, Renoir and Dufy. Conscription for World War I decimated the local population, but the celebrities (including Coco Chanel, see box, page opposite) and tourists returned for a dose of unbridled liberalism in the interwar years, or *les années folles*. These well-heeled foreigners were joined by regular Frenchmen, enjoying a paid state holiday for the first time in 1936. But in the distance, the drums of World War II were already beating the time.

France surrendered six weeks after hostilities began in mid-1940, when the allegedly impregnable Maginot Line near St-Agnès collapsed. Italian soldiers occupied the Riviera as some of its celebrity residents, including Somerset Maugham, were evacuated by coal barge. While the Italians proved a light touch, patently ignoring calls to round up Provence's Jewish population, the collaborationist Vichy regime, which ruled the non-German occupied part of southern France, did not. Thousands were deported to concentration camps in Germany and Poland, although many Jewish children found refuge in Monaco.

As the Germans formally occupied Provence in late 1942, many locals were driven to the resistance. The communist party, with its heartlands in the docks of Marseille and Toulon, was a chief player in the movement. Toulon suffered a double blow during the war: the French fleet was scuttled by its commanders before it could fall into German hands, then the town was blown to bits a few months later as Allied bombs hit Nazi positions in the bay. General Patch (see box, page opposite) led

the Allied army landings on the beaches of St-Tropez in 1944 and headed for Manosque and Gap, while General Vigier of the Free French Forces liberated Avignon and Arles.

Provence's post-war recovery was sluggish. Blocky, stocky buildings took the place of bombed-out residences in the larger cities. Yet more flats shot up to house the migrants from France's Asian, African and Maghreb ex-colonies, not least the *pieds noirs* from Algeria, a million of whom were left homeless after the French withdrawal in 1962. Both state and US Marshall Plan aid got the region moving again, but these handouts combined with a slow pace of success bred corruption, particularly along the coast, of which Nice's Médecin clan is the most oft-used example. But with grand projects like the Paris-Marseille *autoroute* in 1970, the Riviera's Sophia Antipolis technology park and the Paris-Aix TGV line in 2001, things were looking up. The final foreign invasion – this time of sun-seeking tourists – has been heartily welcomed by the locals in most cases. After 27,000 years of action, they could probably do with a holiday too.

Five people who changed Provence

William 1st of Provence (950-993)
Born Count of Arles, William was Provence's first champion, reintroducing vines, agriculture and transportation links to the entire region. The local population was outraged when the Saracens, who occupied much of the Massif des Maures, kidnapped and ransomed the Abbot of Cluny. William defeated them in six straight battles and pushed them from Provence, earning the sobriquet of 'the Liberator', although he later became a monk.

Raymond Bérenger IV (1195-1245)
This last great Count of Provence clearly adored the region and travelled around much of it. Raymond's two sons were stillborn; fearing invasion from France, Rome or the Catalans, he married his four daughters off very neatly indeed. The eldest, Marguerite, married Louis IX, King of France, Eleanor married Henry III of England, Sanchia married the Earl of Cornwall and young Beatrice married Louis's brother, Charles d'Anjou (see page 30).

Lord Brougham (1778-1868)
Henry Peter Brougham was a former Lord Chancellor, and was instrumental in Britain's abolition of the slave trade. In 1835, he stumbled across the village of Cannes, as his final destination of Nice was under quarantine due to a cholera epidemic. He built a huge villa and spent summers there, encouraging other foreign nobles to do the same. Brougham is buried in Cannes' Cimetière du Grand Jas along with Picasso's first wife, Olga Khoklova, and his statue stands opposite the Palais des Festivals.

Coco Chanel (1883-1971)
The creator of Chanel No 5 may have been born in a poorhouse, but her creation of the 'little black dress' and an affair with the Duke of Westminster brought her Riviera-style riches. The Duke built Villa La Pausa in Roquebrune for her in 1927, although she refused his proposal of marriage: "There are a lot of duchesses, but only one Coco Chanel." Coco herself was refused entry at the time to Juan-les-Pins casino, her trendy new 'beach pyjamas' being too risqué. La Pausa was later used by Winston Churchill in the 1950s as his Côte d'Azur bolthole, and put on the market in 2007 for around €10 million by its German owner. Incidentally, Coco Chanel's interlocked 'CC' logo was borrowed from a frieze on the Château de Crémat, an age-old vineyard in the Bellet wine region (see page 80).

General Alexander Patch (1889-1945)
A plaque on St-Tropez's Plage de Pampelonne marks the 15 August Provence landings, commanded by Arizona-born General Patch. In Operation Dragoon, US and Free French troops, including commando and glider squadrons, also stormed the beaches of St-Raphaël, Ste-Maxime, Cap Nègre and Cavalaire-sur-Mer. The Germans had razed the forests below Ramatuelle to withdraw cover from a potential invasion – an area now covered with vineyards – but their manpower was not up to the defensive task, and Hitler ordered a withdrawal. By 28 August, French troops had liberated Toulon and Marseille; a third of all Allied supplies eventually arrived through the latter's port.

Left: A familiar 'CC' logo at the Chateau de Crémat, Bellet vineyards.
Opposite page: TGV Station, Aix-en-Provence.

Art &
architecture

Provence's quality of light, combined with the intensity of its coastal and countryside colours, has long acted as an irresistible magnet for artists. Claude Monet may have dipped his toes off the shores of Antibes in the late 1880s, but it was Vincent Van Gogh, Paul Cézanne and Pierre-Auguste Renoir who truly earmarked Provence as a place of modern art pilgrimage.

Art

Van Gogh arrived in the South of France in 1888. During the final two years of his life, the artist painted with a prolific intensity, turning his attention first to colourful Arles, depicting all its vigorous vibrancy. Like Impressionists before him, Van Gogh focused less on replicating what he saw; he instead channelled his creativity into use of colour and bold strokes, getting an image's personal effect onto canvas. These methods, and their results, were rarely embraced and frequently abhorred, emotions that played on Van Gogh's fragile mental stability.

Fellow artist and friend **Paul Gauguin** soon joined Van Gogh in Arles for a period of two all-consuming months. Together they painted Van Gogh's yellow house, the Roman necropolis of **Les Alyscamps** (see page 259), the Night Café and each

Above: Monastère Saint-Paul de Mausole, Saint-Rémy-de-Provence.
Opposite page: Atelier de Cézanne, Aix-en-Provence.

other. But they were both toeing their own abyss of depression, and frequently fought. One quarrel ended with Van Gogh taking a razor to his ear, landing him in the Hospital Hôtel-Dieu (now **Espace Van Gogh**, see page 258).

The Dutchman soon left both Gauguin and Arles in favour of the **Monastère St-Paul de Mausole** (see page 255) in St-Rémy-de-Provence. Staying at the monastery for over a year, Van Gogh created an incredible 143 paintings, including his famous *Starry Night* and *The Olive Trees*, before abandoning the south altogether later that year.

A bastion of tranquillity by comparison, Pierre-Auguste Renoir made his definitive move south to Cagnes-sur-Mer, just west of Nice, in 1903. He constructed a spacious home, Les Collettes, alongside an old farmhouse on a hill just outside town; in 1907, he and his family moved in. Painting with Monet during the 1880s, Renoir moved away from pure Impressionism, focusing his attention not just on landscapes but also on the female form. Today, Les Collettes is home to the **Musée Renoir**, (see page 97), showcasing the artist's studio and exhibiting ten paintings and 12 of his sculptures.

Cézanne was born, raised and died in Aix-en-Provence, spending but briefs periods outside of Provence.

But more than anyone else, It was Paul Cézanne who acted as a trailblazer for most 20th-century artistic trends. His brushstrokes and his simple shapes are sometimes seen as a precursor to pointillism and most often cubism. Cézanne was born, raised and died in Aix-en-Provence, spending but brief periods outside Provence. Places painted by the artist are thick on Aix's turf, including his **Atelier** (see page 222), where he finished the masterpiece *Grandes Baigneuses*, former home **Jas de Bouffan** (see page 223) and the **Bibémus Quarries** (see page 223). Always hovering on the horizon is **Mont Ste-Victoire** (see page 222): Cézanne was devoted to depicting the unspoilt mountain for decades.

At the turn of the century, in the lonely fishing village of St-Tropez, Paris-born **Paul Signac** painted the bay, boats and hills beyond in his dotty signature style. Friends and fellow artists joined him, emulating his technique, including **Henri Matisse**. Period works can be seen at St-Tropez's **Musée de l'Annonciade** (see page 132). Not far away, artists flocked to the town of L'Estaque, including the Fauvist **Georges Braque** and **Raoul Dufy**, while Amedeo Modigliani, Tsuguoharu Foujita and Chaïm Soutine shared a home, and inspiration, in hilltop Haut-de-Cagnes (now the restaurant **Josy-Jo**, see page 120). Ethereal **Pierre Bonnard** intertwined figurative and natural images at his home in Le Cannet near Cannes.

However, it's **Matisse** who is widely touted as the Riviera's biggest and best artist. Not too shabby a title for a boy from the overcast and gloomy environs of Picardy, beetroot country in northern France. From his first visit to Nice, staying at the Beau Rivage Hotel in 1917, to his death in 1954, Matisse was overwhelmed and inspired by the French Riviera. One of his most enduring creations is the **Chapelle du Rosaire** (see page 100) in Vence. Built between 1947 and 1951, the three-dimensional artwork is simple and utterly bold, glowing beneath its yellow, blue and green stained-glass windows.

On **Marc Chagall**'s first visit to Nice, in 1925, the artist exclaimed "Ici je vois le monde à travers un bouquet de fleurs!" ("Here, I see the world through a bouquet of flowers!"). Chagall spent almost half of his lifetime in the South of France, his well-established artistic style flourishing in the bright colours and tropical landscapes. In Nice's residential Cimiez suburb, the **Chagall Museum** (see page 79) was purpose-built for the artist's interpretation of the Old Testament, which includes 17 large paintings illustrating the first two books of the Bible and the *Song of Songs*, all created between 1954 and 1967.

political chapel murals **La Guerre et la Paix** (see page 96) and ceramics in Vallauris, then basing himself and his entourage in Cannes and Mougins. Around the same time, artist and poet **Jean Cocteau** decorated the **Chapelle St-Pierre** (see page 103) down the coast in Villefranche-sur-Mer, as well as the town hall in Menton (see page 111).

Over the course of the century, a little spot in St-Paul became a Mecca for all. First opened by

On Marc Chagall's first visit to Nice, in 1925, the artist exclaimed "Ici je vois le monde à travers un bouquet de fleurs!"

Arguably the 20th-century's greatest artist, playboy **Pablo Picasso** was almost always at the heart of the action, painting in Antibes (at the **Château Grimaldi**, now the **Musée Picasso**, see page 92), creating his

Not so funny

On April Fool's day 1960, a portion of La Colombe d'Or's artworks were stolen, including Matisse's *Portrait of a Woman* and Léger's *Grand Vase*. All the works were recovered less than a year later, but from that day forth, coach loads of tourists began to pitch up, wandering through the building and terrace as if it were a free museum. Yvonne and Francis Roux soon chose to close their door to all but paying patrons.

Paul Roux under the name 'A Robinson', in 1931 the restaurant and its three *chambres* became **La Colombe d'Or** (see page 120), a seductively beautiful place for artists to meet and exchange ideas. In its early days, starving painters were encouraged to swap room and board for artworks, and Roux's collection quickly grew. Big name artists began to frequent this former artichoke patch, including Dufy, Signac, Soutine, Matisse, Braque, Picasso and cubist **Fernand Léger**. Celebrities like Jean-Paul Sartre, Simone de Beauvoir, Brigitte Bardot, David Niven, Orson Welles and Cary Grant, as well as stars attending the Cannes Film Festival, joined them.

During the 1960s, artists who formed the core of the Ecole de Nice movement – **Yves Klein**, **Niki de Saint-Phalle** and **César** included – spent their days at La Colombe d'Or, eventually donating works to the ever-expanding collection. Art dealers Aimé and Marguerite Maeght opened the **Fondation Maeght** (see page 99) down the road in 1964, housing their remarkable private haul of modern art there.

Although Provence continues to cultivate artists, arrange exhibitions and stimulate creativity, today it is not a bastion of contemporary culture. The region tends to reflect on its past triumphs, emulating the 20th-century heroes, rather than gazing towards a cutting-edge future. Marseille is the one centre that bucks this trend, particularly with the shows held at **La Friche Belle de Mai** (see page 189).

Architecture

Encompassing Roman ruins, glass skyscrapers and a hundred over-the-top follies in between, Provence and the Côte d'Azur have enough highlights to keep any aspiring architect enthralled for weeks.

During the Roman Empire's heady heyday, the Via Aurelia swept through the heart of Provence, linking Nice, Aix-en-Provence and Arles. This trade route served corners of the empire with local

Above: Thermes de Constantin, Arles.
Opposite page: Musée de l'Annonciade, St-Tropez.

produce such as wine and olive oil. Provence is dotted with aqueducts and bridges, plus well-preserved Roman theatres, including the **Théâtre Antique** in Orange (see page 248), Arles's **Amphithéâtre** (see page 257) and Cimiez's stone auditorium in Nice; still enviable acoustics mean they're all choice locations for annual al fresco music festivals.

Saracen and Goth invasions rippled through the region as the first millennium AD drew to a close, leaving a legacy of defensive fortifications. Perched villages and hilltop castles drew ramparts around themselves, keeping aggressive armies out and protecting riches within. Still shining examples of self-containment include the isolated **Château des Baux** (see page 253), the drawbridge-access-only **Entrevaux** (see page 165) and **Eze**'s (see page 105) towering mass. Forts, such as Vauban's 16th-century star-shaped **Fort Carré** (see page 92)

About the region

Above: Skyscrapers lining Plage Larvotto, Monaco.
Opposite page: Monument Porte de l'Orient, Marseille.

in Antibes, plus the defences at Toulon and St-Tropez, were also essential defence systems.

The Middle Ages heralded an era of religious architecture. Following the papal move to Avignon, austere Cistercian **Abbaye de Sénanque** (see page 226) near Gordes and the Massif des Maures's **Chartreuse de la Verne** were superseded by more ornate edifices. The Gothic **Palais des Papes** (see page 243) acted as a precursor for affluent houses of worship, sedate chapels culminating centuries on in creations like Marseille's opulent 19th-century **Basilique de Notre-Dame-de-la-Garde** (see page 186).

It was only in 1860 that Nice and its environs passed from Italian to French rule. Nice's **Old Town** (see page 75) and its **Cathédrale Ste-Réparate**, plus Menton's *vieille ville* and its frescoed **Eglise St-Michel** (see page 111), are all fine examples of Italianate architecture, striking in their contrast to contemporaneous buildings further west in Provence.

The Train Bleu connecting Paris and Nice arrived in the region around the same time. A trickle of arriving aristocrats soon became a flood, and wealth poured into developing monuments of leisure, such as the Charles Garnier-designed **Monte Carlo Casino**. Parisian architecture was reflected in Haussmann buildings that sprang up along

Marseille's **rue de la République** (see pages 178 and 183). As the century turned, the belle époque ushered in pleasure palaces like **Hôtel Negresco** (see page 78) on the promenade in Nice and **Hôtel Carlton** (see page 83) on Cannes' Croisette.

Drive along the coast and it's difficult to miss *les années folles*: the merger of decadent creativity and piles of cash defined the 1920s. The result was a bizarre mix of styles: ship-shaped and modern, in the case of Hyères's **Villa Noailles** (see page 139). In Roquebrune, the iconic **Villa E.1027** (see page 106) was designed by Eileen Gray, while nearby is Le Corbusier's tiny cube of a cabin, **Le Cabanon** (see page 107).

Marseille and Toulon both sustained heavy damages during World War II, and much of the population was left homeless. Post-war immigration added to the mix, with thousands of veterans and *pieds noirs* arriving from Algeria in the late 1950s. Architects sought to rectify the housing shortage, of which Le Corbusier's **Unité d'Habitation** (see page 202) in Marseille is a stellar example.

Throughout the second half of the 20th century, architects threw up a mix of styles, starting with 1960s standout, the wacky, wave-like **Marina Baie des Anges** (see page 97) in Villeneuve-Loubet. Down the coast, Monaco was doused in 1980s towerblocks and a cluster of skyscrapers, making for a dramatic contrast with the rest of the Riviera.

Today, Marseille draws renowned architects like Zaha Hadid, Massimiliano Fuksas and Jean Nouvel for the city's ongoing **Euroméditerranée Project** (see page 188). There's also a strong return to the past, with renovations and new takes on historical buildings, placing the new **Musée des Civilisations de l'Europe et de la Méditerranée** (see page 185) within Marseille's 17th-century Fort Jean, reopening Nice's abandoned art deco **Palais de la Méditerranée** (see page 78) and the ongoing refurbishment of Juan-les-Pins's **Le Provençal** (see page 93).

AUX HÉROS DE L'ARMÉE D'ORIENT ET DES TERRES LOINTAINE

Provence & Côte d'Azur today

Green transportation

France generates around 8% of its GDP from tourism. With over 75 million visitors, it's the world's most popular destination. And many of these arrivals choose to visit Provence, where the leisure industry is the principal earner.

Around 10.2 million people arrived in Provence via Nice airport in 2008, together with many millions more by road, rail and boat. The need to move these visitors around, and transport the staff who service the industry, is a key issue. As the Riviera cements its reputation with business conferences and Marseille steps up to be European City of Culture in 2013, visitor numbers are set to grow. Given a topography that blends Alpine peaks, great lakes and limestone cliffs, building new highways is not a viable option. And the fact that a cyclist can travel from Monaco to Nice faster than a Ferrari in summer hints both at the region's problems and at some of the solutions being introduced today.

Top tips from the locals

❶ "The open-air cinema in Monaco (see page 123). It's by the oceanographic museum where a car park on the rock becomes an outdoor auditorium with open-air bar!" **Amy Clarkson**, *The Riviera Comedy Club, therivieracomedyclub.com.*

❷ "Don't bring your damn car in here! I take the ferryboat from Ste-Maxime." **Monique Lieutaud**, *hotel receptionist, St-Tropez.*

❸ "If you're in Vieux Nice and need a drink – either of the quick restorative or lingering people-watching type – then try Les Distilleries on rue de la Prefecture: circular bistro tables, very atmospheric, very French." **Michael Furniss**, *copywriter and marketing consultant, Nice.*

❹ "The €1 ski bus to Auron or Isola 2000 (see page 168). Stay a night for two days of boarding." **Patrick Boino**, *insurance agent, Sospel.*

❺ "Remove your clothes on Plage du Layet (see page 144), it is the most sublime beach of Le Lavandou. But all my beaches are very nice." **Pierre Louvet**, *restauranteur, Le Lavandou.*

Cycling the Promenade des Anglais, Nice.

On your bike

Bikes are an obvious fix. From 2007 to 2009 the Velib' free bike model pioneered by Paris migrated south. Hundreds of electronic grab-a-bike stands now cover four of Provence's largest cities: Avignon (velopop.fr), Nice (velobleu.org), Marseille (levelompm.fr) and Aix-en-Provence (vhello.fr). Easy-to-use and inexpensive (they're normally free for the first 30 minutes), the bikes have been phenomenally successful for riders of all ages, perhaps naturally so given the region's sunny winters and lack of rainfall. The numbers of cycle tracks and bike-mounted police have rocketed in tandem with the scheme. So have more localised two-wheeled projects, like bike-sharing schemes in Sophia Antipolis, Europe's largest technology park. Open-air electric rickshaws now compete with taxis in many coastal resorts.

Vive le Tram

The French state has never shied away from directing micro-economic policy. The antithesis of free-market planning, the government has a history of installing *grands projets* in zones of high unemployment or social exclusion. Two fine examples are the new tram systems in Marsellle and Nice, which provide both sustainable transportation and have established thousands of manual jobs for a decade. Ripped up in the 1940s to make way for the motorcar, then launched again almost simultaneously in the past few years, both tramlines are great ways to get around. Both also link deprived areas with more prosperous ones, ensuring flexibility of labour and the economic boom that goes with it. Line 3 of Marseille's tram system will be completed by 2011. Line 2 of Nice's network should link the city centre with the airport by 2013.

On track

The TGV Méditerranée is Provence's shining emblem of green travel. It opened in 2001, connecting the 750 km of fields between Paris and Marseille in three hours flat, screaming past cars at 300 km/hr and caricaturing the air-link between France's two largest cities as a stressful folly. Avignon and Aix have similar TGV links with Paris,

About the region

but the resorts of the Riviera remain a long, if exceedingly comfy, five-hour journey from the capital. But in 2009 the government decided on a major upgrade, which should wipe cars off the overcrowded A8 highway: a one-hour dedicated high-speed line between Marseille and Nice. This €15 billion plan will be burrowing underneath some of Europe's most vicious terrain around 2020.

Back on the bus

In a world of TGVs and electronic bike stands, buses will never be the hippest green transport solution. But practical they most certainly are. Firstly, and most importantly for Provence, they can run without a proprietary track; no tunnels or rails needed here. Secondly, they can be converted to run on non-polluting fuels: most of Nice's buses run on natural gas, while electronic people carriers – plugged in overnight to France's 90% nuclear-powered grid – could be a vision of the near-future. Experience in Provence has shown that visitors and

locals alike will use public transport if it's cheap and convenient: the local Var and Alpes-Maritimes governments recently reduced the price of most bus journeys to €2 and €1 per ride respectively.

The property market

Until the mid-1990s, a *pied-à-terre* in the South of France was the preserve of few. Transport links put off many prospective buyers. Others who dreamed of 'A Year in Provence' were foiled by a conservative mortgage market, which only lent up to 50% of a property's value to foreign buyers. Boast that you were converting your savings into Francs to buy a pad near Elton John and you'd be laughed out of the building.

The easyJet effect

Commentators also scoffed at the little orange airline easyJet when it started flying to Nice from

Nice's trams provide an excellent way to get around.

Luton in 1996, and from Liverpool a year later. By 2000, it had six routes working around the clock from Provence's principal air hub. As northern European house prices inflated, a place in the sun became both accessible and affordable. "First you had two or three flights a day to London," says Clive Ward, a Cannes-based estate agent. "Then it was 15-20 a day, then 40-50 a day from Manston, Coventry, Glasgow, Leeds and all over." The situation had a domestic parallel in Marseille, where the arrival of the TGV in 2001 suddenly brought 10 million Parisians within three hours of the coast.

In 2002, buyers could get a large one-bedroom apartment in Antibes or Nice for around €90,000. In Marseille, which had its own easyJet link in 2003, similar apartments in the edgy Panier district were €50,000. Inland in the Haute-Var, Roya Valley and Lubéron, ruins with an acre of land were half the price. 'Doing a place up' and selling it on – a process hitherto unknown in France where many properties were still inherited – became commonplace.

The era of cheap credit arrived too, says the estate agent. "We were taken out by the banks for drinks and pushed to lend even more. One bank's staff were on bonuses if they reached the branch's target of lending €50 million every six months: multiply that by just ten branches and it's €1 billion a year." Foreigners could routinely borrow 70%, then 80% of the properties' value: "but we were getting 100% mortgages approved for non-residents by 2005". Local newspapers printed property price rises every few months, which rose around 15% per annum during this heady period.

And the effect? According to many it was a positive one. Old buildings were renewed and money flowed to local builders, restaurants, insurance companies, swimming pool cleaners and DIY shops. The surge in rental accommodation boosted the number of available beds in each town, a blessing in Provence where to open a hotel requires an 'in' with the local mayor. Many locals seemed happy to trade their romantic 'up and coming' quarter with the fitted kitchens and parking spaces of an outlying suburb. But others,

Old buildings were renewed and money flowed to local builders, restaurants, insurance companies, swimming pool cleaners and DIY shops.

especially the young, were priced out of the market, rents rising as fast as the mortgage approvals.

Europe's credit boom forced interest rates up in 2006. The price of mortgages rose, as did the price of the euro vis-à-vis the dollar, the pound and the Russian rouble. Confidence in the property market evaporated quickly as queues formed around Britain's specialist mortgage bank, Northern Rock, in September 2007. Many claimed, however, that the luxury end of the market was 'recession-proof'.

The Villa Leopolda on glamorous Cap Ferrat duly came on the market in 2008. At €500 million, this former Agnelli family home was the most expensive house ever to go on sale. Alas, the purchase fell through as the financial crisis squeezed the buyer, a Russian oligarch, who was forced to walk away from his €39 million deposit. The heart bleeds.

While the French economy weathered the crisis better than most, Provence's foreigner-reliant property market remained at a plateau. By late 2009, some lenders were offering 0% interest rates to induce buyers. Most estate agencies remained open during la crise although casual builders, removal companies and boutique agencies catering to foreign buyers are still feeling the pinch.

And now? All in all it's probably a very good time to buy. But don't go crazy: it's not the noughties!

Nature & environment

The Provence and Côte d'Azur region sits snugly in the country's southeast, covering mountain peaks, verdant valleys and rugged coastlines over more than 30,000 sq km. The River Rhône marks the border to the west, while the Italian frontier marks its eastern edge. To the south, an almost continuous sentier littoral (coastal path) skirts along from Menton to Marseille.

The Côte d'Azur, a broad area that loosely stretches from St-Tropez to Menton, is mild year-round, hovering around 25°C in the summer and rarely dipping below 0°C in the winter. Warm weather is long and lingering. In the area encompassing Marseille and the Lubéron, the biting *mistral* wind heralds cold northern winds, and makeş the weather much chillier through the winter months. Haute-Provence and the Southern Alps receive plenty of snow, and remain a respite of cool, fresh air through the summer season. Like much of the Mediterranean littoral, wet weeks arrive twice a year like clockwork, in mid March or April and in late October or early November. Beware: during these intense periods, days are dreary.

This region is probably best known as a seaside destination. More than 40 km of Provençal seafront is dedicated to beaches, and around a dozen significant islands bob in its coastal waters. The

Above: Ochre cliffs, Roussillon.
Opposite page: The River Rhône, Avignon.

Mediterranean Sea is generally clean. In 2009, 74 of the region's beaches held an eco-friendly Blue Flag award (blueflag.org). Some summers, the coast is swamped with jellyfish, thought to be a side-effect of over-fishing. Stings are very unpleasant but not lethal, and can be treated at any pharmacy. These days, most seaside resorts from Monaco to St-Tropez employ jellyfish barriers far out at sea, blocking the squidgy invaders from getting through.

Provence is home to four regional parks: **Camargue** (parc-camargue.fr, see page 260), **Alpilles**, **Lubéron** (parcduluberon.fr, see page 224) and **Verdon** (parcduverdon.fr, see page 162), and two national parks (parcs-naturels-regionaux.tm.fr): **Mercantour** (see page 167) and **Port-Cros** (see page 141). They make a haven for protected flora and fauna, such as eagles, wolves and rare succulents, as well as migrating species.

Towering mountains cluster around the Mercantour area, while the sky-scraping **Mont Ventoux** is the Lubéron's highest peak, measuring in at a lofty 1900 m. In the southern **Lubéron**, nature is tamer, the natural ochre deposits around Roussillon making a striking natural contrast to the area's cultivated vineyards and thick, fragrant lavender fields. The low-lying **Massif des Maures** (see page143) hills, just inland from Le Lavandou, are carpeted in thick forest. Visitor numbers here are minimal compared to the more frequented ranges and the coast.

The **River Rhône** flows from the Alps southwards, acting for centuries as a major trade route between Lyon, Avignon and Arles. It branches off into the Grand and Petit Rhônes just north of Arles before spilling onwards into the Mediterranean Sea. The rich delta land between its two arms contains the salt marshes of the utterly unique Camargue. Visitors to the region can opt to explore the Rhône on a ferryboat tour, hit the untamed marshland on horseback or spend days spotting the Camargue's elusive sandgrouse and warblers.

As well as the Rhône, the region's major rivers include the **Durance, Sorgue, Var** and **Verdon**. The latter cuts through the **Gorges du Verdon** (see page 162), a deep limestone canyon that forms a 700-m-deep gash into the earth. The river eventually flows into the bright greeny-blue **Lac de Ste Croix** (see page 162). Hiking trails tangle through the surrounding forests, and the sheer limestone cliffs have become a site of pilgrimage for serious climbers.

Festivals & events

January

Monte Carlo Rally
acm.mc.
Jazzed-up road cars whizz from snowy hills to Monaco's sunny port.

Monte Carlo Circus Festival
montecarlofestivals.com.
Wow-factor big top performances from around the world.

February

Fête du Citron, Menton (Lemon Festival)
feteducitron.com.
Giant sculptures made from oranges and lemons, plus parades and markets in France's sunniest town.

Fête du Mimosa, Mandelieu-La Napoule
ot-mandelieu.fr.
Week-long street festival paying homage to the bright yellow blossom.

Carnaval de Nice
nicecarnaval.com.
Two weeks of processions involving papier-mâché sculptures and flower battles along the Promenade.

March

Napoleon's arrival, Golfe Juan (1st weekend)
vallauris-golfe-juan.fr.
Amusingly epic recreation of Napoleon's arrival on Golfe-Juan beach.

Le Paris-Nice
Prestigious eight-stage cycle race passing through Provence (routinely Fayence, Lac de Ste Croix and Manosque) and finishing in Nice in mid-March.

Fête de l'Olivier (Olive tree Festival)
cagnes-tourisme.com.
Late March olive and oil celebration in the gardens of Renoir's house with free nibbles.

April

Féria de Pâques, Arles
arenes-arles.com.
Easter-time programme of bull fighting.

May

Festival International de Mode et de Photographie à Hyères
villanoailles-hyeres.com.
Early May fashion and art photography festival in the art deco Villa Noailles.

The Carnaval de Nice takes place in February.

Fête de la St-Honorat, Agay
agay.fr.
Rosé wine, bread and aïoli eating event to mark St Honorat's arrival on the Iles de Lérins.

Cannes Film Festival
festival-cannes.com.
Mega 10-day movie spectacular; opportunities for star spotting and screenings abound.

Monaco Grand Prix
acm.mc.
The most glamorous three-day event on the F1 calendar; tickets must be booked early.

Le Pèlerinage des Gitans, Stes-Maries-de-la-Mer
saintesmaries.com.
Riotous late May gypsy pilgrimage to parade the statue of their patron saint, Black Sara.

June

Festival des Heures Musicales, Biot
biot.fr.
Six weeks of classical concerts take over tiny Biot.

Fête de la Musique
fetedelamusique.culture.fr.
Provence-wide street concerts on 21 June to mark the longest day of the year.

Fête de la Lavande, Ste-Agnès
sainteagnes.fr.
Lavender production displays and street parades in heady hilltop village.

Fête de la Mer et des Pêcheurs (Festival of the Sea and Fishermen), Martigues
martigues-tourisme.com.
Late June homage to St Peter, the patron saint of fishermen, with street markets and boat-to-boat jousting near the port.

Rose Festival, Grasse
grasse.fr.
Mid May weekend where 50,000 roses cover the Cathedral and Musée Fragonard.

Fête de la Vigne et du Vin (Vine and Wine Festival)
fetedelavigneetduvin.com.
Open cellars and *domaine* tastings throughout France's winegrowing regions on a Saturday in late May.

Bravade de St-Tropez
ot-saint-tropez.com.
Three-day procession marking the arrival of St-Tropez's patron saint.

About the region

July

Festival de Lacoste
festivaldelacoste.com.
Month-long opera, music and dance festival in the rarified surroundings of Pierre Cardin's village.

Avignon Off
avignonleoff.com.
Full month of fringe street theatre and music.

Festival d'Avignon
festival-avignon.com.
Fortnight of theatre and art premieres in Avignon's most evocative locations.

Bastille Day (14)
Fireworks and festivities all over France.

Cannes Pyrotechnic Festival
festival-pyrotechnique-cannes.com.
Every schoolboy's dream: huge weekly firework displays form part of an international competition, from Bastille Day onwards.

Nice Jazz Festival
nicejazzfestival.fr.
A week of al fresco jazz, blues and reggae in the Roman amphitheatre of Cimiez.

Les Suds Arles
suds-arles.com.
Mid-month world music blowout in Roman Arles.

La Marseillaise
petanque.org.
France's biggest *boules* tournament.

Jazz à Juan
jazzajuan.fr.
Late July open-air jazz festival of international repute hosting artists from BB King to Massive Attack.

Chorégies d'Orange
choregies.asso.fr.
Opera performances inside Orange's awe-inspiring amphitheatre.

Jazz à Toulon
jazzatoulon.com.
The coast's only free jazz festival spanning funk to afro-rock.

Festa de San Pèire, Nice
nice.fr.
Late month weekend featuring local maritime culture and free boat rides in Nice port.

Nuits du Château de La Napoule
ot-mandelieu.fr.
Week of jazz, gospel and French comedy at Henry Clews' seaside mansion.

August

Les Rencontres d'Arles Photographie
rencontres-arles.com.
Eight-week long photography exhibition in and around 20 historic sites.

Festival de L'Isle-sur-la-Sorgue
oti-delasorgue.fr.
Races between flower-filled boats plus floating markets.

Fête du Pain (Bread Festival), St-Martin-Vésubie
saintmartinvesubie.fr.
Early August traditional street fair and bread-making day.

Monte-Carlo International Fireworks Competition
visitmonaco.com.
Sit on Monaco's docks and watch millions go up in smoke over the week as competitors battle it out.

Festival de Musique, Menton
festivalmusiquementon.com.
Classical recitals inside and outside Menton's
churches in the first two weeks of August.

Féria de St-Rémy-de-Provence
saint-remy-de-provence.com.
Parades, agricultural displays and shows of local
bulls and horses in the middle weekend of August.

Festival de Ramatuelle
festivalderamatuelle.com.
Week-long theatre festival above St-Tropez.

Seillans Musique Cordiale Festival
musique-cordiale.com.
Great community-spirited opera festival with
concerts in Seillans, Bargemon and Mons.

Opera les Azuriales
azuriales-opera.com.
Mini open-air opera festival in the stunning
gardens of the Villa Ephrussi de Rothschild.

September

Etoiles de Mougins
lesetoilesdemougins.com.
Mid-month foodie event in medieval Mougins; nibbles
made by Provence's best chefs are passed around.

Journées du Patrimoine (Local heritage days)
journeesdupatrimoine.culture.fr.
Open house weekend at many of the grandest
buildings in Provence.

Voiles de St-Tropez (St-Tropez Sails)
societe-nautique-saint-tropez.fr.
Week long end-of-month race featuring the
world's finest sailing boats.

Fête du Port, Nice
nicerendezvous.com.
Late September weekend packed with music
stages, slow food, cheap drinks and dancing.

Monaco Yacht Show
monacoyachtshow.com.
Step aboard the world's coolest yachts and
pretend you can afford one.

October

Fiesta des Suds, Marseille
dock-des-suds.org.
Cutting edge late October week of rock-pop-
techno-dance concerts.

November

Louis Vuitton Trophy, Nice
louisvuittontrophy.com.
High-end yachts in a fortnight of racing off
Nice beach.

Fêtes de la Châtaigne (Chestnut Festival), Collobrières
collobrieres-tourisme.com.
Three Sundays of chestnut recipes, street food
and fun.

December

Fête de la Lumière, St-Raphaël
saint-raphael.com.
A month of ice-skating, concerts and Christmas
markets.

Fête du Millésime, Bandol
On the first Sunday of the month, wine producers
set up stalls along Bandol's port for this annual
wine festival.

Sleeping

For a region that has been welcoming holidaymakers for 150 years, the standard of accommodation in Provence is naturally pretty high. The majority of hoteliers are also very proactive. Most staff can find babysitters, recommend restaurants, advise on parking and much else besides: trainee receptionists at a Travelodge on the M6 they are not.

Accommodation standards

Like many countries, France has a star classification system. Ratings are normally very harsh. Some basic no-star options represent good honest value, while hotels in the newly created five-star range (until 2009 even the venerable Hotel Eden Roc on the Cap d'Antibes was classified as 'four-star L') represent every luxury known to man. However, it's local tourist authorities who award these ratings, so the system can be a little spurious. Use the hotels in this book, or your own two eyes, as a guide: prospective clients are welcome to peek at the rooms.

Tourist offices, especially inland, are a solid source of local accommodation. Many have lists of local homestays, *gîtes* and mountain refuges. Although the musings of holidaymakers cannot always be trusted, the Tripadvisor (tripadvisor.com) website hosts comments on thousands of hotels, B&Bs, *chambres d'hôtes* and self-catering accommodation in Provence. When exploring a new part of the region, it's advisable to look at the archived features from *The Guardian*, *New York Times*, *Daily Telegraph* or any other travel websites, as the odd little-visited hotel frequently pops up.

Only a very few – mainly city – hotels in the budget category have a shared lavatory in the hall. North American guests may find rooms small by US standards. Most rooms have TVs, although international channels are available only in a handful of high-end hotels: it's assumed that guests would rather be eating or sunbathing than watching the box. About 70% of Provence's hotels have free Wi-Fi.

Self-catering

Perhaps the best value method of holidaying in Provence, especially for families. This is particularly true along the coast where B&B-style *chambres d'hôtes* accommodation is thin on the ground. Self-catering gives you the option of making lunch and dinner: even making breakfast for four people can save €30 a day in hotel charges. Prices for a two-person apartment range from around €250-500 per week, with six-person apartments for around €500-1000 per week.

To find a place it's absolutely necessary to go online. Tourist offices have precious little information on rent-by-the-week apartments and villas, which are often owned by families from northern France, or even Brits, Germans and Swedes. A search on holiday-rentals.co.uk or holidaylettings.co.uk will distil the best results according to budget, number of rooms or amenities. And if you need Wi-Fi, a pool, or a parking place, you can search for it. French-run Gîtes de France (gites-de-france.com) is recommended for rural accommodation. Be aware, rental accommodation in Provence books up very fast indeed.

Camping

Pitching a tent or parking a mobile home remains extremely popular in France. Sites range from

Hotels for under €50

❶ **Hotel Paul, Aix-en-Provence** Central & friendly with a little garden, doubles from €45.

❷ **La Bonne Auberge, St-Martin-Vésubie** Countryside inn, fab walking country, from €48 per double.

❸ **Hotel Patricia, Villefranche-sur-Mer** Classy seaside Eden, from €40 per double.

❹ **Villa Saint Exupéry, Nice** Includes big breakfast, from €27 per double.

❺ **La Bienvenue, near St-Tropez** Sun terrace, old-fashioned rooms, nearby beaches, from €46 per double.

Five tips on renting a holiday apartment

From Matt & Gayle Roberts, owners of the Riviera Pebbles property rental agency.

❶ Do your **research online**. Does the apartment have air conditioning, a fully equipped kitchen and Wi-Fi, if this is important for you? Read any website comments from other guests before making a decision.

❷ If you are planning to rent with an agency who looks after several apartments to offer, they can guide you to the right place. A **brief list of your desires** in order of importance can help them choose the best apartment for you.

❸ **Are apartments cheaper than hotels?** Not unless you're staying for more than a few days, in which case they definitely are. Linen changes and cleaning costs more than at a hotel because apartments are bigger and linen is not laundered on the premises.

❹ If you have a late flight, consider **booking an extra night's stay**. Since a proportion of the charge is spent on the cleaning and linen that goes with the rental, an extra night is often not that much more. You can then fully enjoy the last day of your holiday without having to check out earlier than you would like (normally around 1030). But if you're booking in low season, there is a good chance you can stay late.

❺ When choosing an apartment, consider options that fall just **outside the main tourist zones** for a more authentic local experience. These neighbourhoods have their own hidden gems, from shops to locals-only restaurants, all largely undiscovered by travel guides.

Riviera Pebbles have around 80 apartments to rent along the French Riviera. Visit rivierapebbles.com.

massive commercial ones with swimming pools that attract the same families each year, to tiny, more liberal ones hiding in vineyards by a beach. All have washing machines and good bathroom facilities, while even smaller ones have cute (sometimes incredibly so) cabins to rent, most often by the week in high season.

There are literally hundreds of campsites all over Provence, particularly on the coast. The excellent Camping France (campingfrance.com) website has a list of, and a link to, almost all of them. A pitch for two people will cost an average of €15 per night. Most local tourist offices have a list of every campsite in the area, including prices, facilities and number of pitches.

Tight budgets

Budget hostels exist in most cities with beds for around €16 per night including a simple breakfast. Private dorms seem to be friendlier, cheaper, more flexible and much better run than the 15 or so official hostels in Provence, which are sanctioned by Hostelling International (fuaj.org in France). The private options frequently have two, three and four-bed rooms for those travelling as couples or in groups. Travelling off-season, booking in advance and camping are obvious ways in which to slash your budget. Wild camping is not permissible in France, although backpackers have been known to spend the odd night on a quiet beach.

For drivers the scene is positive. Budget motel chains like Formule1 (hotelformule1.com), BB (hotel-bb.com) and Etap Hotel (etaphotel.com) have around 20 hotels each in the region. These clean, basic rooms can be booked for around €35-50 per double. Urbanites can try Couch Surfing (couchsurfing.com): sleeping over at someone's house in the South of France for nothing.

Eating & drinking

Provençal cuisine

In striking contrast to the French stereotype, Provence and the Côte d'Azur is not a traditional land of plenty. Instead, the region's cuisine is a mix of peasant dishes and Italian influences. Recipes were developed to make the most of harvest gluts, and in times of little to make prized ingredients go the distance. Meats are often used to enhance a dish, rather than taking centre stage, and olive oil, not butter, features in pretty much everything.

Fruit and vegetables are really the local stars, and always have been. Unlike other parts of the world, locals here never lost touch with their traditions. Sure, heirloom vegetables are making a comeback, but you can bet that granny (at her market stall stocking just three seasonal items) never stopped growing them.

Swiss chard (*blettes*) is used in everything from savoury bakes to sweet *tourte*. Courgettes, aubergines and peppers are bathed in a garlic tomato sauce in *ratatouille*. Crunchy raw artichokes, peppers, and even asparagus and broad beans headline in *salade niçoise*. A particularly snacky city, Nice residents favour the same salad in its sandwich version, *pan bagnat*, as well as on-the-go favourites, savoury chick pea *socca* and onion-topped *pissaladière*.

Baguettes are a French staple, but the carb of choice varies in Provence. Italian-esque pasta dishes corner the southeast, while in the Camargue locally grown rice is a favourite. Sprinkled with *fleur de sel* from the nearby salt beds, of course.

Mer et Terre

Suspended between the mountains and the sea, Provence's traditional dishes encompass fruits of both the land and the sea, as well as more carnivorous offerings.

Surprisingly for this sea-flanked region, not only can fish be a pricey choice, but what you're eating is not always Riviera-sourced: much of the coast has been overfished, particularly in the southeast. *Soupe de poissons* makes the most of the Mediterranean's indigenous rockfish, while *bourride* and Marseille's famous *bouillabaisse* are more high-end options. Slow-cooked or fried *soupions* are a down-to-earth dish, and the lucky will sample springtime *poutine*, tiny fish at their tastiest when served raw, dressed with olive oil and lemon.

If you're self-catering, source your own local *rouget*, *rascasse* and *dorade* at Marseille's morning market (see page 187) in the Vieux Port or Cagnes-sur-Mer's daily *Marché aux Poissons*. You'll often find stalls selling fish and other seafood, particularly urchins, along the quay in every town on the coast.

From the Alpine hills inland, particularly around Sisteron, comes Haute-Provence's famous lamb. Traditionally, every part of the animal was used,

"

Provence is a country to which I am always returning, next week, next year, any day now, as soon as I can get on a train.

"

Elizabeth David

Cheeses from the French Alps, Arles street market.

What the locals say

Provençal cooking is about the big, intense flavours that come from sun-ripened seasonal vegetables and locally grown olive oil. Though much of Provence is near the sea, there is a strong mountain influence in the cuisine so you can expect rustic, slow-cooked dishes all year round: look for *daube*, a wine-soaked stew made with beef, lamb or wild bull depending on the area.

Rosa Jackson,
Les Petits Farcis cooking school (see page 125).

that big brands such as Evian and Perrier can be very pricey. Most locals will order *une carafe d'eau* instead. Coffee is ordered from dawn until bedtime. The milk-heavy *café crème* is only consumed before lunch: order it after a meal and you'll be marked out as a foreigner for sure. Better for digestion is a simple *café* (espresso) or *noisette* (with a dollop of milky foam on top). It's common to sip wine with your midday meal, and a glass is frequently offered as part of a set menu deal. Dinner is often preceded by an *apéritif* – *pastis* is by far the local favourite – and occasionally, you'll be offered a *digestif* on the house when you finish. The French generally relish alcohol consumption, but drunkenness is always a *faux pas*.

right down to its hooves, a vital ingredient in the Marseillaise dish *pieds et paquets*. Today more mainstream cuts suit our more affluent tastebuds – dishes such as *agneau rôti aux herbes de Provence*. Beef is most commonly found in *daube*, doused in red wine and simmered slowly for hours. There's also plenty of pork, although it's most concentrated in the region's selection of cured *charcuterie*. In Arles and the Camargue, bull is the local speciality, and you'll find it in everything from *taureau tartare* to *saucisson*.

A bountiful harvest

Offered in tiny bowls alongside an aperitif, crushed with capers and anchovies in *tapenade*, pressed to produce oil, olives are a South of France staple. Trees are harvested in the autumn. From November, you'll find market stalls piled high with local mottled green and black olives, both raw (to put up in brine yourself) and already cured. The latest crop of oil will hit shops around the same time. Don't keep your olive oil for longer than a year. Unlike wine, it doesn't mature with age, and should be used (with abandon) from the moment it's pressed. Stop by Nice's **Oliviera** to sample locally produced oils and learn more from olive oil guru, Nadim Beyrouti.

Drinking etiquette

Tap water is clean and safe throughout the region. If you opt for bottled *eau minérale* instead, note

Provençal wines

The South of France's climate – sunny, mild and dry – makes for fertile earth and plentiful vines. The region is known for its reds, both light and robust, and rosé wines in particular. Provence's premier AOCs include:

Bellet (see page 80) One of France's smallest appellations, in the hills just north of Nice. The unique *folle noire* ('crazy black') grape is crushed to create excellent reds and rosés (vinsdebellet.com).

Bandol (see page 197) Around 60 vineyards radiate northwards through the valleys around seaside Bandol. Of particular note are their tasty rosés (vinsdebandol.com).

Cassis (see page 192) Another small appellation, sandwiched between Marseille and Bandol. Cassis's 12 vineyards are renowned for their crisp white wines: perfect cool nectar to accompany local sea urchins.

Châteauneuf-du-Pape (see page 248) Strong, pricey, delicious reds, plus a very small percentage of fine – but much lesser-known – whites, produced in vineyards north of Avignon (chateauneuf.com).

Côte de Provence The Riviera's most widespread wine, produced from Marseille to St-Raphaël. Vineyards include Château Minuty (see page 134) near St-Tropez and Domaine de la Courtade (see page 140) on the island of Porquerolles.

To call or not to call...

If you have your heart set on dining at any of the superb restaurants included in this book, you must call or stop by to reserve a table in advance, particularly during the busy peak season. Don't worry if your French is a little 'rusty' (or even non-existent): most owners and staff will speak some English, and many of the higher-end establishments offer online booking. However limited your language skills may be, remember that *bonjour* and *merci* are always appreciated.

The €10 Picnic

Sunny summers and mild winter days make the South of France an ideal picnic ground year round. Whether you're urban-based or staying at a country cottage, a good local market should be your first stop. At Nice's **cours Saleya** (page 75) Marseille's **cours Julien** (page 186) or along **boulevard Emile Comes** (page 259) in Arles, small producers sell goat's cheese, *charcuterie*, olives and *tapenade*. All bread is not equal: search out a good *boulangerie* and pick up *fougasse*, a local treat stuffed with Roquefort and walnuts, or grilled tomatoes and aubergines. Round out your feast with seasonal fruit: May's first strawberries, melons in July or sticky purple figs in September.

Menu reader

General

petit déjeuner breakfast

déjeuner lunch (restaurants generally serve between 1200 and 1430).

dîner dinner or supper (restaurants serve dinner from 1900-2200; in rural towns it may be difficult to find a restaurant open after 2100).

hors d'œuvre appetisers, many restaurants also offer little *amuse-gueules* or *amuse-bouches* – literally throat- or mouth-teasers – after you've ordered.

entrées starters

les plats main courses

plat principal main course

menu / formule set menu

plat du jour dish of the day

à la carte individually-priced menu items

carte des vins wine list

une carafe d'eau a carafe of water

fait(e) maison home-made

Appellation d'Origine Contrôlée (AOC) label of regulated origin, signifying quality; usually associated with wine, though can also apply to regional foods such as cheeses.

Label Rouge often applied to poultry, label indicates premium quality and standards in production.

Agriculture Biologique (AB) organically-produced product

biologique or *bio* organic

Drinks (*boissons*)

apéritif drink taken before dinner.

digestif after-dinner drink, usually a liqueur or spirit.

eau gazeuse / pétillante sparkling / slightly sparkling mineral water.

eau plate / minérale still / mineral water

bouteille bottle

dégustation tasting

un verre de... a glass of...

un (verre de) vin rouge / blanc / rosé... a glass of red / white / rosé wine.

pichet jug, used to serve water, wine or cider.

sec dry

demi-sec medium dry – or slightly sweet when referring to champagne.

doux the sweetest champagne or cider

kir popular apéritif made with white wine and a fruit liqueur – blackcurrant (*cassis*) is popular.

petit(e) small

grand(e) big, large

pression a glass of draught beer

une bière a beer

demi small beer (33cl)

cidre cider

panaché beer/lemonade shandy

pastis anise-flavoured apéritif from around Marseille

jus de fruit fruit juice. Bars usually have a wide variety of flavours of bottled fruit juice.

orange pressée freshly-squeezed orange juice.

sirop fruit syrup or cordial served mixed with water, sparkling water or soda. Popular flavours are *grenadine* (pomegranate), *menthe* (mint) or *citron* (lemon).

diablo menthe refreshing green drink made with mint syrup mixed with lemonade.

un coca Coca-Cola

glaçons ice cubes

café coffee (black espresso)

un (grand) crème a (large) white coffee

une noisette espresso with a dash of milk

chocolat chaud hot chocolate, can be too sweet for some tastes. *Chocolatiers* will serve the best quality chocolate, and you can sweeten to taste.

lait milk

un thé tea, usually served *nature* with a slice of lemon (*au citron*) – if you want milk ask for *un peu de lait froid*, a little cold milk.

une tisane / infusion herbal tea: *tisane de menthe* (mint tea), *tisane de camomille* (camomile tea) and *tisane de tilleul* (lime blossom) are the most popular.

Fruit (*fruits*) & vegetables (*légumes*)
ail garlic
ananas pineapple
artichaut artichoke
asperge asparagus
blettes Swiss chard
cassis blackcurrants
céleri-rave celeriac, usually served grated in mayonnaise.
cèpes porcini mushrooms
champignons de Paris button mushrooms
châtaignes chestnuts
choux cabbage
citron lemon
citrouille or *potiron* pumpkin
cocos small, white beans
courge marrow or squash
épinards spinach
fenouil fennel
fèves broad beans
figues figs
figues de Barbarie prickly pears
fraises strawberries
framboises raspberries
gratin dauphinois a popular side-dish of potato slices layered with cream, garlic and butter and baked in the oven.
haricots verts green beans, often served as an accompaniment to a main course.
lentilles vertes green lentils
mesclun a mixture of young salad leaves.
mirabelles small golden plums
myrtilles blueberries
noix walnuts
oseille sorrel, often served in a sauce with salmon.
pêches peaches
petits pois peas
poireaux leeks
poires pears
pomme de terre potato, *primeurs* are new potatoes, and *frites* are chips (*chips* being crisps).
pommes apples, the *Reinette d'Orléans* and *Reine des Reinettes* local varieties.
prunes plums
ratatouille summer vegetables cooked in a tomato and garlic sauce.
soupe au pistou a spring vegetable soup with *pistou*.
truffe truffle

Meat (*viande*) & poultry (*volaille*)
agneau lamb
andouillette soft sausage made from pig's small intestines, usually grilled.
au point medium cooked meat (or tuna steak), usually still pink inside.
bien cuit well-cooked
blanquette de veau veal stew in white sauce with cream, vegetables and mushrooms.
bleu barely-cooked meat, almost raw.
bœuf beef
boucherie butcher's shop or display
canard duck
charcuterie encompasses sausages, hams and cured or salted meats.
chevreuil venison, roe deer
confit process to preserve meat, usually duck, goose or pork (e.g. *confit de canard*).
cuisse de grenouille frog's leg
daube marinated and slow-cooked beef, lamb or bull, vegetable and red wine stew; also used to fill pasta in the south of France.
dinde turkey

Below: Colourful varieties of blettes (Swiss chard).
Opposite page: Marseille's daily fish market, Vieux Port.

escalope thin, boneless slice of meat.
faux-filet beef sirloin
foie-gras fattened goose or duck liver.
fumé(e) smoked
géline de Touraine or *la Dame-Noire* grain-fed chicken prized by restaurateurs, awarded a Label Rouge.
gigot d'agneau leg of lamb
jambon ham; look for *jambon d'Amboise*, an especially fine ham.
lapin rabbit
médaillon small, round cut of meat or fish.
mouton mutton
pavé thickly cut steak
pieds et paquets tripe stuffed with pork, traditionally served with lambs' feet, a speciality of Marseille.
pintade guinea-fowl
porc pork
pot-au-feu slow-cooked beef and vegetable stew.
poulet chicken
rillettes a coarse pork pâté.
rillons big chunks of pork cooked in pork fat.
ris de veau sweetbreads
sanglier wild boar
saucisse small sausage
saucisson salami, eaten cold
saucisson sec air-dried salami
veau veal
taureau bull

Fish (*poisson*) & seafood (*fruits de mer*)
aiglefin haddock
anchoïade anchovy-based spread
anchois anchovies
anguille eel
bouillabaisse Marseillaise traditional fish stew from Marseille, served in two courses (first the soup, then the fish).
boulots sea snails
bourride white fish stew, thickened with *aïoli*.
brochet pike
cabillaud cod
calamar squid
coquillage shellfish
colin hake
crevettes prawns
dorade sea bream
homard lobster
huîtres oysters
lotte monkfish

loup de mer sea bass
morue salt-cod
moules mussels
oursins sea urchins
palourdes clams
poissons de rivière river fish
poulpe octopus
poutine very tiny, young sardines, most often cooked in an omelette or served raw.
rascasse scorpion fish
rouget red mullet
Saint-Pierre John Dory
sardines sardines
saumon salmon
soupe de poisson a smooth rockfish-based soup, served with croutons, *rouille* and grated gruyère cheese.
soupions small squid
thon tuna
truite trout

Desserts (*desserts*)
chantilly whipped, sweetened cream
chichi fregi deep-fried, orange-blossom doughnuts from L'Estaque.
clafoutis a fruit tart (usually cherries) covered in a custard-style filling, served hot or cold
compôte stewed fruit, often as a purée.
crème anglaise thin custard; unlike English custard, it is normally served cold.
crème brûlée chilled custard cream dessert with a caramelised top.
crème caramel baked custard flavoured with caramel.
fromage blanc unsweetened dairy product with a refreshing flavour served on its own or offered with a fruit coulis – most people add a little sugar.
glace ice cream
boules de glace scoops of ice cream
coupe glacée cold dessert with ice cream, fruit or nuts, chocolate or chantilly.
le parfum flavour, when referring to ice cream or yoghurt.
île flottante soft meringue floating on custard, topped with caramel sauce.
liègeois chilled chocolate or coffee ice cream-based dessert topped with chantilly.
navettes orange-blossom biscuits from Marseille.
pâtisserie pastries, cakes and tarts – also the place where they are sold.
sabayon creamy dessert made with beaten eggs, sugar and wine or liqueur.

tarte au citron lemon tart, ubiquitous around Menton during winter.
tarte Tatin upside-down apple tart
tourte de blettes sweet, Swiss chard tart from Nice.

Other

aïoli garlic mayonnaise
assiette plate (e.g. *assiette de charcuterie*)
Béarnaise sauce made of a wine reduction with tarragon, shallots & chervil, served hot with grilled beef or fish.
bagna càuda raw vegetables served with a hot garlic, olive oil and anchovy dip, popular throughout the Alps.
beurre butter
beurre blanc buttery white wine sauce often served with fish.
Bordelaise red wine sauce served with steak.
boulangerie bakery selling bread and *viennoiserie*.
brioche a soft, sweet bread made with eggs and butter.
casse-croûte literally 'to break a crust' – a snack.
crêpe large pancake served with various fillings as a dessert or snack.
croque-monsieur grilled ham and cheese sandwich.
croque-madame as above but topped with a fried egg.
croissant rich and flaky crescent-shaped roll usually served at breakfast.
crudités raw vegetables served sliced or diced with a dressing, as a starter or sandwich filling.
en croûte literally 'in crust'; food cooked in a pastry parcel.
escargots snails
fleur de sel speciality salt collected by hand, particularly from the Camargue.
forestière generally sautéed with mushrooms.
fougasse a type of Provençal bread, plain or filled with mushrooms, tomatoes, aubergine or Roquefort cheese.
fromage cheese
fromage de chèvre goat's milk cheese
fromage de brebis ewe's milk cheese
galette savoury filled pancake made with buckwheat flour, served as a starter or main course.
garniture garnish, side-dish
gâteau cake
gaufre waffle, usually served with chocolate sauce
Hollandaise rich oil and egg yolk sauce flavoured with lemon juice
œuf egg
pain bread – choose from a rich variety of flavoured breads as well as the traditional *baguette*.

pain au chocolat similar to a croissant, but pillow shaped and filled with chocolate.
pan bagnat sandwich version of *salade niçoise*, dressed with lashings of olive oil and vinegar.
pâte pastry or dough, not to be confused with *pâtes*, which is pasta or *pâté*, the meat terrine
petits farcis usually small onions, tomatoes, peppers and courgettes stuffed with a mix of veal, Parmesan and vegetables; Niçois.
pissaladière Niçois onion tart, usually eaten as a snack.
pistou a basil and garlic sauce, similar to Italian pesto but without pine nuts or Parmesan.
riz rice
rouille saffron, garlic and paprika mayonnaise, served with *soupe de poisson* and *bouillabaisse*.
salade niçoise salad usually made up of tomatoes, peppers, artichokes, boiled egg, olives, tinned tuna or anchovies; may also include potatoes and green beans.
salade verte simple green salad with vinaigrette dressing.
socca savoury chickpea flour pancake from Nice.
soupe/potage soup
viennoiserie baked items such as *croissants* and *brioches*.
tapenade Provençal olive, caper and anchovy spread.

Entertainment

Bars & clubs

Provence's major towns host a buzzing year-round bar and club scene. This is supplemented each summer not only by legions of fun-loving tourists (where ages from 15-80 are welcome to party) but also by strings of beach bars that line the coast. Local listings' magazines or flyers point to the best urban late-night bars, where friendly locals will always point you to the right nightclub. With a rapidly changing scene, this method really does work.

By and large, clubs value a sexily-dressed, happy clientele rather than formal shoes or expensive accessories. However, the exclusive summer clubbing season in St-Tropez and its winter equivalent in Monaco are laws unto themselves: with €100 cocktails and €1000 bottles of champagne being bandied about, it's a unique anthropological experience, especially if someone else is paying.

Live music remains ever popular across the region, with jazz clubs, several of which are listed in this book, doing a roaring trade. Rock, blues and indie are popular genres, especially in the population-dense Riviera. Marseille is synonymous with hip hop and has a much larger contemporary pop and rap scene. Smaller towns, be they inland like Gordes or coastal like Juan-les-Pins, are alive in summer but die off each winter.

Morning coffee in place Richelme, Aix-en-Provence.

Café gourmand at Les Deux Garcons, Aix-en-Provence.

Summer festival posters, Arles.

Cafés

Local cafés are the scene of more birth, death and marriage announcements than a local newspaper. The centrepiece of neighbourhood life, they are people-watching heaven and an integral part of any day's entertainment. Come summertime, café-dwellers in larger cities are treated to a barrage of live bands, street theatre and other busking troupes.

Cinema

Around 40 cinemas across the region show nightly *version originale* movies: look for the V.O. abbreviation after the title to be sure. By far the best cinema listings are on provence.angloinfo. com and riviera.angloinfo.com. The open-air cinema in Monaco and the buzz of the Cannes Film Festival are lots of fun.

Festivals

The festival season takes place over a short, but electrifying, two-month summer window. Given Provence's status as a multi-lingual destination, it's opera, jazz and fireworks rather than comedy or drama that are the key events, with some of the world's greatest performers arriving en masse to play in the warm night air. Pick of the jazz festivals

are Juan-les-Pins, Nice and Toulon, while the best opera can be found in Orange, Aix-en-Provence and Seillans.

Gay & lesbian

Provence, and in particular the Riviera, is an extremely tolerant corner of a nation at peace with its own sexuality. The scene extends to most of the region's best clubs, while every town has at least one gay bar, gay-friendly restaurant and often a hotel. Saunas exist in all major cities. Openly male cruising spots include Cap de Nice and St-Laurent d'Eze beach, while relaxed gay naturist beaches include La Batterie in Cannes, Mont Rose near Marseille and Le Llouquet near La Ciotat.

Opera, classical music & theatre

Aside from the rash of summer opera festivals, the winter seasons at the grand opera houses of Avignon, Marseille, Monaco, Nice, and Toulon are very well attended. Schedules, which are heavy on classical recital, are available online for each venue; all sell seats from €8 up to €100 or so. The theatre scene is much larger than both opera and classical music, and trickles down to village hall level, although shows may employ a humour and language not immediately accessible to a foreign audience.

Shopping

Foodie favourites

This is a region that takes its food and drink seriously. The following make good presents, or opt instead to keep them for yourself – dipping in makes for a vivid, immediate reminder of time spent in Provence. All items can be purchased at both markets and speciality food stores.

The mighty **olive** grows across all of Provence and along the coast. If you're visiting during November, keep an eye out for the newest crop of **oil**. Jars of *tapenade*, an olive, caper and anchovy paste, are airtight and travel well.

Anise-flavoured **pastis** is Provence's favourite aperitif. Big brands Ricard and 51 can be bought in French supermarkets. Look out too for smaller artisan blends, such as the herby **Henri Bardouin** (see page 235). If you're interested in seeing how the liquor is made, visit a distillery's premises.

Probably the most popular purchase for visitors to the South of France has to be **wine**. Shops offer excellent local selections, stocking AOCs like Bellet and Cassis that can be difficult to find outside of the region. Better yet is an amble around a vineyard and its cellars. There are numerous vineyards in every appellation, from **Châteauneuf-du-Pape** (see page 247) to **Bandol** (see page 196), who will ply clients with tastings and fun facts, under the

unspoken agreement that you'll be purchasing at least a bottle or two on your way out.

Both *fleur de sel*, mineral-rich sea salt, and black, red and white rice are grown and harvested in the Camargue. They can be purchased locally and in Arles. Other foodie finds include *navettes* (biscuits from Marseille, see page 208) and *calissons* (candied fruit sweets from Aix-en-Provence, see page 235).

Tasty they may be, but aged cheeses and *charcuterie* (cured meats) don't travel quite as well; there may also be restrictions on bringing non-packaged foods back to your home country. Be sure to check with your local authorities, as being forced to gift your holiday treasures to customs' officials is bound to dampen your travel experience.

Tip...

Most shops are open Monday to Friday from 1000-1230 & 1430-1930, and Saturday from 1000-1930. In tourist areas, such as resort towns along the coast, hours are extended during July and August. Annual holidays are usually taken during November or during the winter, except in Marseille, when shops tend to close during August. Like all of France, shops will be closed on 1 May, 1 November, Christmas Day and New Year's Day.

Marinated olives, sold by specialists at local produce markets.

Market know-how

Every Provençal town is home to at least one weekly market. Check out our favourites (see Five of the best Marseillaise markets, page 187 and Five of the best Provençal markets, page 229), ask around or simply follow the locals. Markets are by far the best place to pick up seasonal produce, normally sold directly by the farmer who's tended, hand-picked, bottled or cured it, as well as traditional Provençal souvenirs such as soaps or textiles. Most markets are open from around 0730-1230. The best stock sells out early, while the best bargains can often be had as the market draws to a close. Look out for the restaurants that flank the rows of stalls: these low-key spots usually buy directly from the market, serve the stall-holders year round (ensuring quality) and offer excellent value *plats du jour*.

Sunday market in L'Isle-sur-la-Sorgue.

Purely Provençal

Traditional, artisan-produced goods are synonymous with the region. Look out for kitchen items created from olive wood, such as large bowls, salad spoons and chopping boards. Intricately carved *santons*, or Nativity scene figurines, are also a local speciality. Textiles include regional linens, printed tablecloths and napkins. Marseille in particular was famed for its 19th-century hand-stitched bedspreads, and modern variations can be found at many markets today. Note that the quality of Provençal fabrics can swing wildly from exquisite to synthetic: don't be embarrassed to ask questions about your planned purchase.

Artists in Provence create fabulous, functional ceramics. Vallauris has a long history of firing up bright, chunky jugs, mugs and trays (ex-resident Picasso was a big fan), and the town's central street is lined with speciality boutiques. Tiny shops throughout the region carry vibrant pottery produced by talented locals: Nice's Old Town and Aix-en-Provence's rue Gaston de Saporta house some of the best. Delicate faïence pottery can be found throughout Haute-Provence, particularly in Moustiers-Ste-Marie and nearby. In Biot, artisans produce particular coloured glassware, renowned for its tiny bubbles.

As lavender bursts into bloom, the Lubéron hills glow an almost luminescent purple. The fragrant herb is sold in sachets, tinctures and distilled down to a potent essential oil. It's also used to perfume natural soaps, long a Marseille specialty, and other bath products. International retailer **L'Occitane** (see page 237) demonstrates techniques first-hand at their factory (and outlet shop) near Manosque.

One-of-a-kind finds

Provençal antiques markets attract shoppers from Italy and Paris. At Nice's **cours Saleya market** (see page 123), dealers hunt down 1950s furniture, Bakelite jewellery and vintage timepieces. **Forville** (see page 124) in Cannes is a haven for 19th-century walking sticks and 1960s shades. The sprawling market at **L'Isle-sur-la-Sorgue** (see page 250) is the region's biggest, its vendors packing early 20th-century posters and heavy walnut wardrobes alongside ancient maps and 1940s kitchen tins. Many towns and cities – L'Isle-sur-la-Sorgue, Marseille and Nice included – have a *quartier antique*, a neighbourhood where most of the shops sell antiques. With an expertise often passed down through families for generations, owners tend to price pieces higher than those you'll find at markets.

Cutting a fashionable figure

There's nowhere trendier than the Côte d'Azur in August. So it's no surprise that the clothes found in one-off boutiques and designer outlets along this coastal strip in particular are a fashion victim's dream. Pick up handcrafted *tropezienne* sandals (see page 152) in St-Tropez, or hand sewn floaty tops from *Rosalie de Montmartre* (see page 235) in Aix-en-Provence. In bigger cities like Marseille and Nice, look out for French brands agnès b, Kookai, Comptoir des Cotonniers, Repetto and the fabulous Antoine et Lili.

Bargain hunters would also do well to sift through the street markets: stalls in **Antibes** (see page 91) and **Aix-en-Provence** (page 235) stock treasures aplenty for those who have the dedication required to discover them.

Tip...

Many vineyards, wine shops and olive oil specialists can ship your purchases directly home for you for an additional fee. If you'd rather take them with you, packing them into your checked baggage if you're flying, they'll professionally swathe your bottles in bubble-wrap – just ask.

Top: Cours Saleya produce market, Nice.
Opposite page: Designer labels in St-Tropez.

Activities & tours

While many come to Provence to sip *pastis* and play *pétanque*, others revel in a region that boasts ski slopes, scuba dive spots and vineyards, all just an hour apart. From sipping rosé in the sun to driving a 2CV along a country road, here's a lowdown on how to get the most out of the region.

Adventure

Abseiling, parascending and whitewater rafting are popular activities in almost every corner of Provence. Most adrenalin junkies select the Haute Provence region as their base. This area is criss-crossed by *Via Ferrata*, the ancient iron stairways and rudimentary zip lines that were the trade routes of medieval Alpine commerce. The territory's rough diamond is the gaping Gorges du Verdon, the world's second-largest canyon. It's a hikers', climbers' and bungee-jumpers' dream. More sedate pursuits are popular elsewhere inland and all along the coast, such as balloon rides, river canoeing, sea kayaking and birdwatching. Instruction on the majority of tours listed in this book is bilingual.

Boating

Shimmering off the coast are a dozen tranquil islands, namely the Iles de Lérins near Cannes, Embiez, Bendor and Ile Verte near Bandol, the giant Iles d'Hyères chain near Le Lavandou and the Frioul archipelago near Marseille. Day trips run to all of them, and many harbours have small 6hp runabouts that can be hired without a license. Many harbour establishments run two-day speedboat courses in English and in French, should you wish to learn the skills necessary for a meatier craft. The larger beaches between Hyères and Cannes have sailing dinghies, normally Sunfish and Hobie Cats, to rent by the hour. Many 8-12 m yachts are available for a week's hire along the coast. Googling the words *bateau location Antibes* or *bateau location Porquerolles* is the best way to find one: searching for the same term in English will land you with a Roman Abramovich standard superyacht.

Children

France is an enormously family-friendly nation and children are welcome anywhere. Hence most of its

activities, from scuba diving in Le Lavandou to canoeing through the marshy Camargue, are focused on family fun, rather than packing off the kids for the day. Most beaches are sandy, spacious and patrolled by lifeguards, with pedalos and sea kayaks available for hire. The region's botanical gardens, stately homes and walking trails should also appeal to little ones. Activities directed solely for children include the half-dozen water parks and (extremely tame) theme parks spread along the coast.

Cultural tours

Many of the world's most famous artists, writers and architects, not to mention their wealthy patrons, made Provence their home. Their cultural legacy, ranging from museums to elegant mansions, is immense. It's rather surprising that only a handful of private companies ply tours around the residences, galleries and haunts of the likes of Picasso,

Cocteau and Somerset Maugham. Instead, it's local tourist offices that run walking tours of their neighbourhood hero – such as Cézanne in Aix-en-Provence – and offer maps so you can follow the masters' trails yourself. This guidebook offers information for great DIY tours of the region's galleries, artists' residences and architectural gems.

Cycling & driving

Even if you don't have your own vehicle renting anything from a Ferrari to a vintage 2CV, scooter or mountain bike is a cinch. Although we've listed five superb drives on the Riviera (see page 112), the D41, N98 and Corniche des Maures, in the Hyères to St-Tropez chapter, also really stick out, whether on four wheels or two. In this land of the Tour de France, most drivers are extremely courteous to cyclists, and the bike paths and quiet country roads are a delight, especially outside August. On Sunday mornings, bikes literally take over Provence's highways. The main pilgrimages for cyclists are the Col d'Eze near Nice, the Col de Turini near Sospel and the harrowing *hors catégorie* climb of Mont Ventoux north of Gordes, all regular ascents on *le tour*. Bike shops are common in cities, but are seldom seen in the under-populated interior.

Diving

The sub-aqua infrastructure across the region is world-class. Many dive schools or hire joints are bilingual, and most have year-round boats running to the area's islands, peninsulas, drop-offs and wrecks. The warm azure waters are perfect for snorkelers too. Inexpensive masks are available everywhere, with pan-Provence branches of Decathlon offering the best deals. Pick of the

undersea spots are any of the islands (some of which have nature trails that lead under the waves) or off any of the coastal trails, which run essentially from Marseille to the Italian border.

Food & drink

Most culinary tours through Provence involve a Michelin guide and the addition of several kilos to your waistline. This regime works excellently, as many of the region's restaurants are world renowned, purveying specific local cuisines ranging from classic French to Niçois, Provençal and Marseillaise. For those who want to delve deeper there are two broad forms of cooking course. Fairly inexpensive half-day cooking classes take place along much of the coast and normally concentrate on local cuisine. Inland, there are several

professional – and very pricey – week-long lessons, including the Patricia Wells course near Vaison-la-Romaine and René Bérard's cooking school near Cadière d'Azur. There are literally hundreds of excellent wine *domaines* across the region, covering around ten AOC regions, yet very few private wine tours. Instead, the common way to visit the vineyards is simply to call ahead, then pitch up for a (most commonly bilingual) free tour and tasting in exchange for the purchase of a few bottles. Throughout this guide, we've detailed vineyards that stand out in terms of friendliness or quality.

Hiking

Provence is a walker's dream. Well-signed trails link every hilltop town and every coastal village, through lavender-filled mountains or along sandy shores. Better still, every Tourist Information office has a print out of all the local walking routes, which often run to surrounding villages, a ruin or lake. The dozen Rando06 (randoxygene.org) guides given out for free in every office in the Alpes-Maritimes region are highly professional. Tour guides for hardened hikers are listed throughout the chapters, although serious solo walkers can follow the three Grande Randonnée (ffrandonnee.fr) routes that loop through Provence: the GR4 starts in Grasse, the GR9 runs from St-Tropez into the Massif des Maures, and the GR52 from Menton to the Mercantour National Park.

Skiing

The four resorts of Auron, Isola 2000, La Foux d'Allos and Valberg offer excellent skiing around 90 minutes from the coast. Ski buses connect them with Nice airport and bus station each morning: tickets cost €1 each way. Each resort is set up for family-friendly day skiing, with inexpensive equipment hire and hotels, plus kids' slopes and toboggan runs. In summer these resorts become popular climbing, mountain biking and hiking centres, as their individual websites will explain.

Above: Bellet wines, Chateau de Crémat.
Opposite page: Cycling in the Lubéron, Gordes.

Wellbeing

Aix-en-Provence and Digne-les-Bains boast communal bubbly mineral water baths, which have been used since Roman times. Sadly this experience is unique to these towns. Wellbeing along the coast comes in the form of trendy, friendly spas, which offer massage, pedicures and exfoliation packages, and often swimming pool and sauna access. Pseudo-Arabian *hammams* are a more recent and equally welcome introduction: Marseille has several, including Bastide des Bains (bastide-des-bains.com) by the port.

Contents

The port of Monaco.

Introduction

What to see in...

...one day
A mix of art, beaches, coastal towns and hilltop hideaways make a great day's mix. Starting from **Nice**, cruise the **cours Saleya** and **promenade des Anglais**, then catch a fish lunch near **Cocteau's chapel in Villefranche**. Spend the afternoon at a **beach on Cap Ferrat** or take a stroll up in medieval **Eze**. Further west, try breakfast at **Cannes' Forville market**, lunch near the **Picasso museum in Antibes** or a sunset dinner in **Juan-les-Pins**.

The French Riviera is the most visited, as well as the most action-packed, area in the whole of Provence. Its coast is lined with fabulous beaches, while its sun-kissed seaside and historic hill towns have been showered with more culture than many European capitals. Even understated Nice, the capital of the Riviera, has the greatest concentration of museums outside Paris.

Initial Roman colonisation can be relived first hand in the ruined amphitheatre of Cimiez, among the vineyards of Bellet and in the columns and aqueducts around the lofty redoubts of Vence and St-Paul. In the late 19th century, a train line linked Europe's aristocratic *bons viveurs* to the newly built casino in Monaco and belle époque hotels in Cannes. Artists like Picasso, Matisse, Dufy and Chagall arrived decades later, drawn by the magnificent light and *joie de vivre* spirit in the coastal resorts of Antibes, Menton and Villefranche. Post-war, each one sought solace among the magnificent medieval villages set back from the coast: Mougins, Haut-de-Cagnes and Vallauris. Visitors are now gifted with an eyewitness legacy to those glamorous days gone by, ranging from stately homes and world-class art museums to the heaven-sent coastline and picture-postcard interior that inspired it all. Best of all, the entire Riviera is nurtured by a microclimate that promises mild, sunny winters and summer beach scenes lapped by a translucent sea.

...a weekend or more
Cruise the **museums, restaurants and bars** of buzzy **Nice, Cannes** or **Antibes** for a night or two, then pick a more tranquil **hill village** like **Mougins** or **St-Paul**, or a **belle époque resort** such as **Menton** or **Beaulieu** to rest up and relax.

Sunset on Cap d'Ail.

Nice

Nice is justly described as the Queen of the Riviera. The city is blessed with the 4-km-long promenade des Anglais, which runs along the sea. Although it boasts a medieval history and a colourful period of Italian reign, Nice became the tourism capital of the Côte d'Azur at the turn of the 20th century, when Europe's nobility followed Queen Victoria on her long winter vacations in the upmarket suburb of Cimiez. Artists including Matisse and Chagall soon succeeded on to this exclusive stage. Nowadays holidaymakers from the world over pour on to trains, planes and ferries to arrive in the French Riviera's most vibrant gateway.

Nice Old Town.

Essentials

❶ Getting around Walking is a cinch. The promenade des Anglais, place Masséna, the Old Town and many of the shopping streets are pedestrianized. The no 15 bus to Cimiez leaves from rue Sasha Guitry, by Galeries Lafayette (see page 123). Bus tickets can be bought from electronic kiosks at each stop for €1 per journey. Taxis can be ordered via a multi-lingual hotline (T04 93 13 78 78) or picked up at ranks outside the Grand Hotel Aston, Le Méridien, place d'Ile de Beauté in Nice Port, or at other locations throughout the city.

❷ Train station Nice-Ville train station, 3 avenue Thiers, sncf.fr. Recommended for journeys west to Antibes and Cannes. Linked with the bus station by Nice's single tram line (tickets €1 from electronic kiosk).

❸ Bus station Gare Routière, 5 boulevard Jean Jaurès, T04 93 85 61 81. For the **Train des Pignes** (see page 165) into the mountains, the privately run **Chemins de Fer de Provence** (4 rue Alfred Binet, T04 97 03 80 80, trainprovence.com) is a 10-minute walk north of Nice-Ville station.

❽ ATMs Found on most streets in the newer part of town. Old Town locations include place Rossetti, boulevard Jean Jaurès and the Opera house.

⊕ Hospital Hôpital St Roch, 5 rue Pierre Dévoluy, T04 92 03 33 33, chu-nice.fr.

✛ Pharmacy Pharmacie de Paris, 60 avenue Jean Médecin, T04 93 85 12 81.

✎ Post office 23 avenue Thiers (train station), 2 rue Louis Gassin (Old Town), 6 quai Papacino (Port).

❶ Tourist information office 5 promenade des Anglais, daily June-September 0900-2000, October-May 0900-1800; 3 avenue Thiers, June-September Monday-Saturday 0800-2000, Sunday 0900-1900, October-May Monday-Saturday 0800-1900, Sunday 1000-1700; both T08 92 70 74 07, nicetourisme.com.

Nice Vieille Ville

The pastel hues and lavender-blue shutters that colour the Old Town's zigzag streets are a heady reminder of Nice's Italian connections. Those making a *passeggiata* (leisurely stroll) along these narrow lanes may notice other influences from across the border, like local dialect *Nissart*, a Ligurian tongue, shouted from window to window as you wander beneath.

Decades ago guidebooks warned against visiting this area after dark, it being generally perceived as a warren of prostitutes, drug dealers and vice. These seedy elements have slowly been replaced by one-off boutiques and scores of galleries. The best of these art studios line **rue Droite**, which bisects the old city from north to south. Also along this pretty street is the **Palais Lascaris** (15 rue Droite, Wed-Mon 1000-1800, free), one of a dozen palatial dwellings that once belonged to local nobles, and the only one open to the public. Inside the restored mansion are frescoes, statuary and 17th century objets d'art. .

Marking the border between the Old Town and the promenade des Anglais is the venerable **cours Saleya**. This avenue of ostentatious mansions starts with the gold façade of Matisse's former home at the eastern end. Heading west to the flower market (Tue-Sun 0730-1800) shoppers pass through a line of fruit and vegetable stalls, all covered with stripy awnings (Tue-Sun 0800-1300). At lunch these picture-perfect market pitches give way to the *al fresco* tables of the surrounding restaurants, which in turn become aperitif spots in the evening, and dining terraces at night. This entire street is cleaned with seawater at dawn before the shop-eat-drink-stroll cycle revolves once again.

Promenade des Anglais & beach

The **promenade des Anglais** is the wide esplanade that runs along the entire length of Nice's pebbly beach. The view from the eastern end, over the 4 km of beaches, hotels, restaurants and mountains on the horizon, formed the backdrop for paintings

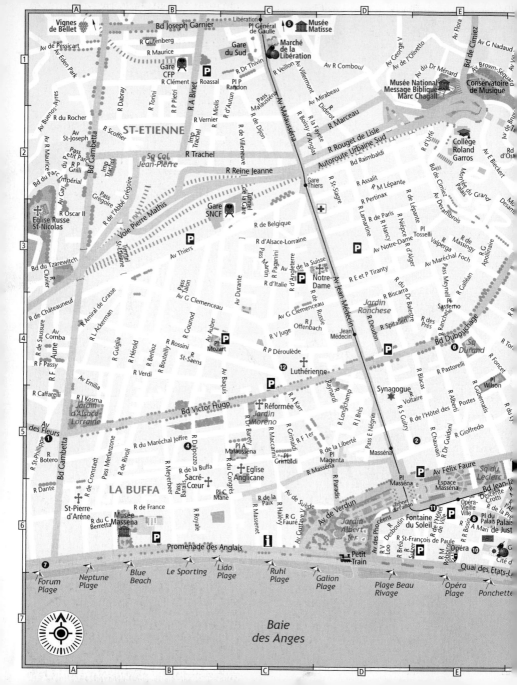

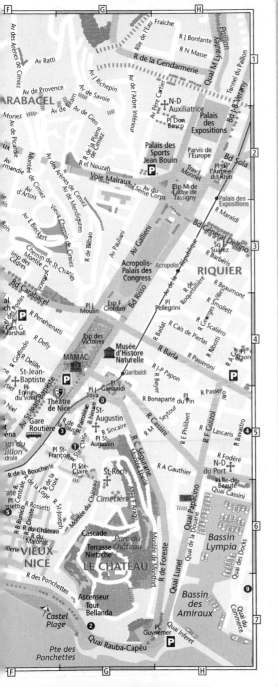

Nice listings

① Sleeping
1 Hi Hotel *3 avenue des Fleurs* A5
2 Hôtel Suisse *5 quai Rauba Capéu* G7
3 Hôtel Villa La Tour *4 rue de la Tour* F5
4 Hôtel Windsor *11 rue Dalpozzo* B5
5 Villa St-Exupéry *22 avenue Gravier* C1

① Eating & drinking
1 Bar de la Bourse *rue Pairolière* G5
2 Brasserie Flo *2 rue Sacha Guitry* E5
3 Café du Turin *5 place Garibaldi* G5
4 Chez Pipo *13 rue Bavastro* H5
5 Fennochio *2 place Rossett* F6
6 Flaveur *25b rue Gubernatis* E4
7 Hi-Beach *47 promenade des Anglais* A6
8 La Merenda *4 rue Raoul Bosio* E6
9 La Tartane *44 boulevard de Stalingrad* H7
10 La Voglia *2 rue St-François de Paule* E6
11 L'Univers de Christian Plumail
   54 boulevard Jean Jaurès E6
12 Les Viviers *22 rue Alphonse Karr* C4

Promenade des Anglais and city beach, Nice.

by Matisse and Dufy, both of whom lived nearby. On the beach below is **Castel Plage**, the most showy of Nice's waterfront clubs, where celebs like Emma Watson and local resident Elton John have been known to hang out. Continuing west along the perimeter of the Old Town are several **Vélo Bleu** bike stands and a rollerblade rental store (see page 125). Those hoping to emulate the 'bladers, bikers and occasional poseurs who gather on the Promenade daily can get kitted out here. Also in this zone are the **Galerie de la Marine** and the **Galerie des Ponchettes** (59 & 77 quai des Etats Unis, Tue-Sun 1000-1800), two small fine art galleries across from the beach.

Heading further west the Promenade widens and becomes palm-lined. A volley of beach clubs appear below, the best of which are the low-key **Opéra Plage**, family-friendly **Blue Beach** and ultra-cool **Hi Beach** (see page 119). Each has private sunbeds, waiter service and sun-kissed holidaymakers, all tanning in neat rows. To the north is Nice's rococo **Opéra** (Opera House, see page 122), facing majestically out to sea. Further along one passes the **Palais de la Méditerranée** and the **Negresco**, both landmark hotels and great

places for a swanky cocktail. The latter played host to The Beatles in 1965 shortly after they received MBEs from the Queen – they stood on the balcony waving at fans below. The esplanade and cycle tracks continue down to the airport, which marks the western end of the Prom'.

Musée Masséna

65 rue de France, gardens entrance on promenade des Anglais by the Negresco, T04 93 91 19 10.
Wed-Mon 1000-1800. Free.
Map: Nice, B6, p76.

Formerly a neoclassical palace, then a local museum, the Musée Masséna reopened in 2008 as an asset-rich historical study of Nice. The exhibits are bathed in glorious sunlight – the mansion overlooks the sea and Promenade – not to mention varied and fun. The 1920s era is covered by newspaper accounts of parties of the time, menus from dinner dances, and street plans of which buildings were owned by which particular Russian Count or American millionaire. Paintings of Nice from a bygone age and artefacts from the city's famed Carnaval (see page 46) illuminate other periods.

Cimiez

A distinctly bourgeois *quartier*, Cimiez is famed for its Matisse and Chagall museums. The suburb's stock of art deco mansions lies juxtaposed with Nice's original Roman settlement, the ruins of which include paved streets and an amphitheatre; the latter becomes a 2000-year-old stage at Nice's annual jazz festival (see page 48). The city's ancient history is brought to life at the **Musée Archéologique de Nice-Cimiez** (Wed-Mon 1000-1800, T04 93 81 59 57, musee-archeologique-nice.org, €3, €1.50 under 18s) in the same leafy park as the Matisse museum.

Musée Matisse

164 av des Arènes de Cimiez, T04 93 81 08 08, musee-matisse-nice.org.
Wed-Mon 1000-1800. Free.
Map: Nice, C1, p76.

Originally from the Calais region, Matisse had a long-term love affair with Nice. A quote on the wall of this Italianate villa, which serves as France's national Matisse museum, sums up his reason why: "When I opened my window and thought how I was going to have to have the light before my eyes every day, I couldn't believe my luck." Exhibits cover his early Parisian period up to his productive last years in the early 1950s when he lived in the fabulous Palais Regina building, a few minutes' walk west of the museum. Of note are his kaleidoscope models for his masterpiece, the *Chapelle du Rosaire* in Vence (see page 100).

Musée Matisse, Cimiez, Nice.

Tip...

Locals take the tram two stops north of Nice's train station to shop at the **Libération fruit and vegetable market** (Tue-Sun 0700-1230). Not only does it have a huge organic (or *biologique*) section, it's packed with fine French cheeses, fresh fish and flowers, and features several inexpensive restaurants, making for a great morning out.

Musée National Message Biblique Marc Chagall

Av Docteur Ménard, T04 93 53 87 31, musee-chagall.fr.
Wed-Mon, May-Oct 1000-1800, Nov-Apr 1000-1700. €9.50, €7.50 under 18s, EU citizens under 26 free.
Map: Nice, E1, p76.

Russian-born Marc Chagall was a creative and playful artist. In the words of Picasso: "When Matisse dies Chagall will be the only painter left who understands what colour really is." The museum's permanent collection is devoted to biblical themes, a subject the artist returned to frequently throughout his life. The museum is particularly unique as it was the first in France to be designed by a living artist: an artistic vessel created to display a specific set of artworks. The powerful, vibrant paintings are exhibited exactly as Chagall planned to have you see them.

Musée d'Art Moderne et d'Art Contemporain

Promenade des Arts, T04 97 13 42 01, mamac-nice.org.
Tue-Sun 1000-1800. Free.
Map: Nice, G4, p76.

The MAMAC, as it's affectionately known, is a light-filled steel and glass edifice, surprisingly in harmony with the 300-year-old buildings of place Garibaldi and the Old Town immediately south. The permanent collection chronicles the history of Pop Art and French Modern Art. Andy Warhol is represented (not least in his amusing rejection letters from the New York Museum of Modern Art), as is Robert Indiana (LOVE imagery) and Roy Lichtenstein (of cartoon art fame). The collections

What the locals say

If you had €10 to spend in a day, what would you do with it?
Patrick Take a Vélo Bleu (see page 125) bike down the promendae.
Laurence You need a degree in mathematics to take a Vélo Bleu, just rent one from Roller Station (see page 125) instead.

What is the weirdest thing a tourist has ever asked you?
Patrick Where is the castle!
Laurence Where is Monaco please!

Where would you take a friend for dinner?
Patrick Locally, Acchiardo (38 rue Droite, T04 93 85 51 16) or, the best place on the coast, La Cabane (167 promenade Flots Bleus, T04 93 07 07 70) in St-Laurent du Var near Nice, where airplanes land over your head.
Laurence Acchiardo. Or, if you have a lot of money, La Petite Maison (11 rue St François de Paule, T04 93 92 59 59).

If you could spend a weekend anywhere in Provence, where would it be?
Patrick Western Provence is no good, people have a strange mentality. Stay in Vieux Nice.
Laurence Gordes (see page 225), the most beautiful village in Provence.

What advice would you give to anyone who wants to buy an apartment in Nice?
Patrick Come and see us!
Laurence Avoid summer – the whole of France is on holiday.

Patrick Macanda and Laurence Manini, brother and sister owners of real estate agency Palais Immobilier, 23 rue de la Préfecture, Nice.

The Vineyards of Bellet

A 10-minute drive north of Nice airport is AOC Bellet (vinsdebellet.com), one of France's smallest prestige wine *appellations*. The one-off combination of altitude, Mediterranean breezes, winter snow and summer sunshine lends a unique flavour to the product. But the precipitous terrain and necessity of handpicking grapes means that the wine graces only a few top Riviera restaurant tables, as well as the excellent Cave Bianchi (7 rue Raoul Bosio) and Cave Caprioglio (see page 123) wine shops in Nice Old Town. Wine-tasting is possible at most of the *domaines* as long as you call in advance. Particularly welcoming are Château de Crémat (T04 92 15 12 15, chateau-cremat.com) and Clos St-Vincent (T04 92 15 12 69, clos-st-vincent.fr).

of the so-called Nice school of art include Yves Klein and Niki de Saint Phalle, each of whom have a dedicated room; the former includes a video installation of Klein shocking Paris society by daubing naked ladies with paint, while Saint Phalle's is filled with an army of mirror-covered humanoids. The museum is noted for its strong temporary exhibitions that take up the entire first floor: recent highlights have included Richard Long and Arman.

Port & Colline du Château

Château Park.
Daily Apr-Aug 0800-2000, Sep 0800-1900, Oct-Mar 0800-1800. Free.

Nice's elegant Port is home to a historic fishing fleet and more than a few floating gin palaces. Ringed by great restaurants, it's a great place to stroll and generally just hang about on a sunny day. East past the Corsica Ferries terminal, a path descends from the road, leading to a score of sandy coves and grottos on the **Cap de Nice**. Also near the Port is the **Quartier des Antiquaires** (most shops open Tue-Sat), hemmed in by rue Foresta to the west and rue Cassini to the north. Over 100 antique shops trade 1950s Milanese furniture, medieval daggers, vintage musical instruments and contemporary art. The tiny **Marché aux Puces** flea market (Tue-Sun) on place Robilante is less pricey.

Towering above, the **Colline du Château** separates the Port from the Old Town. Formerly the defensive bastion of Nice, a cannon still fires off from the top at midday – be aware, it's deafening if you're nearby. Now the Colline is where locals come to play *pétanque*, read books, jam on guitars and let their children run free in the state-of-the-art playground. The clutch of cafés at the top have cracking views and are a just reward for the climb up from either the Port or the three staircases dotted around the Old Town. Of interest are the flamboyant graves in the **Christian and Jewish cemeteries**: only the rich and powerful made it up here.

Russian Church

Av Nicolas II, off bd Tzarevitch, T04 93 96 88 02, acor-nice.com.
Mon-Sat 0915-1200, 1430-1730, Sun 1430-1730. €3. Map: Nice, A3, p76.

During the late 19th and early 20th centuries, Russian migrants were as common on the Riviera as they are today. One of their legacies is this onion-topped cathedral, dazzlingly high from the outside, intoxicatingly beautiful – and hazy with incense – on the inside. No expense was spared during its construction; the walls are covered with fine frescoes, tiles from Florence and icons from distant Moscow. The leafy grounds hum with Russian voices, descendants of the White Russians who patronised the church after its construction in 1912, mixed with more recent arrivals.

Top: Nice port.
Above: Russian Church, Nice.

Cannes, Grasse & Mougins

British aristocrat Lord Brougham stumbled across sunny Cannes in 1835: the first step of the town's transformation from sleepy fishing village to seaside centre for unashamed fun. The coolest of the cool kept coming, although these days the aristocracy consists of rich Russians shopping on the rue d'Antibes and movie stars in shameless self-promotion mode during the famed Film Festival (see page 47). (In the words of one wag: "Cannes is 10,000 people looking for 10 people who really count.") Its hilltop neighbours, Mougins and Mouans-Sartoux, flipped defensive bastions into rich artist residencies, while hilltop Grasse, the world capital of the perfume industry, has long had a nose for success.

La Croisette

La Croisette is Cannes in a nutshell. A dream mile of palm trees and ostentatious hotels, it's at once playful and elegantly over the top. Those promenading along the seafront are a mirror of the average visitor: doggy-carrying Parisiennes stride alongside swaggering Russians, stately Brits and the odd lost backpacker, all overtaken by holidaying Americans on a morning powerwalk. Cannes' premier 'sight' doesn't disappoint.

All are welcome for a cocktail at any of the majestic hotels along the strip, including the **Martinez** (see page 114) at no 73 and the **Carlton** at no 58. The **beach bars** just south of this main drag are more popular still and constitute a day of eating, relaxing *and* sightseeing for most tourists based in town. Expect to pay around €20/day for a sun-lounger and prime patch of sandy real estate at any of these private *plages*. Great **free beaches** exist at **Palm Beach** at the eastern end of the Croisette, and at **Plage du Midi**, west of the town centre.

The lumbering **Palais des Festivals** marks the Croisette's western end. Rebuilt in 1982 and given facelifts – not the first seen in Cannes – in both 1999 and 2009, it's monumentally ugly. But the building, complete with casino and nightclub, plays host to a volley of high-earning conventions from the Tax Free World Exhibition to the Film Festival, and is the lifeblood of Cannes' hospitality industry. Visitors can take in the photo portraits of Hollywood's A-list and place their hands in the cement alongside the imprints of George Clooney and gang.

Vieux Port & Le Suquet

Filled with fishing boats together with a line of mega-yachts, the picturesque Old Port is also the place to catch a ferry to the **Iles de Lérins** (see page 94). Backing on to it is the tree-dappled **allée de la Liberté**, home to a carousel, a *pétanque* ground and an antiques (Sat) and flower market.

Essentials

Getting around Walking is the best way to get around each of these towns. For transfers by taxi try Cannes' Allo Taxi, T08 90 71 22 27.

Train station Cannes train station (rue Jean Jaurès, T04 93 99 50 50) is a few blocks inland from La Croisette. Trains run to Nice, Monaco and all stops in between every 30 minutes and up to Grasse and Mouans-Sartoux every hour.

Bus station Next door to Cannes train station, T04 93 36 37 37, regular routes include Grasse (30 mins) and Mougins (15 mins); place Buanderie, Grasse, T04 93 36 37 37, serves Mougins and the surrounding area. A shuttle bus links Grasse train station with the town centre, or it's a kilometre uphill hike.

Hospital Hôpital Les Broussailles, 13 avenue des Broussailles, Cannes, T04 93 69 70 00, ch-cannes.fr.

Pharmacy Pharmacie Centrale, 21 rue Félix Faure, Cannes, T04 92 59 00 19.

Post office 11 square Mérimée by the Palais des Festivals, Cannes; 9 boulevard Fragonard, Grasse.

Tourist information offices Palais des Festivals, 1 boulevard la Croisette, Cannes, T04 92 99 84 22, cannes.com, daily 0900-1900; Cannes train station T04 93 39 40 19; 18 boulevard Georges Courteline, Mougins, T04 93 75 87 67, mougins-coteazur.org, July & August Daily 0900-1900, September-June Monday-Friday 0900-1730, Saturday 0900-1700; 22 cours Honoré Cresp, Grasse, T04 93 36 66 66, grasse.fr, July-mid September Monday-Saturday 0900-1900, Sunday 0900-1300 & 1400-1800, mid September-June Monday-Saturday 0900-1230 & 1400-1800.

Above: Forville Antiques Market, Cannes.
Opposite page: La Croisette, Cannes.

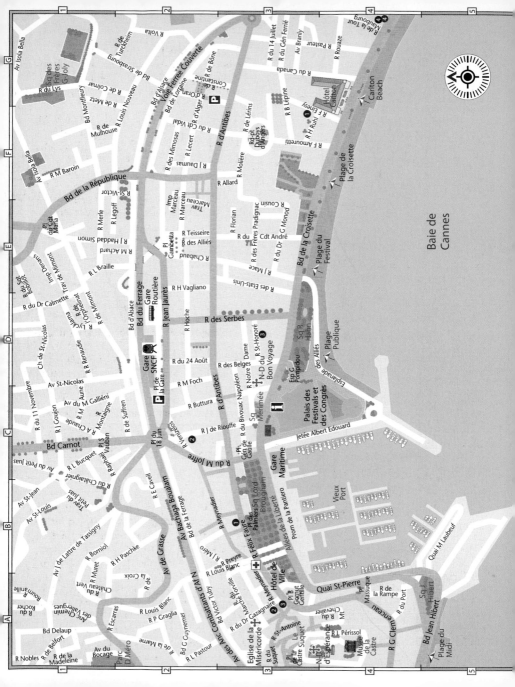

Cannes listings

Dawn on La Croisette, Cannes.

> 66
> So where's the
> Cannes Film
> Festival being
> held this year?
> 99
>
> *Christina*
> *Aguilera, actress*
> *and singer*

Tumbling down the hill from above is **Le Suquet**, the old town of Cannes, a warren of tiny restaurants, antique shops and real Provençal life. A climb to the park at the top is rewarded by an unparalleled view over the Old Port to the Cap d'Antibes and beyond. Also up here is the **Musée de la Castre** (place de la Castre, T04 93 38 55 26, Jul-Aug daily 1000-1900, Apr-Jun & Sep Tue-Sun 1000-1300 & 1400-1800, Oct-Mar Tue-Sun 1000-1300 & 1400-1700, €3.20, €2 under 25s), an ethnographic museum containing primitive art, statues and utensils, collected by explorers in the 19th century. The adjoining **Chapelle Ste-Anne** has a 12th-century viewing tower (a heady 109 steps) and an exceptional collection of musical instruments from all over the world.

Mouans-Sartoux

On the rail line between Cannes and Grasse, medieval Mouans-Sartoux is home to the 16th-century **Château de Mouans**. The castle and grounds were reinvented on cultural, rather than defensive, lines in 1990 as the **Espace de l'Art Concret** (T04 93 75 71 50, espacedelartconcret.fr, Jul-Aug daily 1100-1900, Sep-Jun Wed-Sun 1200-1800, free), a modern art museum with a glowing reputation. Their well-endowed Donation Albers-Honegger collection includes furniture, art and sculpture from the likes of Andy Warhol and Jesus Rafael Soto.

Mougins

Picture-perfect Mougins was an obligatory stop on the Riviera artist trail. Most of the greats, including Man Ray, Fernand Léger and Jean Cocteau lived here at one time or another. Picasso left an early mark in the recently defunct Hôtel les Muscadins by painting a mural on his bedroom wall. The owner, who no doubt kicked himself later, angrily whitewashed over the best efforts of his Spanish guest. Shots of Picasso by his friend André Villers, along with portraits from other photographers including Robert Doisneau and Edward Quinn, can be found in the **Musée de la Photographie André Villers** (Porte Sarrazine, T04 93 75 85 67, daily Jul-Sep 1000-2000, Oct & Dec-Jun 1000-1800, closed Nov, free), accommodated in a medieval townhouse in the village centre.

Serious gastronomy is another string in Mougins' bow. Celebrity chefs Alain Ducasse, Roger Vergé and Alain Llorca (all of whom once worked their magic at the **Moulins de Mougin**, see page 119) drew in restaurateurs and consummate diners alike, turning Mougins into the Côte d'Azur's culinary capital. The yearly **Etoiles de Mougins** (see page 49) is a fabulously accessible event each September: foodie pilgrims can watch the greats at work, and eat boatloads of their offerings afterwards.

Grasse

The weight of history hanging over Grasse makes the hillside town feel like a wise grandfather compared to coastal cool kid Cannes. And it certainly has a lot of knowledge to impart. The town is littered with 14th-century fountains and 16th-century towers, radiating out from the pavement cafés of picturesque **place aux Aires**, each one well marked on the free town maps pinned to the city walls and available – in paper form – from the **Tourist Office** (see page 83). Through winding alleys and ochre façades is the town's principal sight, the Romanesque **Cathédrale Notre-Dame-du-Puy** (free). This soaring edifice boasts a haunting trio of Rubens paintings on the right-hand wall.

Those who have seen the film *Perfume* will be aware that Grasse built its fortunes on scent. In the words of *Time* magazine: "Grasse is to fragrance what Wall Street is to finance." Today busloads of sightseers trip around the excellent **free museums** of **Fragonard** (20 bd Fragonard, T04 93 36 44 65, fragonard.com, daily 0900-1800) and **Molinard** (60 bd Victor Hugo, T04 92 42 33 11, molinard.com, Apr-Sep daily 0900-1830, Oct-Mar Mon-Sat 0900-1200 & 1400-1800) for a sniff of perfume and the chance to purchase soaps, scents and gift boxes at factory prices. But perfume alone cannot mask Grasse's seedy side: poorer North African immigrants live in the tatty back streets while wealthier ex-locals have boxed themselves off in the surrounding countryside.

International Perfume Museum

2 bd du Jeu de Ballon, T04 97 05 58 00, museesdegrasse.com.
Jun-Sep daily 1000-1900 (Thu until 2100), Oct-May Wed-Mon 1100-1800. €3, €1.50 under 25s, under 18s free.

This space reopened in late 2008 as a living, breathing history of the perfume industry, by way of India and Arabia all the way to London and Paris. Scent is traced through the ages as a means of trade, communication, medicine and seduction. Older children will be amused by the touchy-feely-smelly games, while little ones can content themselves in the play area.

Villa Jean-Honoré Fragonard

23 bd Fragonard, T04 93 36 01 61, museesdegrasse.com.
Jun-Sep daily 1000-1900, Oct-May Wed-Mon 1100-1800. Free.

As most visitors sniff their way around the town centre, this elegant Provençal villa, ringed by gardens dotted with modern sculpture and sea views, is left curiously tourist-free. After many of his well-to-do pals lost their heads in the revolution, artist Jean-Honoré Fragonard decamped here in 1790. An informative handout takes visitors on a tour of the painted panel salons, trompe l'œil staircase, French country scenes and portraits of *Grassois* nobles.

The Molinard Perfumery, Grasse.

Walking on Ile St-Honorat

Essentials

Getting there
Planaria (T04 92 98 71 38, cannes-ilesdelerins.com) runs the sole service (€12 return) from the western end of Cannes harbour to Ile St-Honorat. It departs 10 times daily in summer, seven times daily in winter.

Eating As picnic spots go, St Honorat is unsurpassed. A selection of cheese and ham from Cannes' **Marché Forville** (see page 124) is recommended over the island's sole eatery, the chic but pricey restaurant **La Tonnelle** (T04 92 99 18 07).

When the hermit St Honoratus hopped off his boat in AD 410, he had this mini-Eden and its Thai-style waters all to himself. But, like any speck of paradise, word spread fast. A decade later Honoratus was joined by a burgeoning monastic fraternity whose ilk included St Patrick. Barring the odd Saracen raid, a community of monks has lived here ever since.

Ferry services to Ile St-Honorat have been curtailed in recent years lest hordes of holidaymakers bare their bits and spoil the silence. The visitors that do arrive disembark at the island's southern harbour. Little more than a jetty, it stands in stark, serene contrast with the plastic-fantastic rows of motor yachts a kilometre across the water in Cannes. It's best to note down the times for the return ferries (normally 1800 in summer, 1700 in winter): with no place to stay on the island, being trapped in paradise is an option only for the converted.

From the port, a glimpse down to the blue sea on St Honorat's southern shore lends a sense of scale to the skinny, mile-long island. Heading east for a clockwise tour around, keep the Bahama-blue ribbon of water on your left, and your nostrils on alert for not-so-subtle wafts of scented air: chestnut and honey prevail on this shady northern strip of the walk.

The first point of interest is the crumbling arch and dome of the waterside **Chapelle St-Cyprien**, one of half a dozen ruined religious sites on the island. An intact Virgin Mary on top casts a weary eye over the booby sun-seekers on **Ile Ste-Marguerite** (see page 94), St-Honorat's loose cousin just across the water. Heading further up on the right are several vineyards (Syrah, Pinot Noir, Mourvèdre and Chardonnay) and rows of olives, which the monks cultivate and sell in their abbey shop.

Towards the end of the island pines overhang the path up to the abandoned **Chapelle La Trinité**. Through a thicket is a furnace meaty enough to heat a cannonball to a cherry-red temperature in 30 minutes flat. In Napoleonic times enough of these contraptions were placed over the Iles de Lérins to control the approaches to the Riviera coastline. If one of these fireballs connected with the powder keg of an invading vessel, the whole boat would erupt.

A series of little bays and patches of gravelly sand mark St Honorat's eastern extremity. Snorkelling here is among the best on the entire Riviera, with stony outcrops and waves breaking over submerged reefs marking the best spots. Strong swimmers can make for the uninhabited **Ile St-Féréol**, bobbing 150 m off the coast.

Walking westwards, the horizon is dominated by an evocative sight only visible from the island's southern shores: a **fortified monastery** (free) pokes four storeys skyward, perched on its own rocky plinth. An open-air courtyard floods natural light into the abandoned edifice. Up a spooky steep stairway, past various cloisters, work rooms and dormitories, is a stupendous roof terrace overlooking the golden-stone abbey, with its black and white cassocked monks. A translucent sea and the Alpes-Maritimes mountains, which are snow-capped from October to May, lie beyond.

Heading back out at ground level, the working abbey complex is fronted by a parade-ground line of palms, under which rows of lavender grow. These fragrant plants provide the scented honey and a host of lavender products (soap, oil, liqueurs) found in the monastery shop (T04 92 99 54 30, abbayedelerins.com, daily 0900-1230, 1330-1630); rows of pricey island wines, olive oil, almond pâté and jams are also sold. The monks' private domain is down a gated pathway, strewn with bougainvillea and wild geraniums.

From the monastery a track bisects the island back to the ferry terminal past several hectares of Chardonnay vineyards. A full circumnavigation of the island takes in another 30 minutes of coastal path and the rockier, quieter western extreme of the island, which ends with another cannonball heater and the ruins of the **Chapelle St-Caprais**.

Antibes & around

From its roots as a Greek trading post, Antibes, or Antipolis as it was known in antiquity, has long been familiar with foreigners. Groups of young thrill-seekers hit neighbouring Juan-les-Pins in the 1920s and '30s; Picasso, Léger and friends, who decamped to the hilltop retreats of Vallauris, Biot and Haut-de-Cagnes in the post-war period, soon followed them. The more recent additions of British holiday-homers, Italian tourists and Russian bling on the ritzy Cap d'Antibes have added another facet to the town's liberal, colourful mix. And if the huge array of museums and sights becomes exhausting, then the sub-tropical Iles de Lérins beckon off the shore at Golfe-Juan.

Antibes Old Town.

The old city of Antibes is a living, breathing tumble of Provençal architecture. The combination of turquoise blue shutters against the flash of colour from a window box – an everyday mixture in this part of the world – is serenely alluring.

A dozen of these hushed backstreets lead east off **place Nationale**, a big workaday square lined with plane trees, cafés and restaurants (some excellent, some not, see page 119). Heading west towards Antibes' showiest street, **boulevard d'Aguillon**, these lanes become more vibrant and wider, and are scattered with boutiques and *gelato* outlets to cater for visiting Brits and Italians who love this old-fashioned slice of the Riviera more than any other. Heading 100 m due south from place Nationale down **rue Georges Clémenceau** things get classier still: at the junction with **cours Masséna** is the colourful **Cathédrale d'Antibes**, the imposing **Mairie** and the raucous **Marché Provençal**, a covered market featuring photogenic rows of *saucissons*, organic produce, oils, flowers and pastries.

A block further south, towards the water, all roads lead to **Château Grimaldi**, a tall sandy seaview tower housing the **Musée Picasso**. The lanes around here are older and prettier (if that's feasible) than anywhere else in *vieil Antibes*. Waves crash into the ramparts that lead from the museum through parks, fortifications and along the sea all the way to sandy **plage du Ponteil** at the foot of the Cap d'Antibes. In the other direction, these ancient sea walls lead east to **Port Vauban**, once an awesome defensive harbour overlooked by the menacing **Fort Carré**; now the biggest pleasure harbour in Europe. It costs nothing to gape at the gizmo-crazy competition of fibreglass, satellite antennae and jet-ski contraptions bobbing in the bay. Follow the harbour wall to the so-called **Millionaires' Quay** (or should that be Billionaires'?) to find the biggest boats. Regular visitors include Microsoft founder Paul Allen's *Octopus*, Roman Abramovich's *Ecstasea*, and *Al Salamah*, owned by the Saudi Royal family (check out the all-male crew). A hole in the harbour wall leads to **plage de La Gravette**, a protected, sandy beach ideal for kids.

Essentials

➊ Getting around The coastal train is good for hops between Antibes, Juan-les-Pins and Marineland, while the no 100 bus links Antibes bus station with Cagnes-sur-Mer. Envibus (T04 89 87 72 00, envibus.fr) routes to Biot (nos 7 & 10), Vallauris (no 5), Juan-les-Pins (no 3) and the Cap d'Antibes (no 2) also depart from here. For a slower tour of the Cap, there are plenty of bike rental joints in Antibes and Juan-les-Pins.

➋ Bus station Place Guynemer, Antibes, T04 89 87 72 01.

➌ Hospital Centre Hospitalier, avenue de Nice, by Port Vauban, Antibes, T04 97 24 77 77, ch-antibes.fr.

➍ Pharmacy Pharmacie Centrale, 48 rue de la République, Antibes, T04 93 34 00 23.

➎ Post office 5 avenue Robert Soleau, Antibes.

➏ Tourist information offices 11 place de Gaulle, Antibes, T04 97 23 11 11, July & August daily 0900-1900, September-June Monday-Saturday 0900-1230 & 1330-1800, Sunday 1000-1230 & 1430-1700; 51 boulevard Guillaumont, Juan-les-Pins, T04 97 23 11 10, July & August daily 0900-1900, September-June Monday-Saturday 0900-1200 & 1400-1800, Sunday 1000-1230 & 1430-1700; both antibes-juanlespins.com.

Old street in Antibes.

Musée Picasso

Château Grimaldi, T04 92 90 54 20,
antibes-juanlespins.com.
Mid Jun-mid Sep Tue-Sun 1000-1800 (Wed & Fri until 2000), mid Sep-mid Jun Tue-Sun 1000-1200, 1400-1800. €6, €3 concessions.

Picasso moved into the damp Château Grimaldi in 1946 and set about transforming it into one of the loveliest studio spaces on the Riviera. In his words: "I'm not only going to paint, I'll decorate the museum too." Such was the penury in war-ravaged France that he used house paint for colour and even ceramic plates (plus the walls) as a canvas. He created *La Joie de Vivre* and countless frenzied sculptures, all of which he left as a gift to the Antibes municipality.

The Picasso collection was embellished further in the following decades, and added to with works by Yves Klein and Francis Picabia, among others. Out on the sunny outdoor terrace is a permanent exhibition of sculptures by Germaine Richie, with several Miró pieces besides. Fresh from a five-year renovation completed in 2008, this is one of the Riviera's must-see museums.

Fort Carré

T06 14 89 17 45, antibes-juanlespins.com.
Mid Jun-mid-Sep Tue-Sun 1000-1730 (free access plus obligatory free tour for upper levels), mid Sep-mid Jun Tue-Sun 1000-1600 (obligatory free tour every 30 mins). €3, €1.50 under 25s, under 18s free.

Commanding the sea and harbour from a 26-m-high elevation, Fort Carré could cannonade any vessel threatening Antibes harbour. Originally constructed by Henri II, it was remastered in the 17th century as an impregnable four-pointed star by the military architect genius Vauban, who fortified La Rochelle, Dunkirk and dozens of other French towns. A path runs along the outside, but the real action is inside along the ramparts and around the prison, lodgings, medieval bread oven and stone toilet.

Motorboat hire on the Riviera

Chartering a 10-m motor yacht with a captain and crew costs around €1500/day from almost any harbour on the Riviera, a feasible treat for a group of 10 or so. Villefranche and Antibes harbours are the centres for DIY motorboat hire: try Dark Pelican (T04 93 01 76 54, darkpelican.com) and ABS (T06 15 75 44 36, antibes-bateaux.com) respectively, which rent 6hp five-person boats – good enough for a run to Nice and back – for around €120/day. No permit is required for such a small vessel. Those with a speedboat licence can take out something meatier: a 140hp eight-person Cap Camarat will let you cruise in style for around €500/day.

Above: Yachts in Port Vauban, Antibes.
Opposite page: Fort Carré, Port Vauban, Antibes.

Cap d'Antibes

At the very tip of the Cap d'Antibes lies the **Hôtel du Cap Eden Roc** (hotel-du-cap-eden-roc.com). It's this glamorous kernel that seeded many a raucous Riviera season. Back in 1923, American socialites Gerald and Sara Murphy persuaded the proprietor, Antoine Sella, to keep the hotel open throughout the summer, a concept hitherto unheard of. The Murphys' *beau monde* pals, including Zelda and Scott Fitzgerald, joined the party, the latter immortalising the Murphys in his novel *Tender is the Night*, for which the Cap d'Antibes formed the backdrop.

The sexy, celebrity-infused beauty of le Cap is still legendary. Its Californian-style coastline takes in one of the Riviera's most beautiful walking trails and curves past several obscure beaches including boisterous **plage de la Salis** close to Antibes, chichi **plage de la Garoupe** and tranquil **plage les Ondes** on the peninsula's western side. Iconic pieces of far-out playboy architecture – very little of which is screened off behind security gates – dot the Cap's

Le Provençal building

No other building mirrors the highs and lows of the Riviera jet-set like Le Provençal. Contrived as a 290-room luxury hotel, it played host to the Fitzgeralds and Murphys of the roaring 1920s, the Chaplins and Churchills of the plush 1930s, plus Ray Charles, Frank Sinatra and Edith Piaf in the Côte d'Azur's booming post-war era. Fast-forward to the oil shocks of the 1970s and Le Provençal's eccentric owner Alexandre Reza shut up shop, letting this art deco gem run to seed. Reza was purportedly happy to leave the building graffiti-strewn and crumbling, holding out for a deal nearly three decades later. Monaco-based developer Cyril Dennis is now turning the building, regarded by many as the 'last remaining jewel on the French Riviera', into 56 state-of-the-art apartments. Fittings come courtesy of Armani Casa and Porsche, and the complex boasts tennis courts, a private beach, plus shared helicopter and yacht. Fancy a piece? Prices ranging from €2 million to €40 million and owners can pick up their keys in late 2011 (provencal-residence.com).

interior. Crowning the Cap is the **Chapelle de la Garoupe**, with a lighthouse, viewing platform (the panorama can take in Italy to St Tropez) and a peaceful church café that serves a nice cup of cider.

Close to the Eden Roc is the **Villa Eilenroc** (T04 93 67 74 33, obligatory guided visits Wed 0900-1200, 1330-1700, free), a palatial residence designed by Charles Garnier, of Monte Carlo Casino and Paris Opera House fame. Its enchanting tropical, Mediterranean and rose gardens were fashioned by Jacques Gréber, landscape consultant to New York's Great Exhibition in 1939. The **Jardin Botanique de la Villa Thuret** (90 chemin Raymond, T04 97 21 25 00, jardin-thuret.antibes.inra.fr, Jun-Sep 0800-1800, Oct-May 0830-1730, free) is a similarly magical collection of olives, eucalyptus and Asian exotic fauna. The **Musée Napoléon** (bd Kennedy, T04 93 61 45 32, mid Jun-mid Sep Tue-Sun 1000-1800, mid Sep-mid Jun Tue-Sun 1000-1630, €3, €1.50 under 25s, under 18s free) has model ships and artefacts relating to the pint-sized emperor.

A couple on the waterfront, Juan-les-Pins.

Juan-les-Pins

'JLP' is not a culture-rich destination, more a sandy state-of-mind. After seeing a movie containing a party on Miami Beach in 1924, Niçois restaurateur Edouard Baudoin contrived to imagine something similar on this stretch of the Riviera's sandiest shore. The resort flourished, with American millionaire property developer Frank Jay Gould adding the jaw-droppingly glamorous Le Provençal (see box on page 93) hotel in 1927. Waterskiing was invented at the Belles Rives hotel, and lounging around in beach pyjamas was popularised by the likes of Coco Chanel.

Still a centre of abject hedonism, JLP has seaside promenades, nightclubs, toes-in-the-sand restaurants and boutiques galore, the latter with outrageous names that sum up the resort's OTT nature: *55°*, *Hot Hot Hot* and *Juanita Banana* among them. A world-renowned Jazz Festival, **Jazz à Juan** (jazzajuan.fr, see page 48), is held every July under the pine trees off place Gould; a children's play park is just nearby. A line of friendly, trendy beach clubs stretch all the way to **Golfe Juan**, where Napoleon landed in 1815 to start his march to Paris, before meeting his Waterloo three months later.

Iles de Lérins

Pointed out gleefully from an aeroplane window and gazed at longingly from the beach at Juan-les-Pins, the Iles de Lérins are simple to reach yet seldom visited, especially outside summer. Both islands are national parks, which means no smoking, excellent walking and crystal clear water for snorkelling.

Naturalists visiting **Ile Ste-Marguerite**, the larger of the two islands, will be intrigued by the well-signed aromatic and tropical flora surrounding the pristine shore. Naturists will be pleased at the scores of tiny sunbathing coves. The excellent **Musée de la Mer** (T04 93 38 55 26, Jun-Sep daily 1000-1745, Oct-May Tue-Sun 1030-1315, 1415-1645, €3.20, €2 under 25s, under 18s free) in the former military bastion of Fort Royal, the island's only

Fort Royale, Ile Ste-Marguerite.

settlement, traces the history of Mediterranean trade and contains the spooky cell which once held the infamous Man in the Iron Mask.

A working monastic settlement still exists on **Ile St-Honorat**, by far the quieter of the two islands. Its Eden-esque shores are ringed by an exquisite 90-minute hike (see page 88).

Trans Côte d'Azur (T04 92 98 71 30, trans-cote-azur.com) runs 10 daily ferries from Cannes to Ile Ste-Marguerite year round (€11 return, €5.50 child (5-10), under 5s free). Regular daily departures run from Juan-les-Pins from March to November and from Nice and St Tropez from mid June to mid September.

Vallauris

High on the hill above Golfe Juan, Vallauris (T04 93 63 82 58, vallauris-golfe-juan.fr) is a must-stop on the Picasso trail. The artist's revitalisation of the town's ceramics industry six decades ago adds sheen to an otherwise down-at-heel destination. After Picasso's Antibes sojourn in 1946, the Spaniard visited Vallauris' **Madoura** workshop and was soon enamoured with the fine art of spinning clay. The workshop is now a gallery selling Picasso editions, its walls lined with photographs of Picasso at work and with fellow ceramic enthusiast Chagall. It's located just off **avenue Georges Clemenceau**, where 30 or so shops ply locally produced wares.

Vallauris' highlight is Picasso's 1952 masterpiece, **La Guerre et la Paix** (T04 93 64 71 83, musee-picasso-vallauris, Jul-Aug Wed-Mon 1000-1900, Sep-Jun Wed-Mon 1000-1215, 1400-1700, €1). Picasso had originally planned for visitors to discover this vivid mural depicting war and peace by feeling their way through the ex-chapel that houses the work. Outside on place Paul Isnard is an *Homme au mouton*, a **bronze sculpture** of a man with a sheep, another gift from Picasso to the village.

Biot

The Riviera's glass-blowing capital owes its popularity, if not its bucolic town square, to the **Verrerie de Biot** glass workshop (chemin des

Sunset over Ile Ste-Marguerite.

Combes, T04 93 65 03 00, verreriebiot.com, Jun-Sep Mon-Sat 0930-2000, Sun 1030-1330, 1430-1930, Oct-May Mon-Sat 0930-1800, Sun 1030-1330, 1430-1830, €3, €1.50 under 25s). By providing apprenticeships for the local youth, the Verrerie has secured Biot's status as a 'proper' Provençal village, rather than a spot solely allied with sun and souvenirs. The town's other magnet is the shockingly vibrant **Musée National Fernand Léger** (chemin du Val de Pome, T04 92 91 50 30, musee-fernandleger.fr, Wed-Mon 1000-1800, €5.50, €4 concessions), a kilometre south of town. Fresh from a renovation in 2008, a fabulous calendar of temporary exhibitions is shown alongside the large, bold paintings from Léger's Cubist, New York and later French period.

Marineland

When *another* art gallery or pavement café becomes too much for Riviera juniors, the **Marineland** (T08 92 30 06 07, marineland.fr, daily Jul-Aug 1000-2200, Sep-Jun 1000-1730, closed Jan, €35, €27 child under 1.2 m) aquarium and dolphinarium could be the magic potion: leaping dolphins and killer whales are on display in a massive stadium. On the coast by Biot-sur-Mer train station, Marineland is surrounded by the **Aquasplash** water park, which has a mammoth 2 km of slides, and the **Far West** children's theme park. Hideously expensive combined tickets (or cheaper single entry tickets) are available for both.

Haut-de-Cagnes

Aptly named Haut-de-Cagnes sits gracefully above the more everyday town of Cagnes-sur-Mer. With an eye on the sea towards the south, the mountains to the north and the River Var just east, Haut-de-Cagnes was a former frontier town, sitting on the split between the Kingdom of Savoy and Provence proper. Removed from the commercial intensity of the Riviera, its olde-worldly lanes leading uphill from **montée de la Bourgade** and looping around **rue du Pontis Long** have the town's 700 years of history

etched all over them. The **Grimaldi Château-Museum** (T04 92 02 47 30, May-Sep Wed-Mon 1000-1200, 1400-1800, Oct-Apr Wed-Mon 1000-1200, 1400-1700, €3, €1.50 students under 26, under 18s free) on café-lined place du Château was built around 1300 and contains an **Olive Tree Museum**, the **Solidor Donation** of portraits, the small **Musée Mediterranée d'Art Moderne** and a tourist office (T04 92 02 85 05, cagnes-tourisme.com) inside its crenelated castle walls.

A kilometre to the south are the tranquil gardens of the **Musée Renoir** and the **Hippodrome Côte d'Azur** (hippodrome-cotedazur.com), where chariot-style *le trot* races are held most summer evenings. Just to the east, the Riviera coast becomes a tacky splodge, the three nondescript towns of Cros-de-Cagnes, St-Laurent-du-Var and Villeneuve-Loubet Plage merging into one another. The bizarre yet riveting 1960s wave-like apartment blocks of the **Marina Baie des Anges** hem in the latter part of the conurbation. Things get better inland: **Villeneuve-Loubet Village** tucks away three or four restaurants inside its pretty, petite old town.

Musée Renoir

Chemin des Collettes, T04 93 20 61 07.
Wed-Mon 1000-1200, 1400-1700 (until 1800 Jun-Aug). €4, €2 students under 26, under 18s free.

Renoir purchased the Domaine des Collettes, including three acres of olive trees, in 1907 on the advice of his doctor, who suggested that the rheumatoid artist move to warmer climes. It certainly worked. Surrounded by his own citrus groves and vegetable garden, Renoir found a new lease of life on his sunny hillside, painting and sculpting with glee, despite his failing health. He had a fine house and studio space built; it now acts as a gallery for the colour-rich works painted during his final years. The studio replicates the decor and layout as it was when the artist was alive. Gazing up to Haut-de-Cagnes, Renoir's lavender-scented gardens are a pleasure to lounge in.

Vence & St-Paul

Where medieval fortifications once drove away coastal raiders, these enchanting walled towns attracted artists by the dozen during the 1920s. Today it's St-Paul (also known as St-Paul-de-Vence) that trades most on its legendary art connections, including La Colombe d'Or restaurant (see page 120), where once penniless artists like Picasso, Léger and Braque paid for their keep in canvases. This hilltop redoubt now boasts a dining and boutique hotel scene to suit the wallets of those browsing the gallery-lined streets. A five-minute walk from town is the magical, maze-like Fondation Maeght, one of the most prominent modern art spaces in France. Nearby, Vence is built of the same honey-coloured stone as St-Paul, and blessed with pretty piazzas, a visible history and Matisse's final masterpiece, the Chapelle du Rosaire. Yet the town has an understated, lived-in feel, far removed from its chi chi cousin St-Paul.

St-Paul

'Elegant' and 'dynamic' aptly describe this monumental museum-piece town. A common route is to tour the **ramparts** from the **Porte de Vence**, then delve into the ivy-strewn streets past churches and art stores to the **Porte de Nice** on the far side of the village, where a magnificent panorama overlooks the cemetery and the tomb of artist Marc Chagall below. The **Grande Fontaine** back up rue Grande, St-Paul's principal artery, is like a bubbling Rosetta Stone, with the voices of tourists from Japan to Brazil chattering around it.

Fondation Maeght

T04 93 32 81 63, fondation-maeght.com. **Daily Jul-Sep 1000-1900, Oct-Jun 1000-1800. €11, €9 students, under 10s free.**

One of France's key collections of 20th-century art. Pieces on display are rotated; some of the permanent artworks are literally woven into the museum's box-like structure, such as Matisse mosaics, Miró-designed gardens and Giacometti sculptures. Each summer, the Fondation is home to a large-scale temporary exhibition.

Vence

History is visible at every turn in unassuming Vence. From **place du Grand Jardin**, a loop of 25 points of historic interest are waymarked around town, many clustered around place Clemenceau with its awesome fourth-century **Cathedral** and Roman column dating from AD 230. Most visitors enter the *vieille ville* through Porte du Peyra, one of five original gates into the city, where the towering 17th-century **Château de Villeneuve** now houses the **Fondation Emile Hughes** (T04 93 24 24 23, museedevence.com, Tue-Sun 1000-1230, 1400-1800), a contemporary exhibition space with one of the Riviera's best modern art bookshops. The pretty villages of **Tourrettes-sur-Loup** and **Ste-Jeanette** nearby are famous for fine dining and wine production respectively.

Essentials

❶ Getting around Both towns can only be explored on foot. The No 400 bus runs between them.

⊕ Pharmacy Pharmacie du Grand Jardin, 30 place du Grand Jardin, Vence, T04 93 58 00 39.

❷ Post office Place Clemenceau, Vence.

❶ Tourist information offices 2 rue Grande, St-Paul, T 04 93 32 86 95, saint-pauldevence.com, June-August daily 1000-1900, October-May daily 1000-1800; place du Grand Jardin, Vence, T04 93 58 06 38, vence.fr, July-August Monday-Saturday 0900-1900, Sunday 1000-1800, September-October & March-June Monday-Saturday 0900-1800, November-February Monday-Saturday 0900-1700.

Above: Cathedral, place Clemenceau, Vence.
Opposite page: Playing petanque in St-Paul.

Walking between the towns

Locals have been walking the 90 minutes from Vence to St-Paul for centuries. The most direct route runs from Vence bus station down boulevard Emmanuel Maurel to Chapelle Ste-Anne. From here, allée des Bois leads steeply right to a route marker where precipitous steps head down to the valley floor. A small bridge crosses Le Malvan stream. Carrying on right uphill, a signpost indicates left towards St-Paul. After 500 m, the rough track becomes the asphalt chemin des Cèdres; another 500 m and a sign points walkers left to a trail that runs parallel to the asphalt road, winding along with stunning views over St-Paul. Follow the aqueduct downhill, and you'll arrive at a waterwheel and the bus stop for Nice. Vence Tourist Office has further details of this and several similar walks to the Château de la Reine Jeanne, Tourrettes-sur-Loup and the northern rocky hill of Le Baou.

Chapelle du Rosaire

466 av Henri Matisse, T04 93 58 03 26.
Tue & Thu 1000-1130, 1400-1730, Mon, Wed, Fri & Sat 1400-1730, closed mid Nov-mid Dec. €3, €1.50 under 26.

Often considered Matisse's masterpiece, the petite Chapelle du Rosaire was inspired by Monique Bourgeois (later Sister Jacques-Marie), Matisse's former nurse and model who later joined the Dominican order. Stepping inside Matisse's three-dimensional artwork is unique. Blue, green and yellow stained glass windows reflect off black line drawings (*The Stations of the Cross, St Dominic, the Virgin Mary and Child*) on pale tiled walls. There's a small museum at the chapel's exit, which catalogues the artist's preparatory sketches and his designs for colourful Dominican robes.

St-Paul.

The Corniche coast road

The Corniche coast road dips effortlessly through this stylish chunk of the Riviera. The five seaside villages of Villefranche-sur-Mer, St-Jean, Beaulieu-sur-Mer, Eze-sur-Mer and Cap d'Ail are a picture of unhurried elegance, a far cry from the new-money hotspot of neighbouring Monaco. They are blessed with the prettiest beaches, cutest cafés and some of the finest restaurants on the entire coast. Cruising through in a Ferrari would be considered *parvenu*, but a burn along the coast in something less ostentatious, or walking the coastal path that leads from Villefranche past the gardens of Cap Ferrat and into Cap d'Ail, would let you feel at one with the artists, actors and millionaires who made this one of Europe's coolest bits of coast.

Plage du Paloma, Cap Ferrat.

And on the seventh day God created Villefranche. Even the oft-overused phrase 'picture-perfect' understates the beauty of this low-key resort, nuzzled in the crook of a magnificent natural harbour. The lanes of pastel-coloured buildings and shuttered windows date from a period of House of Savoy suzerainty in the 18th century. The cafés sprinkled around the mini-piazzas still lend an Italian feel. An aimless wander around is heartily recommended.

As an age-old fishing port, Villefranche's quay is lined with an esplanade, piles of fishing nets and a church dedicated to St Peter, the patron saint of fishermen. This **Chapelle St-Pierre** (daily Apr-Sep 1000-1200, 1500-1900, Oct & mid Dec-May 1000-1200, 1400-1800, €2) was daubed inside and out by Jean Cocteau in 1957, a happy homage to doe-eyed mermaids and angels. Cocteau, like many visitors in the 1920s, '30s and '50s, found Villefranche a liberal retreat, an air that it retains today, although few would follow the artist's example of chasing young men around the opium-infested bedrooms of the **Hôtel Welcome** (see page 116), now the town's principal hostelry.

A dozen or so fishing boats still line quai Courbet to the north of Cocteau's church. These mainly supply the strip of great seafood restaurants, including **La Mère Germaine** (see page 120), on the other side of the street. Walk further north along the quay to the long **Plage des Marinières** and the poorly marked train station.

Back in town, the action centres around the pavement cafés and restaurants of **place Amélie Pollonais**; a weekend antiques market enlivens the square even more. The palm-lined harbour setting has been used as a backdrop for countless films, including Steve Martin's *Dirty Rotten Scoundrels* and Robert de Niro's *Ronin*.

Just south is the 16th-century Citadelle St-Elme. A little-used coastal path skirts the seaward side of its castle walls to Villefranche's final attraction, the pretty **Port de la Darse** with its bobbing boats and locals-only cafés. Head through a hole in the

Essentials

❶ Getting around The no 100 bus stops in Villefranche, Beaulieu, Eze-sur-Mer and Cap d'Ail. The coastal train makes the same stops, and in all cases drops you at a similarly convenient spot. Bus no 81 runs from Nice bus station to St-Jean village on Cap Ferrat, while bus no 112 links Nice with Eze village. Surprisingly, parking is not too much of a problem anywhere on this stretch of coast, although summer traffic jams are frequent. Most of the towns are a pleasant 30-minute walk from each other.

✚ Pharmacy Pharmacie de la Paix, 6 place de la Paix, Villefranche, T04 93 01 70 42; Pharmacie Internationale, 38 boulevard Marinoni, Beaulieu, T04 93 01 01 39.

❓ Post office 6 avenue Albert 1er, Villefranche.

❶ Tourist information offices Jardin François Binon, Villefranche, T04 93 01 73 68, villefranche-sur-mer. com, July & August 0900-1900, September & June Monday-Saturday 0900-1200 & 1400-1830, October-mid November & mid February-May Monday-Saturday 0900-1200 & 1400-1800, mid November-mid February Monday-Saturday 0900-1200 & 1300-1700; place Général de Gaulle, Eze village, T04 93 41 26 00, eze-riviera. com, April-October daily 0900-1900, November-March Monday-Saturday 0900-1830; mobile office next to Beaulieu train station, T04 93 01 02 21, times vary.

harbour wall to pebbly **Plage de la Darse** (see box page 104), one of the Riviera's quietest beaches.

Citadelle St-Elme

T04 93 76 33 27.
Jun-Sep Tue-Sat 1000-1200, 1500-1800 (until 1900 Jul & Aug), Sun 1500-1800, Oct & Dec-May Tue-Sat 1000-1200, 1400-1700, Sun 1400-1700. Free.

The drawbridge, cannons and summer-long season of open-air movies at this former defensive bastion will appeal to kids and adults alike. Housed inside are three free museums including the **Musée Volti**, containing the curvy bronze nudes of local sculptor Antoniucci Volti. The **Musée Goetz-Boumeester** is filled with the paintings of New York-born Henri Goetz and his wife Christine Boumeester, along with minor works from their celebrity pals Picasso and Miró, among others. The smaller **Collection Roux** features centuries old ceramics and manuscripts.

Cap Ferrat

Europe's richest promontory is the embodiment of 20th-century celebrity and wealth. Jutting out from the coast between Villefranche and Beaulieu, it was once the stamping ground of Somerset Maugham, who drank at the aptly named **Grand Hôtel du Cap Ferrat** at the northern tip of the peninsula. Ian Fleming and the Aga Khan were one-time guests at Maugham's villa, La Mauresque, on boulevard Général de Gaulle.

A well-signed **coastal path** weaves around these billionaire residences, stretching 7 km along the prime coastline and specked with four great **beaches** (see Walking the Caps, page 106). What action there is happens in the sleepy **port of St-Jean**, an unpretentious fishing harbour surrounded by several great restaurants and accommodation options.

Villa Ephrussi de Rothschild

T04 93 01 33 09, villa-ephrussi.com.
Mid Feb-Oct daily 1000-1800 (Jul & Aug until 1900), Nov-mid Feb Sat & Sun 1000-1800, Mon-Fri 1400-1800. €10, €7.50 students/under 17s, under 7s free. Optional guided visits at 1130, 1430, 1530 and 1630, €3.

Cap Ferrat's must-see is a priceless 'folly', built in 1905 for Baroness Ephrussi de Rothschild, an avid art collector and *bonne vivante*. Her Italianate mansion is a 10-minute walk up the hill from St-Jean village. The baroness decorated most of the rooms herself in Louis XV and Louis XVI style, befitting of an aristocrat whose heroine was Marie Antoinette. (Like her heroine, she hosted a good party and played poker on the ex-Queen's own card table.) The Baroness would also send for piles of porcelain, paintings and objets d'art, which she would then pick through and purchase on the platform of Beaulieu train station. The villa's

Five of the best

Riviera's secret beaches

While most visitors will be content in Villefranche's sandy bay or on Nice's 4-km public beach, these heaven-sent secret coves are the Riviera at its most relaxed.

❶ **Plage du Paloma, Cap Ferrat** Half private and cool, half public and family-friendly, with great snorkelling for all.

❷ **Plage Port Crouton, Juan-les-Pins** A totally public sandy arc, lapping up the sun of JLP's famous microclimate.

❸ **Plage St-Laurent, between Eze-sur-Mer and Cap d'Ail** Total seclusion, a steep walk down from the Eze-St-Laurent bus stop.

❹ **Plage des Ondes, Cap d'Antibes** A chilled mix of sun-seekers and millionaires on the Cap's western side.

❺ **Plage de la Darse, Villefranche-sur-Mer** Clear blue water and the chance to swim southwards up Villefranche's protected bay.

surrounding gardens (a rose garden, a formal French garden, a Japanese garden, a musical fountain garden and several others) are sublime.

Beaulieu-sur-Mer

A favourite of European royalty and fronted by belle époque buildings, Beaulieu is stately and sedate, and great for a mooch around. Many wealthy visitors flock to the grand Hôtel La Réserve on the seafront. Legendary British restaurant critic Michael Winner ran up a bill of £58,123 here during a 21-day sojourn in 2009, although it's possible to cruise the town's boutiques, cafés and morning vegetable market on place du Marché for just a shade of the price. An all-public beach west of the harbour, **La Petite Afrique**, has palms, protected bathing and diving platforms.

The best glimpse of town is from the **sentier Maurice Rouvier**, a serene promenade that backs on to Beaulieu's other public beach, **Plage du**

Fourmis. The recently restored casino and a line of outdoor bars lend the area a real buzz, especially in summer. The coastal path continues to the village of St-Jean on Cap Ferrat, passing David Niven's palatial pink former home on **place Niven**. Other famous residents have included Isaac Singer (of sewing machine fame), Gustave Eiffel (of the tower) and archaeologist and ardent Hellenophile Théodore Reinach, who was responsible for Beaulieu's cultural gem, the **Villa Kerylos**.

Villa Grecque Kerylos

Impasse Gustave Eiffel, T04 93 01 01 44, villa-kerylos.com.
Mid Feb-Oct daily 1000-1800 (Jul & Aug until 1900), Nov-mid Feb Sat & Sun 1000-1800, Mon-Fri 1400-1800. €8.50, €6.30 students/ under 17s, under 7s free.

Théodore Reinach's love of all things Greek led him to build this faithful reproduction of a second-century BC luxury Grecian villa, on a spit of Beaulieu coast that reminded him of the Aegean. The gardens are typically Greek: oleanders, pomegranates and vines set against whitewashed walls. The interior of the villa is specially constructed to let in natural light and sea breezes, and features wonderful mosaics, a throne room, a marble bathroom and various statues of the Gods.

Eze Village & Eze-sur-Mer

The term *village perché* could have been created just for oh-so-pretty Eze, literally perched on an outcrop of rock, 430 m above the sea. A former Saracen stronghold, the village is now right on the beaten track: hordes of coaches inundate it on a daily basis, its winding lanes a dodge of art galleries, souvenirs and soap shops. But the **views over Cap Ferrat** and the Corniche are breathtaking – nip into the famous (and very expensive) Château Eza or Château de la Chèvre d'Or hotels for a *jus d'orange* if you'd like to enjoy the view in peace. Various 'contemplative areas' are dotted around for those who prefer to take in the panorama for free.

The **Jardin Exotique** (rue du Château, T04 93 41 10 30, daily 0900-sunset, €5) cactus garden at the very peak of the village is worth a visit.

The **sentier Frédéric Nietzsche** leads back down to the Corniche. It was on this path that the German philosopher composed the third chapter of *Thus Spoke Zarathustra*, a read some believe as tortuous and twisting as the path's hour-long descent to the coast. The sight of **Eze-sur-Mer's** long public beach is the reward at the bottom; you may even catch a glimpse of U2's Bono, whose villa backs on to the *plage*.

Cap d'Ail

Little more than a collection of villas clinging to an azure coast, Cap d'Ail has long been a hidey-hole for celebrities, politicians and those seeking solace from the Côte d'Azur bustle. With few shops and no actual sights, the main attraction is **Plage Mala**. This exclusive sandy stretch has top snorkelling and kayaks for hire (€10/hr), plus two cracking – if pricey – beach bar restaurants, **Eden Plage** and **La Réserve**. The beach is a steep 10-minute downhill hike from the 'Edmonds' bus stop on the Corniche, which renders it essentially a child-free zone. It's also very trendy to boot. Those hankering after total seclusion can walk down from the Corniche to naturist **Plage des Pissarelles** or hard-to-reach **Plage St-Laurent** (see box opposite) further west. Both are visible from Plage Mala and can be swum to by the seriously energetic.

Despite its exclusivity, Cap d'Ail is remarkably accessible in other ways. Arrive by train and you are right on the rocky waterfront, wedged above a row of seafront villas. A well-signed **coastal path** leads off in two directions. It's a precipitous five-minute walk westwards to Plage Mala. In the other direction, the 3-km route loops along a photo-shoot coastline, alive with climbing flowers, figs and rock samphire. It passes sandy swimming coves to the long stretch of **Marquet Plage**, before arriving into Monaco's Fontvieille harbour.

Walking the Caps

Two of the world's richest spits of land are firmly in the public domain in egalitarian, socialist France. Cap Ferrat and Cap Martin may stir up visions of villas, aristocrats and Russian *nouveaux riches*, but they are surrounded by astoundingly beautiful public footpaths with views that even an oligarch can't fence off. These routes were originally *sentiers des douaniers*, customs officers' trails, where local officials on the lookout for smugglers would patrol. Varying in degrees of accessibility and ardour, they are so well waymarked that walkers don't need a map: just keep the sea on your right and you'll be fine. A similar, although more arduous, trail encircles the **Cap d'Antibes** further west along the coast.

Cap Ferrat
Time 4 hours
Difficulty level Hard
Accessibility Moderate
Start point Cap Ferrat Passable bus stop
End point St-Jean village

This route takes in four brilliant beaches – along with acres of palms, figs, Aleppo pines, cactus and wild herbs – along the way. Start at family-friendly **Plage Passable**; the garden dripping into the sea 200 m to the right is that of Nellcote, rocker Keith Richards' former home and a renowned den of vice throughout the 1970s. The coastal pathway signposts begin at the end of the beach. A lazy 3 km of paths dip up and down all the way to **Pointe St Jean**, with rocky coves for bathing and snorkelling to

the right. However, as Villefranche's Genoese castle is lost from sight, the water deepens considerably: it's one of the Riviera's best dive spots but can be a scary prospect for swimmers.

A towering *phare*, or lighthouse, marks the end of the Cap. The sexy cabanas of **Club Dauphin** – beach club of the luxury Grand Hôtel de Cap Ferrat – are a few hundred metres further on. Here the ground has been swept raw with salty spray and the going is tough. Follow the signs for **St-Jean Village** past villas so modern that you wonder how they ever got planning permission (hint: they may have 'friends' on the local council). To walk around the entire cap, peel off to **Point Paloma** before you reach town, passing the wild, tranquil beaches of **Plage des Fosses** and **Plage des Fossettes** on the way. Italy, Monaco and Beaulieu come into view as you walk around to tree-dappled **Plage Paloma** and into St-Jean village 10 minutes further on. Fancy going further? An easy asphalt path carries on all the way to Beaulieu town centre.

Cap Martin
Time 2 hours
Difficulty Moderate
Accessibility Excellent
Start point Roquebrune-Cap-Martin train station
End point Menton Carnolès train station

The quietest of the caps in terms of both visitors and wealthy oddball residents, Cap Martin starts in the shingle of **plage de la Buse**, just below Roquebrune-Cap-Martin train station. The trail runs first past the architecturally iconic **Villa E.1027**,

built in 1929 by furniture designer Eileen Gray and under long-term renovation. Nearby, Le Corbusier built **Le Cabanon** (guided visits Tue & Fri courtesy of Roquebrune tourist office, T04 93 35 62 87), a 3.66 x 3.66 m sq cabin, which was a birthday present for his wife Yvonne.

Crossing a raised walkway high above the sea – the only 'scary' bit of the walk – the view takes in the skyscraper skyline of Monaco. Pathways lead down to various **swimming coves**, or carry on to the 'cap' of Cap Martin itself. Walking along the bare moonscape edge of the promontory, Italy and Menton come slowly into view. The path ends at the bust of Charles Edouard Jeanneret, as 'Le Corbusier' is better known. From here it's a 10-minute walk along the seaside promenade of avenue Winston Churchill (so-called as the big fella used to come here to paint and read) to the no 100 bus stop at Menton Carnolès train station. Those wanting to loop back to the walk's starting point can do so by heading west uphill and on to avenue de la Semaphore (private security barriers are vehicle restrictions only). This avenue in turn runs past the olive-strewn **Parc du Cap Martin**, eventually returning to the trail near Le Cabanon.

Monaco

Monaco's Casino Square is just one of a dozen upscale car parks in the postage-stamp-sized Principality. Each one is an open-air car showroom with the latest Bugattis, Lamborghinis and Bentleys complete with quarter-million-euro price tags. The provenance of their licence plates – Frankfurt, Milan, Moscow – tells of old and new world money distilled into a glam sham corner of Europe. What Somerset Maugham described as "a sunny place for shady people" is governed by the most benevolent of business-friendly dictatorships, the ruling Grimaldi family, known locally as Monaco Inc. and personified by the current Prince, Albert II. Billionaires can, and do, flaunt their wealth in safety, with banks of CCTV cameras capable of stopping crime virtually before it happens. But dare to stir the pot, stand out or even dress like a hippy, and you may be firmly ejected from this rich man's club.

This rocky outpost hasn't always been Singapore-on-Sea. After losing control of neighbouring Menton (together with its lucrative tax on lemons) in 1848, Monaco stared bankruptcy in the face. Enter the world-famous casino in 1856, just as Victorian morals closed down gambling dens operating in other parts of Europe. Add the extension of the railway line a decade later and Monaco had a licence to print money; or at least casino chips. By abolishing both military service and most taxes, the Grimaldis ensured their own popularity and that of their Lilliputian nation for banking, insurance and finance industries.

Visitors are more than welcome to lap up this fancy farce. It's lots of fun just to look, especially inside the recently renovated casino (passport required, entrance free, or €10 to enter the gaming rooms). With heaps of cafés harbourside and by the casino, including the chic Café de Paris (see page 122), it's also a great place to say you've been to. To put a trip to Monaco into the words of a recent visitor: "the (public) beach at plage Larvotto is nothing special but a Facebook photo of me lying there was mint".

Palace hill

Almost all of the Principality's sights are high up on the hill above the port. It's a splendid, if tiring, walk up here, and a footpath-cum-park rings the whole rocky promontory. The daily **changing of the guard** (1155) at the **Prince's Palace** is pompous fun. The royal family's *grands appartements* (palais.mc, daily Apr & Oct 1030-1730, May-Sep 0930-1830, €8, €3.50 students/under 14s, under 7s free) can be visited in all their over-the-top Regency-style glory. Looking down to the west is **Fontvieille**. This new port and mini-suburb were built almost entirely from reclaimed land during the later reign of Rainier III. The so-called 'Builder Prince' added 20% to his territory during his 55-year reign through tunnelling and burrowing, but plans to add another 12 hectares of land to the nation were put on hold by Prince Albert II in 2009 due to the stormy economic climate.

Musée Océanographique de Monaco

Av St-Martin, T00 377 93 15 36 00, oceano.org. Apr-Sep 0930-1900 (Jul & Aug until 1930), Oct-Mar 1000-1800. €13, €6.50 students/under 18s, under 4s free.

This mansion of a museum remains gloriously unreconstructed (glass jars of squid, preserved giant crabs) and is primarily a draw for aquarium enthusiasts and children, covering both the Mediterranean and tropical seas. The ground floor is reserved for excellent temporary exhibitions, although the high-ceilinged salons are admirable themselves. Upstairs are scores of intact underwater skeletons, including those of a blue whale.

Essentials

Getting around Either on foot or by using any of Monaco's public elevators and escalators. The Compagnie des Autobus de Monaco (T00 377 97 70 22 22, cam.mc) runs five routes. Buses nos 1 and 2 run from the port to the Palace hill, No 6 runs from the port to Fontvieille, Casino Square and Larvotto beach.

Train station Avenue du Prince Pierre, T04 93 10 60 01, monaco-gare.com. Monaco's high-tech station is five minutes by underground walkway to most of the Principality's places of interest.

Hospital Centre Hospitalier Princesse Grace, avenue Pasteur, T00 377 97 98 99 00.

Pharmacy Pharmacie Aslanian, 2 boulevard d'Italie, T00 377 93 50 64 77.

Tourist information offices 2 boulevard des Moulins, T00 377 92 16 61 16, visitmonaco.com, Monday-Saturday 0900-1900, Sunday 1100-1300.

Above left: Bust of Charles Garnier outside the Monaco opera house.
Above right: The Feet of God on Monaco's seaside promenade.
Right: Multi-million euro yachts in Fontvieille harbour.

To the Italian border

Compared with anywhere west of Monaco, few tourists pound the long sweeps of beach and archaic Old Towns in this pristine part of the Riviera. Roquebrune's ancient amber and orange *vieille ville* is as well preserved, yet infinitely more placid and authentic than either Eze or St-Paul. Cap Martin (see Walking the Caps, page 106) has quiet aristocratic roots: the thinking man's Cap Ferrat. More than anywhere else in coastal Provence, border-bumping Menton owes its heart to *le soleil*. A unique microclimate makes this the sunniest place in the republic – a perfect place for cultivating lemons (celebrated with a procession of oversized citrus sculptures and floats each February, feteducitron.com) and retirees (of which there are proportionally more than anywhere else in the country).

Monaco's Grimaldi family moved out in 1848, only to be replaced by thousands of British consumptives three decades later. The seaside town was, as Mary Blume (see page 22) puts it, "an ideal resting place, in every sense, for the very ill". A visit by Queen Victoria in 1882 put the town firmly on the haughty holiday map, with regency buildings and exclusive hotels to match. Present-day Menton is a royally preserved delight with a rich Italian flavour, ringed by two beaches (long, sweeping **plage du Soleil**, and **plage des Sablettes** by the port) and topped with an ochre-hued **Old Town** and its exquisitely frescoed **Eglise St-Michel**. Several episodes of the 1930s detective drama Poirot have been filmed outside the latter, so undisturbed is the backdrop. The sun shines on a classical **music festival** each summer (festivalmusiquementon.com), but even during spring and autumn, when the **beach bars** hire out their rows of sun-mattresses for a bargain €6 a pop, it's a perfect place to visit.

Musée Jean Cocteau

Bastion du Vieux Port, T04 93 57 72 30, menton.fr. Wed-Sun 1000-1800. €3.

This former defensive bastion, built by the Monegasques to defend Menton's two bays, is home to an outrageous Jean Cocteau love-in. The artist adored Menton, and it features in the background of his *innamorata* collection, a suite of paintings presenting a sly salty fisherman's desire for a voluptuous young maiden, which is housed here. Tiny windows lend a 270° view out to Cap Martin and the Italian border. Lifelong Cocteau fan Severin Wunderman donated 1200 works to the magnificent **new Musée Cocteau**, which opened on nearby quai de Monléon in May 2010.

Even those not tying the knot are welcome in the Cocteau-designed **Salon des Mariages** inside the *mairie* (Town Hall, place Ardoïno, T04 92 10 50 00, Mon-Fri 0830-1230 & 1400-1700, free). The artist's fruitily colourful paintings are guaranteed to inject fizz into any new marriage.

Essentials

☉ Train station Place de la Gare, Menton, T04 92 41 16 00. It's a five-minute walk from here to the port.

⊖ Bus station Avenue Sospel, Menton, T04 92 10 96 24. Terminus of the no 100 Nice-Menton coastal bus. Route no 7 heads north to Gorbio, nos 9 and 10 to Ste Agnès, no 112 to Eze village and no 903 to Castellar.

⊕ Hospital Centre Hospitalier Universitaire, 7 route du Val de Gorbio, Menton, T04 92 10 13 83.

✚ Pharmacy Pharmacie Centrale, 13 place Georges Clemenceau, Menton, T04 93 35 71 52.

❶ Tourist information office 8 avenue Boyer, Menton, T04 92 41 76 76, tourisme-menton.fr, June-mid September daily 0900-1900, mid September-May Monday-Saturday 0830-1230 & 1400-1900, Sunday 0900-1230.

Above: Shopping for antiques in Menton.
Opposite page: The fort that houses the Jean Cocteau collection.

Five of the best

Riviera Roads

On scooter, bike or car, these priceless pieces of tarmac will wow drivers and riders alike.

❶ **Monaco GP circuit** Follow the Ferraris touring the F1 route from boulevard Albert 1er to Casino Square, through the Tunnel, then back to the harbour. Can you beat Felipe Massa's 75-second fastest lap?

❷ **Around the Cap d'Antibes** On two wheels or four, the *tour du cap* is seascapes and wedding cake architecture all the way round.

❸ **The Col d'Eze** A thigh-pumping Tour de France climb attacked by the odd brave amateur, or a heady drive with acres of blue sea below.

❹ **Grande Corniche** See clouds forming in the valleys below on the high road between Nice and the Italian border.

❺ **La Napoule to Agay** Past La Napoule, the coastal D6098 twists through the red rock Estérel moonscape all the way to Agay.

A bamboo-banistered walkway leads you through muggy Amazonian corners and along blossom-scented trails.

Driving into the hills

Tenuously linked to the coast at Menton by twisting back roads, these three hilltop redoubts are assuredly *terroir*, rather than *mer*. Lofty, lovely **Ste-Agnès** (sainteagnes.fr) is perched up at 800 m. It was founded by the Saracens and has a World War II-era bastion and stunning sea view. Heady **Castellar** (castellar.fr) exudes an austere beauty, not least in the drive up there, and boasts just one lone shop. **Gorbio** (gorbio.fr) is super seductive, occupying the visitor with an old mill, several squares and churches. The three villages are linked by well-signed footpaths to each other, as well as to several points over the Italian border (and down to Menton in the case of Ste-Agnès).

Garden Centre

Sun-kissed Menton has seven botanical gardens (jardins-menton.fr) and more tropical trees than you can shake a stick at. The most accessible – and the only one not requiring one's own transport – is the **Jardin Exotique du Val Rahmeh** (T04 93 35 86 71, Apr-Sep Wed-Mon 1000-1230 & 1530-1830, Oct-Mar Wed-Mon 1000-1230 & 1400-1700, €6, €3 students/under 18s, under 7s free). A bamboo-banistered walkway leads you through muggy Amazonian corners and along blossom-scented trails, finishing at a giant lily-pad pond: sitting on these, Alice in Wonderland style, is sadly prohibited. Those arriving on foot pass a public park complete with an olive orchard on their right on the walk up.

The other gardens include balmy, palmy **Jardin Maria Serena**, the **Jardin du Palais Carnolès** by the Musée des Beaux-Arts (free) on the promenade towards Cap Martin, Spanish-styled **Jardin Fontana Rosa** and three other private gardens all regularly open to the public.

Heading towards Gorbio are the **Serre de la Madone** gardens (T04 93 57 73 90, Tue-Sun 1000-1800, €8, €4 students/under 18s, under 12s free), designed by Lawrence Johnston of Hidcote Manor fame. **Giardini Hanbury** (Mortola Inferiore, T00 39 01 84 22 95 07, giardinihanbury.com), 10 minutes over the Italian border, is a magnificent English-Chinese-Mediterranean garden.

Below: Roquebrunes tumbling down into the sea.
Bottom: Menton's garden route.
Opposite page: In Menton's colourful side streets.

Roquebrune

Romantic Roquebrune (roquebrune-cap-martin. com) sticks limpet-like to the rock, a 30-minute uphill slog from the Corniche. Its environs follow a hair-raising footpath down the mountain in a haze of church spires, olive groves, villas and swimming pools. A fairytale **medieval castle** (T04 93 35 07 22, daily 1000-1230, 1400-1800, €3.70, €1.60 students/ under 18s), jazzed up even more by its British owner Sir William Ingram before he donated it to the town in 1921, sits at its crest. Head a few hundred metres east from the central **place aux Deux Frères** to find *l'olivier millénaire*, a thousand-year-old olive tree reputed to be the world's oldest. Visit on a sunny weekend and you're guaranteed to see parascenders (see page 125) arcing past the village on their descent to plage de la Buse.

The beach route into Monaco

Plage de la Buse, right underneath Roquebrune-Cap-Martin train station, and **plage le Golfe Bleu** right next door are off the radar and virtually tourist free. Both sandy, shingly strips have crystal-clear water and a view of Monaco's high-rise glitz if you swim out far enough. La Buse maintains a sole restaurant, **Le Cabanon** (T04 93 28 95 56, open all summer and 'sunny weekends'), a shabby-chic beach cabana in the sand good for char-grilled steaks and salads, while Golfe Bleu has a similar snack spot. Strong swimmers can swim between these two beaches, or you can access both along a poorly marked old customs trail, the *sentier des douaniers*, which eventually takes you right into Monaco, passing a handful of tiny, secluded strips of sand en route.

Sleeping

Nice

Hi Hotel €€€
*3 av des Fleurs, T04 97 07 26 26,
hi-hotel.net.*
Map: Nice, A5, p76.
The contemporary, industrial
style one might expect from a
hotel that boasts its own Twitter
feed. The nine room concepts
– open bathrooms in some,
movie projectors in others – are
a soothing mix of leather, glass
and colourful plastics. Boasts its
own sushi bar and Franco-
Japanese garden.

Hôtel Windsor €€€
*11 rue Dalpozzo, T04 93 88 59 35,
hotelwindsornice.com.*
Map: Nice, B5, p76.
A tropical garden complete with
parrot and a palm-dappled pool
makes for perhaps the most
memorable stay in Nice. The
Windsor's offbeat elegance
includes an Ottoman lounger
in the foyer, one-off luxury
bedrooms designed by local
artists, a hammam, gym and
low-key cocktail bar.

Hôtel Suisse €€-€€€
*5 quai Rauba Capéu, T04 92 17 39
00, hotel-nice-suisse.com.*
Map: Nice, G7, p76.
Panoramas from the Suisse's
balconies – over the Baie des
Anges, Nice Old Town and the
Promenade – mimic the ranging
perspectives portrayed in Raoul
Dufy's paintings; a replica of one
lies across the road from this
refined yet relaxed
establishment. A recent
renovation has rendered the
guestrooms both comfy and
sophisticated.

Hôtel Villa La Tour €-€€
*4 rue de la Tour, T04 93 80 08 15,
villa-la-tour.com.*
Map: Nice, F5, p76.
A friendly, family-run guesthouse
named for the landmark tower
that marks the quietest and most
authentic part of the Old Town.
Rooms range from romantic to
simple; many look out over
red-tiled rooftops. A buffet
breakfast (€8.50) is frequently
served outside on the pretty
square, a five-minute walk from
the Promenade and beach.

Villa Saint Exupéry €
*22 av Gravier, T04 93 84 42 83,
vsaint.com.*
Map: Nice, C1, p76.
An award-winning hostel laying
claim to every conceivable
luxury. A host of complimentary
facilities include Wi-Fi, parking,
all-you-can-eat breakfast, towels
and luggage storage. Other
goodies include BBQ area,
state-of-the-art kitchen and a €1
drinks menu. Comfy single, twin
and triple rooms also available.

Self-catering
Riviera Pebbles
*20 rue de l'Hôtel des Postes,
rivierapebbles.com.*
Purveyors of over 50 magnificent
apartments in Nice (plus others
in nearby towns), all of which can
be booked online. These upscale
properties (from around €55 per
night) are uniformly well located
and well equipped. Ranging
from one-bedroom modern
apartments in the Old Town to
three-bedroom villas in the Port,
the entire selection fills up fast.

Cannes

Hôtel Martinez €€€€
*73 La Croisette, T04 92 98 73 00,
hotel-martinez.com.*
Map: Cannes, G4, p84.
You know you've made it when
you gaze out onto the Croisette
from the art deco splendour of
the Martinez. Graceful yet
playful, its large size affords a
glam pool area, a world-class spa
with its own seventh-floor sun
terrace, and a fitness centre. Non-
guests can lord it up in luxury at
ZPlage, Cannes' coolest beach
club, just across the road.

3.14 €€€
*5 rue François Einesy, T04 92 99
72 00, 3-14hotel.com.*
Map: Cannes, F3, p84.
If it's *de rigueur* for a design hotel
in Cannes to have a private
beach club and über-trendy bar,
3.14 goes one step better by
offering its guests a rooftop pool
and the optional extra of adult
toys. Each storey's rooms are
themed to a continent; America
boasts Disney kitsch, Africa a
Moroccan tent theme.
Unforgettable.

Hôtel America €€-€€€
13 rue St-Honoré, T04 93 06 75 75,
hotel-america.com.
Map: Cannes, D3, p84.
Small but perfectly formed.
A block behind the Croisette, yet
away from the noise, the America
offers friendly, unfussy comfort.
There's blanket Wi-Fi coverage,
modern bathrooms and a
refreshing mix of antique and
modern furniture. Great
off-season rates.

Hôtel Alnea €-€€
*20 rue Jean de Riouffe, T04 93 68
77 77, hotel-alnea.com.*
Map: Cannes, C2, p84.
An inexpensive delight that
constitutes a real find. The loud
colours and chintz may smack of
trendy teenage bedrooms to
some, but the Alnea is ever-
popular, not least thanks to its
gregarious owners. Guestrooms
are small, but as a cute crash pad
equidistant from the sea and
train station it has it all.

Grasse

La Bellaudière €-€€
78 av Pierre Zille, T04 93 36 02 57.
A little cracker of a hotel, 2 km
north of Grasse. Both cheaper
and friendlier than anything
to be found in town. Part of
the *Logis de France* chain –
unfussy, Frenchy inns – the
dozen or so rooms are two parts
Provençal romantic, one part
Granny's spare room. Own
transport a must.

Antibes

Hôtel La Jabotte €€-€€€
*13 av Max Maurey, T04 93 61 45
89, jabotte.com.*
Brilliantly executed boutique
hotel midway along the Cap
d'Antibes, 100 m from
chic'n'sandy plage du Salis.
Surrounded by chaotic gardens
– a score of aromatic plants and
antique outdoor furniture –
guestrooms are simple and calm,
and come with a top breakfast.
Three- and four-bedded rooms
available.

Le Bosquet €€
*14 chemin des Sables, T04 93 67
32 29, lebosquet06.com.*
Heaven-sent B&B with four
1920s-style rooms, a 10-minute
walk from both Antibes and
Juan-les-Pins. Fittings include art
deco sinks, marble fireplaces and
wrought-iron loungers. Take
breakfast (included) inside the
bastide's herby gardens.

Relais du Postillon €
*8 rue Championnet, T04 93 34 20
77, relaisdupostillon.com.*
Well located rustic-trendy treat.
Rooms are individually styled in
soft southern French colours.
Breakfast (€8) is served from a big
wooden bar in a homely dining
room, or on the outdoor balcony,
one of the sole outdoor terraces
on place des Martyrs.

Camping
Eden Camping
*Chemin de Pôme, T04 93 65 51
56, sunhatfrance.com.*
Fine British-run camping site. It's
paradise, but book well ahead in
summer. Large swimming pool,
pétanque courts and table tennis,
with shop, washing machines,
cosy bar and restaurant. Mobile
home rental (from €300 per
week) also available. On the bus
route between Antibes and Biot,
within walking distance of
Marineland.

Juan-les-Pins

Hôtel La Marjolaine €€
*15 av Docteur Fabre, T04 93 61 06
60, jabotte.com.*
In a charmingly dated Provençal
villa, 100 m from JLP's train
station and long sandy beach.
Rooms aren't large, but have old
wooden beds, exposed beams
and air-conditioning. Breakfast is
extra and can be taken al fresco
on the south-facing terrace, by
the hotel's private car park.

St-Paul

Hostellerie les Remparts €-€€
72 rue Grande, T04 93 32 09 88.
St-Paul's least expensive inn (and
boy can they be pricey here) is
filled with antiques and period
furnishings. Small, neat rooms
reside smack bang in the historic
town centre. Simple dinners can
be taken on the terrace looking
out onto the Cap d'Antibes.

Listings

Vence

Le Provence €-€€
9 av Marcellin Maurel, T04 93 58 04 21, hotelleprovence.com.
Doesn't look like much from the outside, but push through the great wooden doors to reveal a secret garden of yuccas, geraniums, palms, jasmine, garden chairs and sturdy wooden breakfast tables. Rooms could do with updating, but are a clean, tidy place to rest a head.

Villefranche-sur-mer

Hôtel Welcome €€€
3 quai Amiral Courbet, T04 93 76 27 62, welcomehotel.com.
The Welcome is as close as sleepy Villefranche gets to a *grande dame* hotel, where each and every modern room boasts a balcony and a fine sea view. This seafront spectacular still trades on its associations with Jean Cocteau and other louche Riviera characters, but with a location to die for and a waterfront 'wine pier', it's undeniably popular.

Villa Vauban €€-€€€
11 av Général de Gaulle, T04 93 55 94 51, hotelvillavauban.com.
A British-run, nine-bedroomed guesthouse with lashings of Parisian charm. Two of the four bedrooms in the main villa have views over Villefranche bay, while the five in the garden annex lead out on to a flower-filled patio. All have calm, classic, tasteful decor.

Free parking, a rarity along the Corniche, is just around the corner.

Hôtel Patricia €
Av de l'Ange Gardien, T04 93 01 06 70, hotel-patricia.riviera.fr.
A veritable – and shockingly cheap – Eden. Past the friendly welcome (the street name translates as Guardian Angel Avenue) are a dozen or so unique bedrooms: some (recommended) with stupendous sea views. There's also a sun-terrace of boutique hotel standards, complete with loungers, marble tables, citrus groves, mobiles and Moroccan lamps. The downside? The local train rattles past every hour.

Cap Ferrat

Hôtel Brise Marine €€€
58 av Jean Mermoz, St-Jean village, T04 93 76 04 36, hotel-brisemarine.com.
A sumptuous yet unpretentious hotel stunningly located five minutes from St-Jean village and Plage Paloma. Guests can lounge on the sun terrace (view to Monaco and Italy beyond) or in the gardens. Bedrooms are sunny and simple. Trade the pricey breakfast for a morning *café* in St-Jean town.

Beaulieu-sur-mer

Le Havre Bleu €-€€
29 bd Maréchal Joffre, T04 93 01 01 40, lehavrebleu.com.

An unpretentious blue and white clapboard façade hides a truly excellent hotel, with as many facilities as Beaulieu's legion of 5-star establishments. The 20 rooms feature Wi-Fi and air-conditioning, private parking and a sun-terrace outside. Beaulieu's casino, beach and train station are a few minutes' walk away.

Eze

Camping
Les Romarins
250 av des Diables Bleus, T04 93 01 81 64, campingromarins.com, €26 per two person tent.
Up from Eze village, not only is this one of the Côte d'Azur's few campsites, it also offers some of the finest views – over Cap Ferrat and Villefranche bay – on the entire Riviera. Open from mid-June to late September, there's space for 40 tents among the olive and citrus groves; bungalows (from €400 per week) are available for the week. Good showers, toilets and bar on site.

Cap d'Ail

Hôtel Miramar €€
126 av du 3 Septembre, T04 93 78 06 60, monte-carlo.mc/ hotel-miramar-capdail.
A double room with private sun terrace, stupendous sea view and complimentary breakfast 10 minutes from Monaco for under €70. Pinch yourself. Perched on the *basse corniche*, 10 minutes

Eating & drinking

from Cap d'Ail's exclusive Mala Plage. The less expensive rooms on the ground floor lack view; there's a book swap spot on the first-floor landing.

Monaco

Hôtel de France €€
6 rue de la Turbie, Monaco, T00 377 93 30 24 64, monte-carlo.mc.
Not to be confused with the venerable Hôtel de Paris on Casino Square 10 minutes away, this bright, clean hotel underneath the train station is a boon in this pricey Principality. Standard guestrooms with baths or showers, plus a bar downstairs.

Menton

Hôtel Napoléon €€-€€€
29 porte de France, T04 93 35 89 50, napoleon-menton.com.
A slick, sea-facing hotel; the minimalist bedrooms, white leather lobby and hip bar have benefited from a funky style overhaul. Extra-posh sunloungers and a line of fancy gym equipment ring the outdoor pool. Enter via an evergreen lavender-scented walkway just by the port. Private beach club over the road.

Royal Westminster €€
1510 promenade du Soleil, T04 93 28 69 69, hotel-royal-westminster.com.
A belle époque seafront gem decked with tiny balconies. Sip

a €2 beer in the comfort of a lounger in the south-facing hotel gardens and be the envy of passers-by. Around a hundred fancy rooms in modern 1990s style are set over six floors: the higher up, the sunnier they are. Breakfasts are a little institutional but can be taken in-room. Amazing value.

Roquebrune

Villa la Quinta €€€
Escalier Saft, plage de la Buse, T04 93 35 19 97, villaquinta.free.fr.
Hiding splendidly a five-minute walk above Roquebrune's plage de la Buse is this kick-back-and-relax B&B. Views pan out to sea from the 75 sq m private terrace. An advance booking, plus the ability to nip up a few flights of stairs to get here, is an absolute must.

Hôtel Les Deux Frères €€
1 place des Deux Frères, T04 93 28 99 00, lesdeuxfreres.com.
Roquebrune's fabulous landmark hotel, based in a 150-year-old former schoolhouse. Ten individually themed rooms (*écologique, flower power, 1001 nuits*); some have sea views over Cap Martin and Monaco. Lovingly decorated apartments in the village are also available. Superb gourmet southern French restaurant attached.

Nice

Brasserie Flo €€€
2-4 rue Sacha Guitry, T04 93 13 38 38, flobrasseries.com.
Daily 1200-1430, 1900-2400.
Map: Nice, E5, p76.
A former theatre with service (silver salvers, bow ties) and OTT decor (red banquettes, chandeliers) that wouldn't look out of place on an Orient Express dining car. Great value *prix fixe* lunches, heavy on raw seafood from the onsite *fruits de mer* counter, plus classic bistro dishes.

Café de Turin €€€
5 place Garibaldi, T04 93 62 29 52.
Daily 0800-2200.
Map: Nice, G5, p76.
Le Turin is the literal first port of call for most visiting seafood fans. The plastic tables are served by a team of 20 or so waiters, oyster-shuckers, barmen and *fruits de mer* platter platers: the latter being giant *assiettes* of sea snails, urchins, crab, prawns and clams on ice. A Niçois institution for over a century.

La Voglia €€€
2 rue St Françoise de Paule, T04 93 80 99 16, lavoglia.com.
Daily 1200-1430 & 1900-2300.
Map: Nice, E6, p76.
There are no reservations at this cours Saleya favourite, so give your name to the young Maitre d' and stand by. It's well worth it. Serving bowls of spaghetti with clams, platters of *antipasti* and Italian desserts of mammoth

Listings

proportions that simply blow diners away. Formal service in an atmosphere of noisy bustle.

L'Univers de Christian Plumail €€-€€€€
54 bd Jean Jaurès, T04 93 62 32 22, christian-plumail.com.
Tue-Fri 1230-1430, Tue-Sun 1930-2130.
Map: Nice, E6, p76.
Upmarket, with a summer dining terrace on place Masséna. By night, the single Michelin-starred cuisine is extravagant: dishes based around foie gras, truffles and line-caught seabass abound. Lunch is lighter and features the excellent value €20 two-course *menu de la semaine*.

Les Viviers €€-€€€€
22 rue Alphonse Karr, T04 93 16 00 48, restaurant-gastronomique.fr.
Daily 1200-1400 & 1930-2200 (restaurant closed Sat eve and Sun).
Map: Nice, C4, p76.
Two highly regarded seafood restaurants in one: a *restaurant gastronomique* and a less formal bistro next door. The former serves up fresh lobster, crab and fine wines; the latter plates of oysters, fish stew and a €15 lunchtime set menu.

Flaveur €€
25 rue Gubernatis, T04 93 62 53 95, flaveur.net.
Tue-Fri 1200-1400 & 2000-2230, Sat 2000-2230.
Map: Nice, E4, p76.
In 2009, three young chefs hailing from Nice's grander establishments set up this hip restaurant. The result: Provençal dishes modernised with a hint of Far Eastern flavour. *Prix fixe* lunches with wine are a steal at €15.

La Merenda €€
4 rue Raoul Bosio, no tel.
Mon-Fri 1215-1400 & 1900-2200.
Map: Nice, E6, p76.
Award-winning chef Dominique Le Stanc left his Michelin stars at the venerable Negresco hotel to take over this hole-in-the-wall eatery. It's tiny, and there's no telephone for reservations or credit cards. Authentic local dishes, from salt cod to chickpea chips, make this a site of foodie pilgrimage.

La Tartane €€
44 bd Stalingrad, T04 93 89 66 91.
Mon-Sat 1230-1430 & 1900-2200.
Map: Nice, H7, p76.
Nothing changes at La Tartane, not the inexpensive handwritten menu, nor the kindly waiter-cum-owner – not even the jokester manning the wood-fired pizza oven. Dishes are comprised of 30 mouth-watering pizzas and succulent char-grilled meats.

Bar de la Bourse €
15 place St François, T04 93 62 38 39.
Mon-Sat 1200-1430.
Map: Nice, G5, p76.
An Old Town favourite, frequented almost exclusively by locals. The €11 four-course menu is a rollercoaster of regional flavours: a kir aperitif to start, followed by grilled sardines, beef stew or grilled rabbit, topped off with a rich dessert. No nonsense *plat du jour* dishes around €8 each.

Chez Pipo €
13 rue Bavastro, T04 93 55 88 82.
Tue-Sun 1800-2230.
Map: Nice, H5, p76.
The sole three items on Chez Pipo's menu are all Niçois classics: *socca* (a chick-pea pancake), *pissaladière* (a local onion and olive pizza) and *anchoïade* (an anchovy laden dip). Tables are communal, house wines inexpensive and tasty.

Cafés & bars
Fennochio
2 place Rossetti & 6 rue de la Poissonerie, T04 93 80 72 52, fenocchio.fr.
Daily 1000-2400, place Rossetti closed Nov-Feb.
Map: Nice, F6, p76.
Nice's most celebrated *glacier* is excitement in a cone: the 92 all-natural flavours include thyme, tomato & basil, orange flower and cookies.

Hi Beach
T04 97 07 26 26, hi-beach.net.
Daily 1100-2400, closed
Oct-Apr.
Map: Nice, A6, p76.
Super-cool offshoot of the Hi
Hotel (see page 114), and Nice's
trendiest – but possibly most
relaxed – beach club. Lounge on
swing chairs, hammocks or
sun-loungers. Sushi and
Mediterranean dishes are all
organic. Playroom, library and
concept shower rooms to boot.

Cannes

La Palme d'Or €€€€
*73 bd la Croisette, T04 92 98 74
14, hotel-martinez.com.*
Wed-Sat 1230-1400 & 2000-
2200.
Map: Cannes, G4, p84.
Basking in two Michelin stars
under the stewardship of
Christian Sinicropl, La Palme d'Or
is a Film Festival favourite, when
Messrs Eastwood, Coppola and
Penn drop by. Seasonal modern
French gastronomy (sea bass and
squid with sorrel, frogs' legs with
banana mousse) in polished
surroundings.

Caveau 30 €€-€€€
*45 av Félix Faure, T04 93 39 06 33,
lecaveau30.com.*
Tue-Sun 1800-2400.
Map: Cannes, B3, p84.
Strictly no-nonsense service
adds to the classic atmosphere at
this 1930s-era super-bistro. While
budgets can be blown on

towering ice-trays of crab, lobster
and snails, the two all-day
prix-fixe menus (€24 and €36)
brim with oysters, *fruits de mer*
and succulent fish.

Chez Vincent et Nicolas €€
92 rue Meynadier, T04 93 68 35 39.
Tue-Sun 1800-2400.
Map: Cannes, A3, p84.
Dishes at this highly
recommended, gay-friendly
restaurant are meatier and more
inventive (foie gras hamburger)
than others in Cannes. Awesome
desserts, bubbly atmosphere
and cracking outdoor terrace.

La Piazza €
*9 place Cornut Gentille, T04 92 98
60 80, resto-la-piazza.com.*
Daily 1200-1430 & 1930-2330.
Map: Cannes, A3, p84.
Bustling Italian on the corner of
the old port. No prizes for
service, but full marks for
wood-fired oven-baked pizzas,
hearty meats (*osso bucco*,
scaloppine Milanese) and pasta.
Similarly well-regarded Italian
restaurant 50 m away at **Ciro**
(28 rue du Suquet).

Grasse

La Grignote €€
2 rue de Thouron, T04 93 09 91 45.
Mon-Sat 1200-1430 & 1930-
2230, closed Nov.
The shining star of an otherwise
disappointing selection on pretty
place aux Aires. Dishes like duo of
salmon and sea bass, and a light

curry of *gambas* with herbs, are
served on the trendy piazza tables.

Mougins

Moulin de Mougins €€€€
*Ave Notre Dame de Vie, T04 93 75
78 24, moulindemougins.com.*
Wed-Sun 1230-1330 &
1930-2130.
A gloriously inventive restaurant
under chef sensation Sébastien
Chambru. The world's finest
ingredients do not come cheap
(*wagyu* beef in salt seaweed,
monkfish fillet with *shitake*
mushroom compote) but the
two-course business lunch (€39)
is culinary art on a budget.

Antibes

Auberge Provençale €€
Place Nationale, T04 93 34 13 24.
Tue-Sat 0800-1300 & 1800-
2300, Sun 0800-1300.
A chilled cabinet brimming with
crabs, langoustine and *crevettes
grises* at the entrance is the source
of most of the Auberge's starters.
Arrive before 2030 and grab a
glass of wine plus oysters, snails
or prawns for €10. Lovely leafy
terrace to the rear. Simple guest
rooms available upstairs (€€).

La Taverne du Safranier €€
*Place Safranier, Antibes,
T04 93 34 80 50.*
Daily 1200-1430 & 1900-2230,
closed mid Nov-early Feb.
Hip street restaurant liberally
sprinkled over place Safranier.

Colourful menus hung from the square's walls are chalked up with solid, unshowy dishes: grilled bream with garlic, *gambas à la Provençale*.

Le Rustic €
33 place Nationale, T04 93 34 10 81.
Daily 1200-1430 & 1800-2300.
Few of the restaurants on bustling place Nationale are any good. Le Rustic is the least expensive and it is truly outstanding. Perfectly executed cuisine comes direct from the 1980s: bouquet of prawns, salad with *lardons, entrecôte grillée* and *crème brûlée*.

Juan-les-Pins

Le Perroquet €€€
13 av Georges Gallice, T04 93 61 02 20.
Daily 1200-1400 & 1900-2230, closed Nov-mid Dec.
The sublime dining favourite of most JLP locals. Upmarket interior plus laid-back summertime terrace on the square. Slick Provençal specialities include beef *daube* and local red mullet. Inexpensive lunch menu focuses on a new main dish each weekday.

Biot

Le Jarrier de Laurent Broussier €€€€
30 passage de la Bourgade, T04 93 65 11 68.
Wed-Sun 1200-2000.

Top chef Laurent Broussier arrived in Biot from Nice's Michelin-starred Palais Maeterlinck in 2009. Over six set menus, all around the €50 mark, he takes diners on a fancy foodie journey by way of lobster salad, aubergine *confit*, scallop risotto and rabbit *bouillabaisse*. A blow-out to remember.

Haut-de-Cagnes

Josy-Jo €€-€€€
2 rue du Planastel, T04 93 20 68 76, restaurant-josyjo.com.
Mon-Fri 1200-1400 & 1930-2200, Sat 1930-2200, closed Nov.
Refined Provençal-Niçois cuisine from a chef with more than 30 years experience, a hop away from the ramparts of Haut-de-Cagnes. Try stuffed *farcis, beignets de courgettes*, local calamari and an excellent selection of char-grilled meats.

St-Paul

La Colombe d'Or €€€€
Place Général de Gaulle, T04 93 32 80 02, la-colombe-dor.com.
Daily 1200-1400 & 1900-2200, closed Nov-mid Dec & 2 weeks Jan.
St-Paul's must-eat restaurant and high-end hotel (rooms €€€€) where the likes of Picasso and Matisse once paid for their keep in canvases. Wonderful stone dining terrace where friendly, suited-up waiters serve the house aperitif,

peach bellinis, and their speciality, roast chicken.

Café de la Place €
Place Général de Gaulle, T04 93 32 80 03.
Daily 0800-2000, closed Nov.
Unhurried café-bar with *plat du jour* lunches like chicken *chasseur* and steak *brochettes*, in front of St Paul's premier *pétanque* ground. Step inside for marble tables, a polished steel bar and bags of old-style class.

Vence

La Litote €€€
5 rue de l'Evêché, T04 93 24 27 82, lalitote.com.
Tue-Sat 1230-1400 & 1930-2200, Sun 1230-1400.
Spread casually over one of Vence's tranquil old town squares, Litote puts rich starters (lobster and crab cakes, *foie gras poêlé*) with meaty mains (*filet de veau à la planche*, beef with a red wine reduction and organic chips).

Villefranche-sur-Mer

La Mère Germaine €€€
Quai Courbet, T04 93 01 71 39, meregermaine.com.
Daily 1200-1430, 1900-2130, closed mid Nov-Dec.
So-called after the chef-cum-momma who fed officers from the US Navy's 6th Fleet during sojourns in Villefranche. Elegantly presented seafood including

oriental octopus, Italian-style shellfish stew and marinated tuna.

Le Cosmo €€
11 place Amélie Pollonais, T04 93 01 84 05.
Daily 0800-0300.
In Villefranche's buzzing main square, with a seaview terrace that serves cappuccinos at breakfast and pastis at sundown. Lunch and dinner are happy and snappy: *moules et frites*, tuna *tartare* and Cosmo's famous *anchoïade* crudités dipping plate for sharing.

Cap Ferrat

Restaurant du Port €€
7 av Jean Mermoz, St-Jean, T04 93 76 04 46.
Daily 0800-2200, closed Nov.
Only a fool couldn't eat well in the dozen restaurants ringing St-Jean port. Join locals here on plastic chairs for beer and exquisite seafood, including local sea bass and bream. Lobster and prawns seared on grill.

Beaulieu-sur-Mer

Les Agaves €€€
4 av Maréchal Foch, T04 93 01 13 12, lesagaves.com.
Daily 1930-2230, closed Nov.
A heartily recommended modern French restaurant, discreetly frequented by A-list celebrities and local gastronomes. Dishes are not a departure from the norm

(braised sweetbreads, rack of lamb, Charolais beef) but there's a hint of luxury at every turn (truffle shavings, lobster and truffle sauces).

African Queen €€-€€€
Port de Plaisance, T04 93 01 10 85.
Daily 1200-2400.
On a row of great restaurants in Beaulieu marina, which range from pricey down to dirt cheap as you wander from left to right. The African Queen may be celeb-showy (Stallone and Bono are regular diners) but this Riviera institution knocks out fancy salads, char-grilled burgers and pizzas with aplomb.

Eze

Le Pinocchio €€
1 av du Jardin Exotique, T04 93 41 16 42.
Daily 0900-2200.
Most diners spend five times as much in Eze's twin towers of fine dining: the nearby **Chèvre d'Or** and the **Château Eza**. Dishes on this seaview terrace are cheaper and simpler: steak *tartare* and chips, chunky vegetables and cod with aïoli, grilled shrimp salad and pizzas.

Cap d'Ail

Le Cabanon €€€
Pointe des Douaniers, T04 93 78 01 94, capresort.com/cabanon.
Daily 1200-1500 & 1930-2330 (2200 in winter), closed Nov.

A 15-minute walk east of Cap d'Ail train station on the coastal path, Le Cabanon is a shade overpriced. But its impossibly romantic jumble of lampstands, wooden tables and parasols stuck out on a rocky peninsula is hard to beat. Southern French bistro fare: duck *cassoulet*, red mullet lasagne and beef stew.

Monaco

Yoshi at Le Métropole €€€€
4 av de la Madone, T00 377 93 15 15 15, metropole.com.
Tue-Sun 1215-1400 & 1930-2230.
Inside the incredibly glamorous Métropole lies Joël Robuchon's top-notch Japanese restaurant; the renowned 'chef of the century' also houses his eponymous restaurant in the same hotel. Lunchtimes feature sushi and sashimi Bento Boxes from €29 up to an ouch-inducing €90. Dinner is jaw-dropping, and pricier still.

Amici Miei €€€
16 quai Jean-Charles Rey, T00 377 92 05 92 14.
Daily 1200-1600 & 1900-2330.
Home-spun Italian restaurant plucked out of central Italy and plonked in gleaming Fontvieille harbour. Photos of 1980s celebrities line the walls of the dining room, where a fish-rich set menu (*branzino alla griglia, spaghetti ai frutti di mare*) is dished up. The terrace overlooks the marina and Palace hill.

La Salière €€€
*14 quai Jean-Charles-Rey,
T00 377 92 05 25 82.*
Daily 1200-1430 & 1930-2300.
Another highly recommended
Fontvieille harbour spectacular.
The trendy Mediterranean
specialist is popular with hip
locals and stars (ex-racing driver
David Coulthard among them).
Scallops with sage, crispy
Tuscan-style pizzas and *osso
bucco* are all cooked to
perfection.

Cafés & bars
Café de Paris
*Casino Square, T00 377 98 06 76
23, montecarloresort.com.*
Daily 0800-0200.
Monaco's best known 'see and
be seen' joint is still frequented
by the stars. A Parisian-style
brasserie with tables on the
square. (Alain Ducasse's
wallet-busting **Restaurant Louis
XV** resides through the Hôtel de
Paris' nearby gilded doorway.)
Diners breakfast on smoked
salmon, lunch on moderately
priced bistro classics, or sip
cocktails in the evening.

Menton

Basilico €€
1 square Victoria, T04 93 35 76 04.
Thu-Tue 1900-2230.
Italian-run pizzeria and grill
reassuringly packed with *signori*
from over the border. Crisp,
simple pizzas (Parma ham,
rocket, top grade mozzarella),

great meats (*escalope à la
Milanese*) and fish (*fritto misto,
gambas grillées*) inside or on the
terrace.

Braijade Méridiounale €€
66 rue Longue, T04 93 35 65 65.
Daily 1930-2130, Thu-Sun
1200-1400.
Hearty carnivorous cuisine
tempered by platters of
vegetables, all served in a
medieval-style wooden-beamed
cave. House special are the
skewers of marinated prawns,
lamb and beef, which arrive
suspended over your plate.

Brasserie le Brazza €
*2 place Georges Clemenceau,
T04 93 35 73 12.*
Daily 0700-2000.
Ignore the plastic tables. This
neighbourhood brasserie
covering the *place* whips up
delightful *tajines, steak-frites* and
moules marinière. Open all hours,
making for a good tree-dappled
coffee and snack spot.

Cafés & bars
La Cigale
7 av Carnot, T04 93 35 74 66.
Wed-Mon 0700-1930.
A *citron*-centric *pâtisserie* and
salon de thé hooked on locally
sourced Menton lemons. Try
*crème brûlée au citron, tarte au
citron* and home-made *pâte
de citron*.

Entertainment

Nice

Cinema
Cinéma Mercury
16 place Garibaldi, T04 93 55 37 81.
Original language art house
movies shown thrice daily.

Cinémathèque Acropolis
*3 esplanade Kennedy, T04 92 04
06 66, cinematheque-nice.com.*
Original language classic films.

Bars & clubs
Bliss Bar
12 rue de l'Abbaye, T04 93 16 82 38.
Daily 1800-0100.
Trendy DJ and cocktail bar, open
late in Nice Old Town.

Wayne's
*15 rue de la Préfecture,
T04 93 13 46 99, waynes.fr.*
Daily 1200-0100.
Raucous dancing on the tables
to international cover bands.

Music
Opéra de Nice
*4 rue St-François-de-Paule, T04
92 17 40 00, opera-nice.org.*
Superb calendar of opera, ballet
and recitals in rococo seafront
opera house.

Festivals & events
Riviera Comedy Club
*Antibes, Cannes, Monaco & Nice,
T06 71 49 79 12,
therivieracomedyclub.com.*
Weekly program of comedians
plucked from the Edinburgh
Festival and British TV.

Shopping

Bars & clubs
Palais
1 La Croisette, T04 92 99 33 33,
palais-club.com.
Daily 2200-0400.
Summer-only celeb-spotting
superclub.

Music
Made in Cannes
Various locations, T04 97 06 44
90, madeincannes.com.
Theatre, ballet, modern dance and
circus troupe. More performances
at Théâtre de Licorne.

Bars & clubs
Le Village Voom Voom
1 bd de la Pinède, T04 92 93 90 00.
Jul-Aug daily 2200-0400,
Sep-Jun Fri & Sat 2200-0400.
Hot disco destination for hip
tourists.

Cinema
Monaco Open-air Cinema
Parking du chemin des Pêcheurs,
T08 92 68 00 72,
cinemasporting.com.
Summer-long al fresco
auditorium with English-
language blockbusters; set
up by Le Sporting cinema in
Casino Square.

Bars & clubs
Stars'N'Bars
6 quai Antoine 1er, T00 377 97 97
95 95, starsnbars.com.
Tue-Sun 1200-0200.
Fun, cheesy pub that kicks off
many a rowdy Monaco evening.

Music
Opéra de Monte-Carlo
Grimaldi Forum, T00 377 98 06 28
28, opera.mc.
Celebrity-orientated but expertly
produced opera performances.

Festivals & events
Festival de Musique
T04 92 41 76 95,
festivalmusiquementon.com.
A fortnight of open-air classical
concerts in August.

Red hot chilli peppers in Nice's flower market.

Art & antiques
Rue Delphy
Most open Tue-Sat 1000-1230,
1430-1800.
An entire street of antique maps,
objets d'art, sculptures and
editions near the MAMAC.

Nice Antiques Market
Cours Saleya.
Mon 0900-1800.
Cutlery, linen, 1950s Milanese
furniture, €10 stalls and much else.

Books
Librairie Masséna
55 rue Gioffredo, T04 93 80 90 16.
Mon-Sat 1000-1900.
Elegant selection of English-
language books and travel
guides.

Department stores
Galeries Lafayette
6 av Jean Médecin,
T04 92 47 64 54.
Mon-Sat 0900-2000.
Designer labels, luggage, linen
and terrific twice-yearly sales.

Food & drink
Cave Caprioglio
16 rue de la Préfecture,
T04 93 85 71 36.
Tue-Sun 1000-1300, 1500-1900.
Wine store *par excellence*
featuring Bellet (see page 80)
and rare Southern vintages.

Boulangerie Hervé Martinez
24 rue Cassini, T04 93 55 32 75.
Tue-Sat 0700-1900, Sun
0700-1300.
Award-winning croissants,
pissaladière (Niçoise onion pizza)
and deluxe sandwiches to go.

Terres de Truffes
*11 rue St-François de Paule, T04
93 62 07 68, terresdetruffes.com.*
Mon-Sat 1200-1400 & 1900-2100.
Raw truffles and truffle products
fit for the Gods, from expert
Bruno Clément.

Souvenirs
L'Atelier des Cigales
13 rue du Collet, T04 93 85 70 62.
Mar-Oct & Dec Fri-Wed
1000-1800, Nov & Jan-Feb
Wed-Sat 1000-1800.
Lead-free, oven-proof Provençal
pottery, beautifully hand-
painted.

Bérénice & Eglantine
*15 rue de la Préfecture, T04 93 79
69 12, berenice-eglantine.com.*
Tue-Sat 1030-1900, Sun
1400-1900.
Spa and bath treats from Dr
Hauschka to local organic
goodies.

Cannes

Books
Cannes English Bookshop
*11 rue Bivouac Napoléon,
T04 93 99 40 08.*
Mon-Sat 1000-1845.

Thousands of titles. Hosts local
expat authors including Peter
Mayle and Carol Drinkwater.

Beachwear & clothing
Bathroom Graffiti
52 rue d'Antibes, T04 93 39 02 32.
Mon-Sat 1030-1900.
Sassy souvenirs, vintage airline
luggage, bikinis and shorts.

Food & drink
Marché Forville
Tue-Sun 0730-1230.
Organic section, fish, cheeses:
picnic heaven.

Antibes

Books
**Heidi's English Language
Books**
24 rue Aubernon, T04 93 34 74 11.
Tue-Sun 1000-1900.
New books upstairs, huge range
of second-hand downstairs, €1
slush pile outside.

Beachwear & clothing
Antibes Clothes Market
*Behind Post Office and on place
Nationale.*
Thu 0700-1200.
Second-hand and last season
designer goodies. Attracts savvy
shoppers from all over, including
the author's mother.

Monaco

Beachwear & clothing
Lull
*29 rue de Millo, T00 337 97 77 54
54, lull.mc.*
Mon-Sat 1000-2000, Sun
1400-2000.
Graffitied motorbike helmets,
funky jackets and a clothes
deconstruction atelier.

Outdoor equipment
Decathlon
*Fontvieille Commercial Centre,
T00 377 92 05 01 50, decathlon.fr.*
Mon-Sat 0900-2000.
Packed high with swimming
trunks, fishing gear, surf boards,
snorkels and much else.

Menton

Food & drink
Au Pays du Citron
*4 rue St Michel, T04 92 09 22 85,
aupaysducitron.com.*
Daily 1030-1230 & 1430-1830.
Lemon-crazy family outlet in
Menton for jam, citron olive oil,
limoncello and orange wine.

St-Paul

Souvenirs
Galerie Joel Guyot
*11 rue Grand, T04 94 32 80 60,
galerie-joelguyot.com.*
Hip gallery for Niçois art from
Ben, Arman, Bernard Reyboz
and others.

Activities & tours

Adventure
Air Odyssey
Cannes-Mandelieu Airport, T06 09 56 06 54, air-odyssey.com.
Panoramic flights in light aircraft over the Iles de Lérins, Gorges du Verdon and St-Tropez.

Eze Astrorama
Route de la Revère, Eze, T04 93 85 85 58, astrorama.net.
Peek at the stars from the Eze observatory on weekend evenings; €9, €7 concessions.

Monaco F1 Racing
Monte Carlo, T06 28 34 62 15, f1monaco-racing.com.
Tour the Monaco GP circuit in a rented Ferrari 430 F1 Spider; €50, or €100 to drive yourself.

Nature Elements
Roquebrune, T06 29 33 23 15, naturelements.com.
Tandem paragliding for beginners and school above Roquebrune village; €130/lesson.

Diving
Nice Diving
14 quai des Docks, Nice, T04 93 89 42 44, nicediving.com.
Undersea explorations and qualifications in English and French.

Food & wine
Confiserie Florian
14 quai Papacino, Nice, T04 93 55 43 50, confiserieflorian.com.
Daily 0900-1200, 1400-1830.

Famous candied fruit factory on Nice port; free.

Les Petits Farcis
Nice, petitsfarcis.com.
Gourmet Provençal cooking classes and market tours with chef and long-time Nice resident Rosa Jackson; lessons from €195 per person, market tours from €120 per person.

Bike/rickshaw/rollerblade
Holiday Bikes
holiday-bikes.com.
The first choice for scooter and bike rental. Nine Riviera bureaus including Beaulieu (T04 95 85 84 94), Cannes (T04 97 20 90 20) and Nice (T04 93 16 01 62).

Nice Cyclo
T04 93 81 76 15, cyclopolitain. com/nice.
Electronic rickshaws for hire (1030-1900) and tours.

Roller Station
49 quai des Etats Unis, Nice, roller-station.com.
Daily Apr-Sep 0930-2000, Oct-Mar 1000-1830.
Bike, skateboard and rollerblade hire on the Promenade.

Vélo Bleu
200 points around Nice, velobleu.org.
Electronic rent-a-bike system all around town; free for 30 minutes, €1/hour thereafter.

Transport

A car is often a hindrance in terms of traffic jams and parking. Conversely, public transport along the Riviera is world-class.

Bus
The no 100 bus (lignedazur.com) runs from Nice's bus station every 15 minutes during peak times to every coastal resort on the way to Monaco and Menton; no 200 runs every 30 minutes at peak times (very slowly) down the coast in the other direction, passing through Nice Airport Terminal 1 (0800-2200), Cagnes-sur-Mer, Antibes, Cannes and making a hundred other stops in between. From Nice airport (nice.aeroport.fr) the no 98 bus (0605-2350) departs every 20 minutes during business hours for Nice bus station, the no 99 (0755-2055) for Nice train station. Route no 110 (0845-2115) is an express service to Monaco and Menton. Other lines head north to the ski resorts of Auron and Isola 2000 (see page 168).

Train
The speedy coastal train service (sncf.fr) stops at 27 stations from Grasse to the Italian border every half hour or so, including almost all of the destinations in this chapter. A summer train pass (Carte Isabelle, valid Jun-Sep) grants unlimited access along this route.

Contents

Sunset over the Iles d'Hyères.

Port Cros, Iles d'Hyères.

Introduction

This most beguiling and varied area of Provence started from humble beginnings. The saltpans between La Capte's 4-km-long beaches were the primary source of income for Hyères' residents, while those living on Porquerolles Island and the Massif des Maures hill stations scratched a living from piracy and herding respectively, both of which likely vie for rank of the world's second oldest profession.

Aristocratic consumptives provided a wealthy fillip in the mid-1800s, but the economy of this stunningly beautiful region found itself best suited to the pursuit of pleasure. In the decades following painter Paul Signac's 'discovery' of the quaint charms of St-Tropez in 1892, other artists and celebrities glamorised the region with fiery canvases and architectural follies.

By and large, the area's magnificent beaches (Le Lavandou alone boasts 12) went untouched until they were invaded by US troops in 1944. Post-war, it was the French, not foreigners, who colonised the resorts of Ste-Maxime, Giens and Théoule, with quaintness unseen elsewhere in Provence. But as the luxury of leisure grew – and with it, the sexy decadence of St-Tropez and gastro-greatness of Bormes-les-Mimosas – so did the demand for escape. The unpretentious headed to the romantic hill villages of Gassin or Ramatuelle, or joined the island communities on Port-Cros and Levant: the former a nature reserve, the latter a reserve for naturists. The lonely D41 and N98 wind through the unruly Massif des Maures, while the Corniche de l'Esterel corkscrews through cliffs too precipitous to build on. And if the mountain trails and rigours of the GR9 don't tempt, perhaps the coastal paths around St-Tropez's peninsula and St-Raphaël will.

What to see in...

...one day
In **St-Tropez**, the canvases of the **Musée l'Annonciade** and the promenades of **place des Lices** and the **quay** best evoke the fishing-village-to-hedonist-hotspot story. An afternoon in nearby **Ramatuelle** or **Gassin**, or on a nearby white-sand beach, offers sweet respite. A day **snorkelling** on the **Iles d'Hyères**, or **hill town** hopping in the **Massif des Maures**, is equally appealing.

...a weekend or more
The **dozen beaches of Le Lavandou** warrant exploration, be it by car, scooter, kayak or speedboat. The region's **vineyards** drip down to the sea further east and west, while the hilltop redoubts of **Grimaud** and **La Garde-Freinet** could be explored in a full day.

The St-Tropez peninsula

To condemn this sun-kissed part of Provence as a mythical rich man's playground is naïve. While St-Tropez and its vine-and-pine patchwork peninsula can be expensive, it's also unassuming, friendly and more than a little bit fabulous.

In summer the epicentre of St-Tropez is molten. Its energy encourages eating, drinking and partying with abandon, and makes the old feel young again (although the odd sugar daddy can take this maxim too far). For a tranquil escape, some of Provence's best beaches are strung along the peninsula's hundreds of acres of protected coastline, while its most important modern art museum, the Musée l'Annonciade, is a haven of peace. Visit in winter and you'll be an honorary citizen, with low prices, empty beaches and some of the region's best restaurants all to yourself.

St-Tropez's glamorous harbour.

A commentator who coins any glitzy resort as the 'St-Tropez of such-and-such a place' is badly missing the point. Rather, this souped-up seaside village is the shabby-chic capital of understated elegance. The odd footballer who pitches up in a Hummer is scoffed at, his ton of ego snarled up in the savage summer traffic. More subtle visitors cruise around in a Mini Moke (see page 153), while millionaire locals arrive for lunch by scooter, with a battered Panama hat and big glasses for protection.

A **walking tour** (see page 136) of the town confirms St-Tropez's status as an overgrown fishing village, albeit a very trendy one. Fishermen once pulled their boats up to the town beach of La Ponche, where locals still take a dip each morning. Rows of brightly painted boats now share space in the harbour with dozens of floating motor yachts – plus a similar number of more low-key sailing craft – and their daily catch continues to make its way on to the marble slabs of the age-old fish market at the corner of the quay.

It was courtesy of the sea that St-Tropez got its name. When the Christian martyr Torpes was beheaded at Pisa, his torso was placed on a raft with a rooster and a dog, who were expected to devour the corpse as a final humiliation. Instead, St Torpes' unchewed (and unpecked) body floated into St-Tropez harbour smelling of roses, while the rooster flew to **Cogolin** (see page 142) and the dog fled to **Grimaud** (see page 143).

Further flotsam arrived in 1892 in the form of impressionist painter Paul Signac, whose boat *Olympia* sheltered from a storm in the bay. Enamoured with the unfussy resort, he bought a villa and was later joined on an artistic voyage by Matisse, Derain and Dufy. Known as *Les Fauves*, or the 'wild beasts', their use of strong colour and powerful portraits led to Fauvism, an artistic movement highlighted in glorious Technicolor inside the excellent **Musée l'Annonciade**.

Even St-Tropez's towering Citadelle could not forestall the flood that followed. The wealthy came

Tip…

Do not arrive anywhere on the peninsula in summer without a reservation. Book any of the recommended hotels (see page 146), or restaurants with attached accommodation (see page 148), as far in advance as possible.

Essentials

❶ **Getting around** Good roads and cycle tracks cover the entire peninsula. Most visitors bring or hire a set of wheels (see page 152), which can range from a mountain bike to a 4WD.

❷ **Bus station** Local bus services fan out from place des Lices, with services to Gassin, Ramatuelle, La Croix-Valmer and further afield leaving the small bus station on avenue Général Leclerc.

❸ **Hospital** Hôpital du Golfe de St-Tropez, Gassin, T04 98 12 50 00, ch-saint-tropez.fr.

❹ **Pharmacy** Pharmacie du Port, 9 quai Suffren, T04 94 97 00 06.

❺ **ATMs** All over St-Tropez and one in La Croix-Valmer, but none in Gassin, Ramatuelle or Plage Gigaro.

❼ **Post office** Place Alphonse Celli, St-Tropez.

❶ **Tourist information offices** Le Port, St-Tropez, T08 92 68 48 28, ot-saint-tropez.com, July-August daily 0930-1330 & 1500-2000, April-June, September-October daily 0930-1230 & 1400-1900, November-March daily 0930-1230 & 1400-1800; place de l'Ormeau, Ramatuelle, T04 98 12 64 00, ramatuelle-tourisme.com, July-August daily 0900-1300 & 1500-1930, April-June, September-October Monday-Saturday 0900-1300 & 1500-1900, November-March Monday-Friday 0900-1230 & 1400-1800.

to gaze at the landscape immortalised on the canvases. They were followed by the not-so-wealthy, buying postcards of the villas of the wealthy that sprang up out of nowhere along the coast.

Nowadays the local *Var Matin* newspaper publishes photos of the famous arrivals each summer, from Keith Richards to Jay-Z, as they tour around town or cruise to the beach clubs of **Plage de Pampelonne**, by far the peninsula's coolest beach. St-Tropez's narrow streets have long been accustomed to this A-list clientele, and a high-end array of restaurants and hip hotels has grown up around them, pushing prices inexorably upwards. The new mayor of St-Tropez, Jean-Pierre Tuveri, hopes to concentrate on high-end tourism, not least by culling the number of low-spending cruise ship passengers who alight here each year. In years to come, one of the few ways for mere mortals to visit in the pricey summer months may be on a boat trip from neighbouring Ste-Maxime, or on a bus from Le Lavandou or La Croix-Valmer.

While it's free to play *pétanque* in the place des Lices, or to mooch around its Tuesday and Saturday markets, succumbing to this fishing village's manifold charms on a long-term basis may be pushing the boat out too far for many. But committing yourself to a titanic 24 hours of spending is a scintillating insight into the party capital of the rich and famous.

Musée l'Annonciade, St-Tropez's must-see museum.

Musée l'Annonciade

Le Port, T04 94 17 84 10, saint-tropez.fr.
Jun-Sep 1000-1300 & 1500-1900, Oct-May Wed-Mon 1000-1200 & 1400-1800, closed Nov. €5, €3 under 18s.

Gazing over the port from its *emplacement* in the corner of the quay, this tidy summation of Provence's modern art scene is reason enough to visit St-Tropez. The 16th-century former chapel serves as a wonderful whitewashed backdrop for the glowing palettes of the greats, including Derain, Matisse and Marquet, all of whom followed Paul Signac south at the turn of the 20th century. Many of the paintings depict St-Tropez and the coastal Var, including canvases of the harbour outside by Signac.

Citadelle

Daily Apr-Sep 1000-1830, Oct-Mar 1000-1230 & 1330-1730. €2.50, under 8s free.

Wander over the drawbridge and you'll have this naval bastion very much to yourself. Poke about the ramparts, peek at the well and old washing basins, and gaze out over hundreds of square miles of sea: a delight at sunset. A single-roomed museum shows how the Citadelle could command the entire bay, with St-Tropez's sheltered harbour in its lee. The scale relief of the town from 1716 – there's not a villa in sight – shows this high-walled fort as a rough eight-pointed star, a design not dissimilar from the towering naval fortifications of Antibes and Toulon.

Plage de Pampelonne

Pampelonne's 5 km of white sand and lapping waves were the perfect approach for the American landing craft that pulled up here in August 1944. These attributes are similarly suitable for the outlandish revelries that occur here all summer. Prudes look away now.

It was Brigitte Bardot who made the strip famous with a topless excursion during Roger Vadim's 1956 movie *Et Dieu créa la femme*: 'And God created woman'. Nudity and sexual tension

Views from St-Tropez's Citadelle.

still abound on the **two dozen beach clubs** and **public areas** of sand. **Neptune Plage** is fully nudist, **Club 55** is where the A-list flock, while tabs running into tens of thousands of euros are racked up at the **Voile Rouge**, where merchant bankers have been known to spray lines of nubile beauties with jeroboams of vintage champagne. Other *plages*, like Aqua Club, are way more relaxed; all have sun loungers to rent for around €20-30 per day. The above nonsense switches abruptly off around 5pm, when the party people return for a siesta and fiesta back in St-Tropez. An hour later, evening swimmers and a posse of metal detectors arrive en-masse, the latter scanning the sand for lost euros, diamond rings and the odd designer watch.

Ramatuelle

Although popular with celebs who have grown tired of the coastal glitz, buzzing Thursday and Sunday morning markets prove that Ramatuelle is a real-life working town. Hand-painted signs advertising local ceramics, Aleppo soap, eucalyptus honey and *confiture de figues* tempt visitors around this beautifully restored village. But Ramatuelle's pre-chichi history is alive at every turn from the **medieval washrooms** on rue Victor Léon to the **Saracen entrance gate** nearby. The whitewashed **Napoleonic prison** along the road was once thought to be a Turkish-style bathhouse, thanks to its Arab-esque vaulted ceilings.

In a glade of wild olives and oaks five minutes above Ramatuelle by car is a similarly restored wonder: the **Moulin de Paillas** windmill (Mar-Oct Tue & Sat afternoons, free). When open, a wooden mechanism grinds wheat on the millstone. The drive from here to Gassin is bucolic, with the entire coastline, including the Iles d'Hyères, opening up to the left.

Gassin

The sun revolves around hilltop Gassin as if this overgrown hamlet was its own prettified planet. Renowned as one of the most beautiful villages in France (as well as the birthplace of France's most handsome footballer ever, David Ginola), its 360° views take in the Esterel hills and the yacht masts of distant St-Tropez. This playground in the sky played host to a honeymooning Mick and Bianca Jagger in 1971, although modern visitors are content to wander around the ramparts and along pretty rue des Bouchonniers, its name derived from the cork industry, which has its source in the dense surrounding woodland. To pull a *bouchon* or two there are few better cork-popping experiences than **Château Minuty** (T04 94 56 12 09, chateauminuty.com, Mon-Fri 0930-1245 & 1400-1845 Sat & Sun 1000-1215 & 1500-1730), a welcoming vineyard and purveyor of excellent wines 2 km north of the village. Wine-tastings are free and appointments unnecessary, although a minimum purchase is required.

Five of the best

Provençal Vineyard Visits

While you can sip, sample and stamp the grounds of almost all of Provence's vineyards, these five win plaudits for originality and quality. In all cases it's best to call ahead for a tasting.

❶ **Château Minuty** Excellent wine and extensive grounds with chapel, backed up by the massive 19th century château featured on the wine labels. See above.

❷ **Château Crémat** The 2000-year-old centre of viticulture, now a gold medal-winning domain near Nice. See page 80.

❸ **Domaine de la Croix** Cru Classé vineyard that supplies wine for hundreds of southern French restaurants. See page opposite.

❹ **Domaine de la Courtade** All organic vines on the island heaven of Porquerolles. See page 140.

❺ **Château du Pibarnon** Prestigious rosés from near Bandol. See page 199.

La Croix-Valmer & Plage Gigaro

Although built on a pre-Christian settlement, the *croix* in Valmer's name is derived from an apparition of the cross that appeared in the sky over the village in 1893. La Croix-Valmer now has enough picnic supplies to feed the 5000, its main square packed with *boulangeries*, rôtisserie chicken sellers and *charcuteries*, along with the day's international press. It also has a handful of excellent value hotels and B&Bs, of which the tourist office has a complete list.

A kilometre south of town is the welcoming vineyard of **Domaine de la Croix** (T04 94 95 01 75, domainedelacroix.com, Tue-Sat 1000-1300, 1500-1900). Slightly further are two beaches used in the Provence *débarquement*, the seaborne landings of World War II: **Plage du Débarquement** and **Plage Gigaro**. The latter is a chilled, restaurant-lined strip, which melts into the coastal path (see page 137) and deserted beaches of Cap Taillat and Cap Lardier.

Port Grimaud

The utopian vision of architect François Spoerry, Port Grimaud rose up from the sand dunes near St-Tropez in the 1960s. Spoerry envisaged a seaside village of the future: 100% privately maintained with access controlled by a security guard 'drawbridge'. Each property had its own mooring berth. But what could have turned out as a dull Docklands developed into a Little Venice, with the settlement expanding in stages until the 1990s. Cars are left in the parking lot outside, as visitors and residents mooch around the canals on foot or on one of the little four-person **electric boats** (€20/hr from inside the city walls). While tourists are unlikely to stay the night, the **GKL Go-Karting track** (Chemin des Blaquiers, T04 94 56 00 12, gkl-karting.com) on the Grimaud road and the surprisingly good value **Azur Park** (T04 94 56 48 39, azurpark.com, Apr-Sep daily 1200-0100) mini golf/adventure park/water slide complex on the main Port Grimaud-St-Tropez roundabout are great local distractions.

Long, sandy Plage Gigaro.

Exploring St-Tropez & the peninsula on foot

Historical St-Tropez

Like its cuisine, art and style, St-Tropez's history is vibrant, contemporary and visible on every corner. For a tasty sample, exit place des Lices on the northeast corner down rue Gambetta, leaving the *pétanque* players behind (fear not, they'll be in the same position when you return an hour later). Notice the street's intricately carved wooden doors, including those at no 52, behind which hides **Pan Deï**, a discreet €1000 a night celebrity-targeted hotel. Turn right uphill on delightful rue de la Citadelle to the corner of boulevard d'Aumale. (To take in the 17th-century Citadelle, with its cannons and impregnable views, carry on uphill past the two anchors to its entrance gate and drawbridge.)

Follow ivy-strewn boulevard d'Aumale downhill, taking a right turn into rue des Pêcheurs and place Person. At the lamp post at the end of this square, an unmarked *rue* leads left, passing an **oblong entrance door** on the building on your right: this traditional rounded shape allowed St-Tropez's fisherman to slip their boats indoors for storage. Carry on for 20 m to La Ponche, the small town beach where fishermen once hauled their catch.

Retrace your steps back to the oblong doorway and take a right. Walking over place Révélen, turn right into the **Porte de Révélen**, a dark fortified gateway dating from 1550, and come out onto rue de la Ponche. Just ahead is place Hôtel de Ville, hosting the fancy town hall on the right with flapping Tricolour above. At the entrance to the building on the far left is the **Porte de Zanzibar**, a carved wooden door brought back by a Tropezien captain. Head left before this house down rue Commandant Guichard to see the **Notre Dame de l'Assomption** church, its bright steeple St-Tropez's landmark, then return to the square.

Exit under the tree at the far left corner of the square, down rue Portalet. This takes you to **Tour de Portalet**, a 16th-century defensive tower, now lined with benches looking out to sea. The energetic can climb up and walk along the harbour wall, which overlooks St-Tropez's historic fishing fleet. Otherwise, carry on along the boat-lined quay to the statue of **Bailli de Suffren**, a St-Tropez native who rose to be chief commander of France's naval forces (1729-88). Further along is the **Musée l'Annonciade**, the Var's premier modern art stop housed in an ancient chapel. When done, retrace your steps to the Suffren statue, heading past the boutiques on rue Clemenceau back to place des Lices.

The coastal paths

The entire peninsula is circled by a coastal trail stretching 30 km from Cap Cavalaire to St-Tropez itself. It's well marked, takes in around 15 superb beaches and is stupendously beautiful, particularly the area between Plage Gigaro and Plage les Salins.

Those without a vehicle can often hike back to their base from a local bus stop. *Navette* buses run from St-Tropez's place des Lices five times daily to Plage des Salins, Cap du Pinet and other points on the easterly section of the coastal path (€1 each). From La Croix-Valmer, free *navettes* run all summer to Plage Gigaro and Plage du Débarquement on the southern edge of the coastal trail.

Heading anti-clockwise around the peninsula from Plage du Débarquement to Plage Gigaro the going is easy, before the path enters its most beautiful section around Cap Lardier, Cap Taillat and Cap Camarat. The beaches between these outcrops, including La Douane, Cap Taillat Plage and the lagoon of La Crique Canadel are stunning, although the trail can be tricky to navigate.

North of Cap Camarat is the 5-km sandy stretch of Plage de Pampelonne. After this glamorous beach, the trail rounds Cap du Pinet. At Plage les Salins it takes in another 2 km of sandy bays, weaving wondrously around the northeastern edge of the peninsula. The path remains pretty, but soon becomes poorly waymarked. Keep the sea on the right and you'll arrive under St-Tropez's Citadelle roughly 5 km later, passing the sailing boats on Plage des Canebiers and the small town beach of Plage des Graniers on the way.

Hyères & Giens

The South of France is no stranger to health tourism. Like a pioneer Priory Clinic, consumptive celebs including Victor Hugo, Robert Louis Stevenson and Queen Victoria dropped into sunny Hyères in the late 1800s. Some 50 years later the likes of Man Ray and Cocteau partied in the wonderful gardens around the Villa Noailles. But as fashions changed to ray bans and sun tans, the tide went out on hilltop Hyères. Predominantly domestic tourists now hit the beaches of La Capte, or strike out onto the magnificent Iles d'Hyères (see page 140) from La Tour Fondue ferry terminal. At the end of the isthmus, good-looking Giens is a village that guidebooks forgot.

Rascas island off Port-Cros. A snorkeling trail runs under the waves.

The odd belle époque mansion and the casino are visions of Hyères' more illustrious past, but it's the **medieval old town** and its environs that are most accessible. This crumbling *vieille ville* radiates outwards from the pavement cafés of place Massillon. The **Tour St-Blaise** – a tower dating from Templar times – and the **Eglise St-Paul** – stuffed with *ex-voto* paintings – overlook the square.

Hyères' legion of gardens includes the centrally located **Parc Olbius Riquier** (av Ambroise Thomas, T04 94 00 78 65, summer 0730-2000, winter 0730-1700, free), with seven hectares of rare exotic species and palms. Up past Villa Noailles is **Parc Ste-Claire** (T04 94 00 78 65, Jun-Aug 0800-1900, Sep-May 0800-1700, free), a sub-tropical garden which once belonged to the American novelist Edith Wharton. Rounding off the hill are the ruins of the **Vieux Château** (free), a classified 11th-century fortification now punctured with olive trees, pines and scented brush.

Villa Noailles

Montée de Noailles, T0 Villa E.1027 *4 98 08 01 93, villanoallles-hyeres.com.* **Jul-mid Sep Wed-Thu & Sat-Mon 1000-1200 & 1600-1930, Fri 1600-2200, mid Oct-Jun Wed-Sun 1000-1230 & 1400-1730. Free.**

This **modernist villa** and dazzling **cubist garden** could only exist in the South of France. Architect Robert Mallet-Stevens designed the Miami-style main house for art patron the Vicomte de Noailles in 1925. It swiftly became a haven for surrealists and filmmakers, and a party house for the likes of Picasso and Jean Cocteau, with fixtures and fittings courtesy of Giacometti and Eileen Gray. Man Ray's surreal-sexy movie *Les Mystères du Château du Dé* was filmed here, and is played on a loop alongside the other far-out modern art exhibits and photography on display. The attached exotic gardens of **Parc St-Bernard** (Jul-Aug 0800-1900, Sep-Jun 0800-1700, free) still offer visitors fragrant inspiration.

Essentials

⊙ Getting around Bus 67 links Hyères' bus station (T04 94 03 87 03) with La Tour Fondue ferry port via La Capte and Giens. Buses also link Hyères' town centre with its train station, 1 km south.

⊕ Hospital Centre Hospitalier Général, 579 rue Maréchal Juin, Hyères, T04 94 00 24 00, ch-hyeres.fr.

✚ Pharmacy Pharmacie du Fenouillet, 7 avenue Gambetta, Hyères, T04 94 65 01 15.

⌐ Post office 4 avenue Joseph Clotis, Hyères.

❶ Tourist information office 3 avenue Ambroise Thomas, Hyères, T04 94 01 84 50, hyeres-tourisme.com, July-August daily 0830-1930, September-June Monday-Friday 0900-1800, Sat 1000-1600.

Tour St-Blaise, Hyères.

Beautiful villages

From Hyères to St-Tropez there are scores of fairytale *villages perchés* and classic seaside gems. Here's our list of favourites:

❶ **Gassin** Justifiably proud of its official status as one of 'Les Plus Beaux Villages de France'.

❷ **Grimaud** Majestic tumble of flowers and honey-stone buildings, topped with a fairytale castle.

❸ **La Garde-Freinet** Austerely beautiful, with mountain backdrop and great country dining.

❹ **Giens** Knot your sweater around your neck and join France's cultured classes at this ever-so-sweet resort.

❺ **Bormes-les-Mimosas** Flower-filled and elegant; not to mention the regional gourmet capital.

La Capte

Giens is tethered to Hyères' port by two 4-km-long barrier beaches. **Plage La Capte** occupies the sheltered eastern side, awash with sandy beaches and holiday homes. **Plage l'Almanarre** is exposed to *mistral* gales and is a centre for windsurfing and kitesurfing (see page 152). In the middle of the two spits lies a salty moonscape marshland. La Capte becomes one long traffic jam on summer mornings as cars head to La Tour Fondue.

Giens

Tiny Giens is a subtle, attractive place to escape to. Like a fancy Breton port, it laps up French tourists who eschew ritzy holiday bustle for stone cottages and evening promenades around place Belvédère. A coastal path loops around the green peninsula all the way to La Tour Fondue, once a working fortification built by Cardinal Richelieu, now the ferry port for boats to the islands of Porquerolles and Port-Cros.

The Iles d'Hyères

These three show-stopping islands, known locally as *Les Iles d'Or*, or 'The Golden Islands', lumber majestically off the Var coast. Lit up by the morning sun, on approach they appear shrouded in rainforest canopy. Step ashore in summer and the aroma is sub-tropical, the water a light Bahama-blue. Disembark in winter and you can treat half an island as your own private domain.

The massive islands are all owned by the French state and are strictly preserved. Smoking and cars are prohibited, and development is kept to a bare minimum. Only the most westerly island of Porquerolles, with its year-round population of around 350, gets really busy in July and August. Pristine Port-Cros, the middle island, has about 50 residents and revels in National Park status. To the east, Levant has a population of around 100 and is an island of two halves. A tiny chunk is **Héliopolis**, Europe's first dedicated naturist village, while the rest is a French artillery test site: venture off the beaten track and you may get your bits blown off.

Porquerolles

All action centres on Porquerolles' port. A half-dozen beachy eating and accommodation options are lined out, Thai-bungalow style, on the waterfront. **Fort Ste-Agathe** (T04 94 58 07 24, mid May-Sep 1000-1200 & 1330-1700) towering above is a reminder of the islands' former duty as frontlines in the fight against piracy, and also as penal colonies (although being sentenced to 10 years on *les Iles d'Or* hardly seems like punishment now).

Four or five rental spots hire mountain bikes (€12/day), with tandems for those who really want to put their relationship to the test. Little five-person speedboats are available in the port (€100/day, no licence required). The island's best beaches are **Plage d'Argent** on the north coast and 3-km-long **Plage de Notre-Dame** to the east, but jumping of the rocks into the water is pinch-yourself-perfect just about anywhere.

Oenophiles can call ahead and visit the **Domaine de la Courtade** (T04 94 58 31 44, lacourtade.com). The island's vines and tropical flora are the legacy of Belgian-born Francis Joseph Fournier, who is buried in the island's cemetery. Fournier's first payday came by working on the Canadian Pacific railways, then on the Panama Canal and in the California Gold Rush. His own mining company struck Mexico's largest silver deposits at the turn of the century, enabling him to buy the entire island in 1912. Lucky devil.

Port-Cros

Port-Cros is Jurassic Park-like paradise. The roughly 30 km of well-signed trails fan out from the tiny port and take in rare birds, fungi, unkempt shores and aromatic herbs. A 4-hr route covers the island's many ruined forts, by way of the 192-m **Mont Vinaigre** and the cliff-top **route des Crêtes**. For coastal walks, the **sentier des Palmiers** close to the village, and the wild **sentier des Port-Man** on the east of the island, are recommended. The best beaches are the **Plage du Sud** and **Plage Palud**, both 30 minutes from the village, the latter with an undersea trail that follows the buoys out to Rascas island and back. As fishing is banned on the island, the waters teem with life.

Levant

Levant's **Héliopolis** naturist island colony is novel even in liberal Provence. But this nudist settlement is more Garden of Eden than Carry On Wifeswap. Clothes are banned from the **Plage des Grottes** beach, a short walk from the village. The **Domaine des Arbousiers** nature park is alive with exceptional Mediterranean plants and birdlife, including herons, shearwaters and terns. Some 90% of the island is occupied by the French military, although there's local talk of the army handing the island over to the state.

Bormes-les-Mimosas

Seen from afar, Bormes looks like an impressionist painting: a palette of pastel covered buildings tumbling down the hill. The town is so flooded with mimosas, roses, bougainvillea and seasonal

Essentials

❶ **Getting around** Two-island itineraries are possible from May-September when the density of services is highest. All prices are return. **Vedettes Îles d'Or** (T04 94 71 01 02, vedettesilesdor.fr) offers year-round crossings from Le Lavandou (6 daily Jul & Aug, 4 daily Apr-Jun & Sept-Oct, 1 daily Nov-Mar) to Port-Cros and Levant for €24.50, plus more expensive daily summer crossings from La Cavalaire port and La Croix-Valmer beach. **TLV** (T04 94 57 44 07, tlv-tvm.com) has year-round services from La Tour Fondue to Porquerolles (every 30 mins in summer) for €16.50 and from Hyères' port to Port-Cros or Levant for €24.20.

Tip...

Drinking water is available only in the port of each island, so stock up on arrival. A mere handful of bars and restaurants are open in winter.

Picnic on the Porquerolles.

blossom that it has been awarded four *ville fleurie* stars by the French state. Bormes is also a regional dining capital, with a dozen superb restaurant terraces – some on stone stairways, some in their own piazza – emanating out from place Gambetta. As well as hikes outside town, steps lead up to the ruined medieval **Château des Seigneurs de Fos**, which has panoramic views to the Iles d'Hyères.

The D41: The Hairy Road to Collobrières

Peaceful **Collobrières** is 20 km north of Bormes. It's reached by the hairy, scary D41, which bisects the Massif des Maures from north to south. A handsome centre for the cork and chestnut industries, it's also the nexus of a plethora of walking routes, for which the local tourist office can provide more information. Marooned up at 779 m in the Massif's dense woodland, a few kilometres from Collobrières, is the lonely **Chartreuse de la Verne** (T04 94 43 45 41, la.verne. free.fr, Feb-Dec Wed-Mon 1100-1700 (until 1800 Jul-Aug), €6, under 18s €3, under 11s free). A massive monastery dating from 1174, this captivating site contains a restored chapel, prison, bakery, church and refectory hall.

The N98: The High Road to St-Tropez

From Bormes, the N98 skirts through dark cork and chestnut plantations, zigzagging gloriously past mountain streams and Alpine valleys. After 12 km ('country kilometres', mind you) comes **La Môle**, a sleepy village blind to outside influences. Past town, **La Môle Aérodrome** serves the private jets of St-Tropez-bound VIPs. Fierce crosswinds make it a notoriously difficult airport to land at, and many celebrities have arrived in paradise with a bump.

Some 10 km further on is **Cogolin**. The town got its name from the legend of St Torpes (see page 131), when the martyr's rooster allegedly flew here upon arrival: *coq-au-lin*. Still very much a centre for artisanal goods, the averagely pretty streets are lined with carpet shops, pipe stores and vintners. From here, it's a short hop over to Grimaud, or a longer 10-km drive into St-Tropez.

Essentials

❶ Getting around A car, bike or scooter is the best way to travel, although the efficient 7802 bus runs from Bormes-les-Mimosas to St-Tropez via Cogolin and La Môle every two hours, and nos 7701 and 7202 link St-Tropez with La Garde-Freinet via Grimaud. The twice-daily 8803 bus links Hyères with Collobrières.

ATMs, Post office & Pharmacy In all the Massif des Maures villages.

❶ Tourist information offices Place Gambetta, Bormes-les-Mimosas, T04 94 01 38 38, bormeslesmimosas.com, July-August Monday-Saturday 0930-1300 & 1430-1900, Sunday 1000-1300 & 1500-1900, April-June & September Monday-Saturday 0930-1230 & 1430-1800 (until 1830 Jun & Sep), Sunday 1000-1300 & 1500-1800 (until 1830 Jun & Sep), October-March Monday-Saturday 0900-1230 & 1330-1730; place de la Mairie, La Garde-Freinet, T04 94 43 67 41, lagardefreinet-tourisme.com, July-August daily 0930-1300 & 1600-1830 (closed Sun afternoon), April-June & September Monday-Saturday 0930-1230 & 1530-1730, October-March Tuesday-Saturday 0930-1230 & 1400-1700.

Grimaud

One can see the medieval castle that crowns gorgeous Grimaud well before its perched lower village comes into view. This panoramic high point is perfect for a scramble around. The whole settlement is a legacy in both name and design of the Grimaldi family, whose well-heeled heritage lies in elegant piles throughout Provence. Following the village's historic walking tour past its Romanesque **Eglise St-Michel**, fountains and squares is a sweet confusion of flowering cacti, geraniums, citruses and climbing roses. A half-dozen unhurried, upmarket restaurants make this spot ripe for a morning's exploration.

La Garde-Freinet

An unrelenting 10-km uphill drive from Grimaud, handsome La Garde-Freinet welcomes visitors with a light mountain chill. A one-time centre for the cork industry, the local forests' other speciality is chestnuts: a posse of salesmen line the road into town each autumn. Signposts lead visitors up to the crucifix and Saracen fortress that can be seen from the bistro-lined main square. La Garde-Freinet's helpful Tourist Office has details of this walk and nine arduous others, some of which hook up to the GR9, which passes close to town. This bureau is also in possession of a giant accommodation book, filled with country homestays, mountain refuges and local *chambres d'hôtes*.

Le Lavandou

Le Lavandou was once a grand resort, now unashamedly dedicated to eating, promenading and reading a newspaper in a deckchair. Twelve tranquil beaches are scattered like jewels along the D559 Corniche des Maures, which winds slowly eastwards to St-Tropez. Sprinkled along are the easygoing resorts of Cavalière, Pramousquier and Canadel-sur-Mer, where holidaymakers can eat grilled fish and drink rosé until eternity. Yet, perhaps as public transport is limited to a coastal bus every hour, few foreigners visit, keeping prices low and lending a sense of discovery to the area. Such a royally beautiful stretch cannot last forever: it duly descends into tackiness at Cavalaire-sur-Mer.

Fish are still passed from Le Lavandou's working harbour straight to the restaurants that line boulevard Tassigny and the quay. Other than this taste of history, visitors happily trade cultural sightseeing for a day on the beach or a boat trip to the Iles d'Hyères. Behind the Tourist Office is the Lego-smooth cream and white Eglise St-Louis and a maze of tranquil old streets. The latter are ablaze with wood-fired pizza ovens all summer, when getting a table is managed with elbowroom only. In fact, seasonal overcrowding is such an issue that the mayor, Gil Bernadi, made it temporarily illegal to die in Le Lavandou in 2000, as disagreements broke out over the *placement* of a new cemetery.

Above: Grimaud's flower-filled streets.
Opposite page: Bourme les Mimosas.

Essentials

✚ **Pharmacy** Pharmacie Centrale, 21 avenue Martyrs de la Résistance, Le Lavandou, T04 94 71 03 55.

⌖ **Post office** 12 avenue Général de Gaulle, Le Lavandou.

ℹ **Tourist information office** Quai Gabriel Peri, Le Lavandou, T04 94 00 40 50, ot-lelavandou.fr, May-September daily 0900-1900, October-April Monday-Saturday 0900-1200 & 1400-1730.

Domaine du Rayol

Av des Belges, Rayol Canadel, T04 98 04 44 00, domainedurayol.org.
Daily 0930-dusk, €8, under 18 years €6.

The landscapes of the world's Mediterranean-type climatic zones, from Mexico to Chile and Australia, are set over 50 seaside acres. Tropical plants wind themselves along narrow trails, around the organic café, up Inca-like staircases and into moisture-drenched palm plantations. Visitors can don a mask and snorkel on the domain's private beach and follow the *sentier marin* (€17, €14 child (8-16 only), price includes Domaine entrance ticket) nature trail under the waves. Highly recommended.

The 12 beaches of Le Lavandou

According to local authorities, the Corniche des Maures' unique coast boasts 12 magical beaches featuring 12 different kinds of sand. A clever marketing ploy? Nope, they really are that magical. And in the case of Plage de Pramousquier, some do actually shimmer with gold. Most are a short walk down from the D559.

Plage de l'Anglade & Grand Plage Sheltered from westerly winds, L'Anglade turns into Le Lavandou's popular town beach, Grand Plage. Both are child friendly, with toilets, showers and lifeguards.
Plage de St-Clair Cracking beach sheltered by a rocky outcrop, lined with kid-friendly beach bars and a lifeguard.
Plage de la Fossette Small, discreet and magical, with fine soft sand. Sunset-facing.

Plage l'Aiguebelle Refined pine-shaded beach, backed by a couple of high-end beach restaurants.
Plage Jean-Blanc, Plage de l'Eléphant & Plage Rossignol All tiny and peaceful, even during high summer. Sandy-bottomed shallows surrounded by tropical brush.
Plage du Layet Wild and sunrise-facing. Half naturist, half funky beach restaurant. Excellent diving off the wooded outcrop to the right.
Plage de Cavalière Water sport heaven: hobie cats, windsurfers, kiteboards and volleyball, all under the watchful eye of lifeguards.
Plage du Cap Nègre & Plage de Pramousquier Either side of exclusive Cap Nègre, the summer playground of the Sarkozy-Bruni clan. Both feature chic beach bars and sublime swimming. Plage du Rayol Canadel, 1 km further east, is equally awesome.

Ste-Maxime to the Corniche de l'Esterel

Between the old-style resorts of Ste-Maxime and La Napoule is Provence's least pretentious stretch of coast, offering an inexpensive, unhurried comedown after the decadence of St-Tropez. Although sprawling, St-Raphaël is best used as a rail and road junction; adjoining Fréjus is a discovery for archaeologists. The beach-speckled Corniche de l'Esterel, which cuts through the red Esterel hills into Cannes, is of film location standard.

Ste-Maxime

This resort made its name in the 1920s, and is a cheaper alternative to staying in St-Tropez (to which ferries leave every 15 mins in summer). Ste-Maxime's ring of family-friendly Blue Flag beaches are an unfussy joy. The **Aqualand** (T04 94 55 54 43, route Plan de la Tour, aqualand.fr, mid Jun-Aug daily 1000-1900, €24.50, under 12 years €18, under 1 m free) water park just north of town offers such rides as Kamikaze and Free Fall.

Fréjus, St-Raphaël & around

Beguiling Fréjus was once a bustling Roman town with a 10,000-seat **amphitheatre** (rue Henri Vadon,

T04 94 53 58 73). The nearby **Théâtre Romain** (Roman Theatre, av du Théâtre Romain, T04 94 53 58 75) held social, not gladiatorial, events and now hosts summer concerts. Once a haunt of Alexandre Dumas and F Scott Fitzgerald, **St-Raphaël's** glitzy sheen has been subsumed into a working town and ferry port. Those waiting for a fast train to Nice or Marseille can check out the graceful **Eglise Notre Dame**, the basilica of which dominates the skyline. Some 15 km northeast, **Roquebrune-sur-Argens** is a walking centre, with canoes for hire (see page 152) on the lovely Argens river.

The Corniche de l'Esterel

A spectacular 35 km of coast road. Like a sharply edited road movie, the crimson reds of the bulbous Esterel mountains are mashed with deep blues as the rocks crash into the sea. The action sequence is broken up every 5 km or so by a yellow sandy strip.

Opposite the resort of **Dramont** is the private island of **Ile d'Or**. Its mock Saracen castle was built by an oddball physician, Augustus Lutaud. He threw wild parties, declared himself king of the island in 1913 and inspired a Tintin adventure, where our blonde hero chases a mad doctor. A few kilometres on is charming **Agay**, with a string of little beaches before and after.

Midway along the Corniche, **Le Trayas** is the best starting point for jaunts into the Esterel, including the 492-m-high **Pic de l'Ours**, which is signposted from the tiny train station. The beaches of L'Aiguille beaches just west of family-friendly **Théoule-sur-Mer** are among the cutest and most isolated on the coast, although Théoule's town beach is also worthy of a mention. After more cliff-top switchbacks comes La Napoule, home of the **Château de la Napoule** (T04 93 49 95 05, chateau-lanapoule.com, Feb-Oct daily 1000-1800, tours at 1130, 1430, 1530, 1630, Nov-Jan daily 1000-1700 (from 1400 on weekdays), tours at 1430 & 1530). Another preposterous folly, the château was built by former Wall Street banker American Henry Clews in 1918. He hosted fancy dress parties in his flamingo-filled exotic gardens and rarely left his seaside wonderland. The beaches of Cannes are visible after a couple more hairpin bends.

Essentials

➊ Getting around Regular buses to Ste-Maxime, Roquebrune-sur-Argens, Fréjus and La Trayas depart from St-Raphaël's **bus station** on quai Albert, T04 94 95 24 82. The **train station** on place Gallieni is good for coastal hops eastwards to La Napoule, and further afield. A pass to all the sights in Fréjus, including the amphitheatre, the archaeological museum, the Roman theatre, local history museum and an incongruous copy of a Malian mosque, costs €4.60, or €3.10 for over 65 and under 12s. All are open from Tuesday-Sunday 0930-1230 & 1400-1800 (until 1700 mid Oct-mid Apr).

➕ Pharmacy Pharmacie Provençale, 62 rue Général de Gaulle, Fréjus, T04 94 51 28 98; Pharmacie Bausset, 76 avenue Charles de Gaulle, Ste-Maxime, T04 94 96 19 56.

➋ Post office 75 rue Docteur Albert Ciamin, Fréjus; 12 boulevard Frédéric Mistral, Ste-Maxime.

➊ Tourist information office 249 rue Jean Jaurès, Fréjus, T04 94 51 83 83, frejus.fr, June-September daily 0900-1900, April-May Monday-Saturday 0930-1800, Sunday 0930-1200, October-March Monday-Saturday 0930-1200 & 1400-1800, Sunday 0930-1200.

Yacht's lined up in Le Lavandou harbour.

Sleeping

St-Tropez

Pastis €€€€
61 av du Général Leclerc, T04 98 12 56 50, pastis-st-tropez.com. Closed Dec.
Remodelled from a former *hôtel particulier*, or wealthy private home, Pastis still feels like one. Nine wow-factor rooms (high linen counts, marble bathrooms with double sinks) are set around a large black swimming pool, itself framed by striped bathing cabins, cushions, candles and light wood furniture. The bar-cum-library is filled with contemporary art and is for hotel guests only. Amazing.

Hôtel des Lices €€€
Av Grangeon, T04 94 97 28 28, hoteldeslices.com. Closed mid Nov-Mar.
Effortlessly cool. Heavy pink and grey interior with cascading light fittings and a wall of cushions for seats in the lounge bar. Outside is a black tile swimming pool with fountain. Classy garden furniture on each balcony or sun terrace. An eminently affordable treat.

Hôtel Lou Cagnard €€
18 av Paul Roussel, T04 94 97 04 24, hotel-lou-cagnard.com. Closed Nov-Christmas.
St-Tropez's best budget option naturally fills up fast (and employs a week-long minimum stay in Aug). The 19 rooms are set around a fig-, palm-, yucca- and lilac-covered enclave, two minutes from place des Lices. All have cool tile floors and French country furnishings; some have outdoor patios.

Plage de Pampelonne

Camping & self-catering
Tiki Hutte
T04 04 55 96 96, tiki-hutte.com. Closed Nov-Mar.
Luxury Thai-style beach bungalows sleeping 4-6 people (€80-300 depending on season, minimum one week stay) lined

The Pastis pool and terrace, St-Tropez.

up by St-Tropez's longest, coolest beach. Pizza oven for dinner; *babyfoot*, games, beach volley and billiards for additional fun.

Les Eucalytpus
Chemin des Moulins, T04 94 97 16 74, leseucalyptus.com.
Closed mid Nov-Feb.
A heavenly place to pitch a tent (€17 or €27 for 2 persons, depending on season) or camper van (€21 or €31). Five minutes' walk from Plage de Pampelonne. Garden space dotted with chairs, trees and BBQs. Washing machines, ice and hot showers a tad extra. Six blissfully cute studio bungalows with private terraces (around €500/week).

La Croix-Valmer

La Bienvenue €
Rue Louis Martin, T04 94 17 08 08, hotel-la-bienvenue.com.
Shockingly cheap century-old guesthouse with simple tiled-floor rooms in central La Croix-Valmer. Breakfast, taken in the south-facing gravel courtyard, is a treat. Private parking and sea views.

Plage Gigaro

Les 3 Iles €€€
Near Plage Gigaro, T04 93 49 03 73, 3iles.com.
Closed mid Oct-mid Mar.
Impeccably chilled B&B, complete with infinity pool and modern guestrooms. Breakfast is included

in the price and served on the massive terrace. On beach route between Plage Gigaro and La Croix-Valmer, a five-minute drive from each. Les 3 Iles refers to the views over the Iles d'Hyères.

Le Refuge €€
Plage Gigaro, T04 94 79 67 38.
Closed Nov-Mar.
A line of achingly beautiful studios – ground floor with open terrace, first floor with giant balconies – within wave-crashing distance of Plage Gigaro. Classic French furniture inside, shared gravel garden full of succulents outside. Books up months in advance.

Giens

Hôtel Provençal €€-€€€
Place St Pierre, T04 98 04 54 54, provencalhotel.com.
Closed mid Oct-Mar.
A hotel that sums up laid-back Giens: sea views all round with a wooden bar and guestrooms stuck gloriously in the 1950s. Magnificent waterside swimming pool, plus nearby tennis courts. Out-of-season offers.

Port-Cros

Le Manoir €€€€
Port-Cros, T04 94 05 90 52, monsite.wanadoo.fr/ hotelmanoirportcros.
Closed Oct-Easter.
Little can prepare you for the Eden-like glory of Le Manoir, the

only hotel on this sub-tropical nature reserve. Leafy garden for beers, a pool hemmed in by flowers and an obligatory half-board dinner, rich with squid, sea bass and fancy starters. Can arrange speedboat hire (€100/ day) and picnic baskets.

Bormes-les-Mimosas

Hôtel Paradis €-€€
62 Impasse Castellan, T04 94 01 32 62, hotelparadis.fr.
Twenty dated but cosy guestrooms, some looking out to sea, a stone's throw from Bormes' historic village centre. Citrus-covered patio with hammocks and loungers, private parking and Wi-Fi. Family-run and excellent value.

Le Lavandou

Hôtel Espadon €€
2 place Ernest-Reyer, T04 94 71 00 20, espadon-lavandou.com.
Closed Dec-Jan.
Ever-so-friendly central seafront establishment that lends a glamorous touch to Le Lavandou. Twenty slightly dated rooms vary in price depending on sea view, balcony or terrace. Parking, breakfast in bed optional.

Hôtel 'Ilot Fleuri €
Rue Cazin, T04 94 71 14 82, lilotfleuri.com.
Closed mid Nov-Mar.
Excellent little find, 20 m from the sea. The wood and white

Eating & drinking

walls decor are reminiscent of Granny's spare bedroom. Rooms have either balcony and sea view, or feature an outdoor table and two chairs facing the leafy communal courtyard. Book-swap shelf in vintage foyer.

Plage de Pramousquier

Villa du Plageron €€€
Chemin du Plageron,
T04 94 05 61 15, plageron.com.
Closed Nov-Dec.
Out-of-this-world B&B almost falling into the azure sea by Plage de Pramousquier. The main villa hosts several individually designed, yet simple, rooms and suites. Surrounded by a scented Mediterranean garden.

Ste-Maxime

Le Mas des Oliviers €€
Quartier de la Croisette, T04 94 96 13 31, hotellemasdesoliviers.com.
Closed Dec-Feb.
Tranquil hotel centred around pool, *pétanque* ground and

gardens, 1 km from the St-Tropez ferry terminal. The 20 rooms are a charming mix of classic French decor with modern fittings. Plus 12 studios sleeping 2-6 persons with private terraces (€320-780/ week).

Rayol Canadel

Hotel de la Plage €-€€
6 av Colonel Bouvet, T04 94 05 61 22, rayolhotelplage.com.
Closed Oct-Jan.
Excellent value accommodation overlooking the Iles d'Hyères, a quick hike uphill from Rayol Canadel's wonderful beach. Large pool, breakfast terrace, sun loungers and decent on-site restaurant to boot. Rooms very plain.

St-Tropez

Salama €€€
1 rue Tisserands, T04 94 97 59 62.
Jun-Aug daily 1900-2300, Mar-May & Sep Tue-Sun 1900-2300.
This acclaimed backstreet Moroccan restaurant is the real deal. Appetisers include *pastilla* (sweet pastry around fish or meat) and aubergine dips. Couscous with chicken, lemon and olives, and *tagine* with lamb and apricots are classic mains.

La Table du Marché €€€
38 rue Georges Clemenceau, T04 94 97 85 20, christophe-leroy.com.
Daily from 0730 (lunch 1230-1500, dinner 1900-2300).
Moderately priced and exciting bakery/atelier/dining room from star chef Cristophe Leroy. Daily €29 menu with glass of wine, vegetable *velouté* and fillet of cod, plus *tarte tatin* straight from the glass patisserie cabinet.

Le Café €€
Place des Lices, T04 94 97 44 69, lecafe.fr.
Daily 0800-2400, closed 1430-1800 out of season.
Only in St-Tropez could this place des Lices establishment blend a red banquette-lined interior and peeling 1960s film posters with a humidor and space age bathroom. Simple mains on the €18 lunch menu: salmon risotto, artichoke vinaigrette. *Pétanque* balls behind the bar – just ask to borrow for free.

The Ste-Maxime coastline.

L'Orient €€
3 rue St-Jean, T06 03 28 19 84.
Apr-Oct 1200-1430 & 1900-2400.
Surefire Lebanese specialist by
the port. Authentic Eastern
dishes on the tiny menu include
moutabal, shawarma and *warak*,
or eat the entire meze *carte* for
€35. Waterpipes and sweets on
the outdoor terrace for dessert.

Le Sporting €€
Place des Lices, T04 94 97 00 65.
Daily 0630-2400.
Friendly daily stopping point for
St-Tropez locals. Hamburgers,
mussels, club sandwiches and
pizzas, plus wine by the *pichet*,
make for an inexpensive lunch on
the *place*. A café in the afternoon,
cocktail bar after hours.

Le Gorille €
Le Port, T04 94 97 03 93,
legorille.com.
Trusty open-all-hours favourite,
Le Gorille has been serving *steak
tartare et frites* and simple sides
since 1953. New in 2009 was Le
Gorille O'Soleil on place Garonne
behind the port: similarly low key
with pizzas, pasta and grills.

Ramatuelle

La Ferme Ladouceur €€€€
*Quartier La Rouillère, T04 94 79
24 95, fermeladouceur.com.*
Daily 1900-2230, closed
Nov-mid Dec.
Romantically laid-out
underneath the fig trees,
midway between St-Tropez and

Ramatuelle. Chef Jérome Lentz's
inspired single set menu (€42)
changes daily: items include
scallop curry and crusted lamb.
Above the restaurant are six
tastefully traditional guestrooms
(€€-€€€) with tile floors and
stone sinks.

Café l'Ormeau €€
Place Ormeau, T04 94 79 16 78.
Daily 0800-2100.
Old-fashioned café and
centrepiece of Ramatuelle. The
day's local and international press
is lapped up with a *café crème* on
the terrace. Unelaborated solid
lunch dishes: *pavé de bœuf aux
morilles*, fillet of cod.

Gassin

Bello Visto €€€
Place des Barrys, T04 94 56 17 30,
bellovisto.eu.
Daily 0900-1430 & 1930-2300,
closed Nov-Mar.
The €28 set menu of *gambas à la
Provençale*, stewed beef cheeks
and thyme-roasted rabbit is
popular on Bello Visto's
delightful outdoor terrace. Long
marble bar for *pressions* inside.
Upstairs are nine simple rooms
(€€), some with cracking views.

Plage Gigaro

Le Refuge €€
T04 94 54 28 97.
Jul-Aug daily 1230-1430 &
1900-2230, Sep-Oct & Feb-Jun
Fri-Sun 1230-1430 & 1900-2230,
closed Nov-Jan.
Delicious find specializing in
Provençal favourites including
aïoli with cod. Stone's throw from
Plage Gigaro. The eccentric
dining terrace has an unruly
seating plan: school chairs,
wrought iron benches and stools
under parasols and pines.

Hyères

Le Bistrot de Marius €€
1 place Massillon, T04 94 35 88 38,
bistrotdemarius.fr.
Jul-Aug Tue-Sun 1200-1430 &
1930-2300, Sep-Oct & mid
Dec-Jun Wed-Sun 1200-1430 &
1930-2230, closed Nov-mid Dec.
Extravagantly fun cuisine dished
up on the wide terrace or within
a homely interior. Oysters, local
mussels and scallops for starters,
offbeat and classic meat cuts
for mains, Kahlua and liqueur-
based desserts. Well-priced
menus. Superb.

Bello Visto hotel and restaurant, Gassin.

Escoundudo €€€
2 ruelle du Moulin, T04 94 46 42 56, escoundudo.com.
Jul-Aug daily 1900-2230, Sep-Oct & Apr-Jun Tue-Sun 1900-2230, mid Jan-Mar Fri-Sat 1900-2230, closed Nov-mid Jan. Sloping down one of Bormes' picturesque little staircases. Tasty, elaborately presented dishes like foie gras mini-club sandwich, scallop lasagne and chestnut-stuffed chicken.

Grimaud

Café de France €€€
Place Neuve, T04 94 43 20 05.
Daily 0900-1500 & 1800-2000. Purveys a bankrupt aristocracy feel indoors with gilt trays and heavy silverware, outside wooden tables overlook Grimaud's main square. Hearty, unfussy, quality cuisine from *pavé de bœuf* with pepper sauce to duos of salmon and sea bass.

Le Lavandou

Le Pêcheur €€€
Quai Gabriel Péri, T04 94 71 42 48.
Daily Jul-Aug 1230-1430 & 1900-2300, Sep-Dec & Feb-Jun Tue-Sun 1900-2200, closed Jan. Harbour-fresh *brochettes de la mer*, seabream fillet and grilled sardines from this established quayside eatery. Rockfish soup and house aïoli are the specialities: both feature on €23 set menu.

Entertainment

Le Krill €€
22 rue Patron Ravello,
T04 94 46 39 56.
Daily 1200-1430 & 1800-2100.
With a terrace overlooking the
pricier restaurants on the quay,
Le Krill cheerfully bangs out
moules frites, superb steaks,
whitebait platters and *loup grillé*
for €16 as part of a two-course
menu. Good wine by the *pichet*.

Restaurant La Louisiane €€
18 av Président Vincent Auriol,
T04 94 71 24 59, lelavandou-
resto.com.
Daily 1230-1430 & 1900-2230,
closed Nov-mid Jan.
Simple waterfront seafood
and *bourride* specialist, the
latter a creamy Mediterranean
fish stew akin to *bouillabaisse*.
Paella *fruits de mer*, seafood
sauerkraut and stuffed mussels
are other options.

Plage Le Layat

Restaurant Mathias Dandine
€€€€
Av des Trois Dauphins, T04 94 71
15 53, mathiasdandine.com.
Daily 1200-1500, 1900-2300,
Sep-May closed Mon-Tue.
Magnificent signature restaurant
from young super-chef, which
tumbles over the seaside terrace
of the exorbitant **Hôtel Les
Roches** (€€€€). Crunchy, exotic
and playful textures on the €60
evening menu. Accompanying
wine deal available.

Plage de Pramousquier

Akwaba Beach €€€
T04 94 71 23 93,
akwababeach.com.
May-Sep daily 1000-2200.
Trendy beach bar and grill by the
crystalline waters of
Pramousquier. Toes in sand
dining, with coconut juice drinks,
fruits de mer and other classics
from this stretch of coast, plus
Tahitian salad and seared tuna.

Ste-Maxime

La Badiane €€€
6 rue Fernand Bessy,
T04 94 96 53 93.
Mon-Sat 1930-2130, closed
late Nov-mid Feb & mid
Jan-early Feb.
Young super-chef Geoffrey
Poësson cooks his way to
perfection on a street winding
back from Ste-Maxime's
promenade. Formerly of
gastro-pilgrimage site the
Moulin des Mougins (see
page 119), Poësson's original
seafood creations include
crustacean mousse and
gambas skewers.

St-Tropez

Bars & clubs
Chez les Garcons
11 rue du Cépoun San Martin, T04
94 43 68 70, chezlesgarcons.com.
Jun-Aug daily 1800-2400,
Apr-May & Sep Fri-Sat 1800-2400.
Pink, fluffy, miniscule gay-
friendly bar and lounge.

Le Papagayo
Le Port, T04 94 97 07 56.
Jun-Aug daily 2330-0500,
Apr-May & Sep Fri-Sat
2330-0500.
Hip 1970s hangout, now
blistering disco with raucous DJs.

Sénéquier
Le Port, T04 94 97 00 90,
senequier.com.
Daily 0700-2400.
Quayside tea room, pâtisserie
and bar. Locals' and celebs'
hangout. Wearing shades
obligatory.

Listings

Shopping

St-Tropez

Beachwear & clothing
Kiwi
10 rue Commerçants,
T04 94 97 41 67.
Apr-Oct Mon-Sat 1000-1930.
Everyday bikinis, shorts, towels
and bags. Several branches
around town.

Vilebrequin
24 rue Gambetta, T04 94 97 62
04, vilebrequin.com.
Apr-Oct Mon-Sat 1000-1930.
Pricey men and boys' swimming
shorts, synonymous with
St-Tropez.

Food & drink
La Tarte Tropézienne
Place des Lices, T04 94 97 04 69.
Daily 0630-2000.
Inventor of the famous custard
tart and purveyor of St-Tropez's
best sandwiches.

Souvenirs
Rondini
16 rue Georges Clemenceau,
T04 94 97 19 55, rondini.fr.
Tue-Sat 0900-1230, 1430-1900.
The original Tropézien sandal shop:
must-wear footwear from €100.

Ramatuelle

Souvenirs
Alm
25 rue du Centre & 10 place
Gabriel Péri, T06 11 62 01 63,
alm-ramatuelle.com.
Tue-Sat 1000-1300, 1600-1800,
Sun 1000-1300.
Colourful wobbly ceramics
and sexy fabrics.

Activities & tours

Adventure sports
Base du Rocher
D7, Roquebrune sur Argens,
T06 61 41 75 74, basedurocher.fr.
Canoe (€16 half day) and
mountain bike (€8 half day)
hire along the River Argens.

**Baptême de l'Air Flying
School**
Quartier de la Plaine, Fréjus, T06
60 05 49 91, ulmflyingsafari.com.
Light aircraft pilot baptism flights
over the coast (€60/20 mins) and
novice training courses.

Kaupo-Sport
Bd Patch, Plage Pampelonne,
T06 09 21 19 80, kauposport.com.
Hobie cat, windsurf and sailboat
rental.

A quiet day in St-Tropez.

MF Kite

1 allée des Genêts, Résidence les Bleues, Presqu'île de Giens, T06 76 31 89 45, mfkite.com.
Non-macho multilingual kitesurfing instruction on Plage l'Almanarre, €180 for weekend course.

Excursions

Escapa'Deuche

46 av Berthie Albrecht, Ste-Maxime, T06 15 77 67 57, escapadeuche.com.
Hire one of 20 different coloured 2CVs (€100/day) for a jaunt along the coast.

Hrubon Mini Moke

43 route des Plages, St-Tropez, T04 94 54 89 07.
Mini Moke rental. *Très chic* transport for €110/day.

LocAzur

9 route des Plages, St-Tropez, T04 94 97 57 85, locazur83.com.
Smart cars, VW Polos, 125cc and 50cc scooters (€45/day).

Octopussy Boat Rental

Le Port, St-Tropez, T04 94 56 53 10, octopussy.fr.
No-licence 6hp five-person speedboats (€160/day), plus bigger powerboats for hire.

Diving

European Diving School

Kon Tiki, Route des Plages, St-Tropez, T04 94 79 90 37, europeandiving.com.
Debut diving instruction (€25/30 mins, €49/2 hrs) in English and French from St-Tropez, Port Grimaud or Hyères.

Sun Plongée

Port-Cros port, T04 94 05 90 16, sun-plongee.com.
Island accommodation (€€) and day dives around the nature reserve of Port-Cros.

Tours

Taxi Bateau Boat Tours

Le Port, St-Tropez, T06 07 09 21 27, taxi-bateau.com.
Circuits around St-Tropez's celebrity villas (€9/1 hr) and fishing trips (€30/3 hrs).

Wellbeing

L'Institut des Lys

Place des Lices, St-Tropez, T04 94 97 01 02, institut-des-lys.fr.
Facials, hydrations, algae wraps (€50) and hour-long massages (€65).

Transport

Boat

Les Bateaux Verts (T04 94 49 29 39, lesbateauxverts.com) run boats from St-Tropez to Ste-Maxime every 15 minutes in summer, less frequently in winter. Harbour tours and trips to Port Grimaud, Port-Cros, Cannes and the Iles de Lérins are also offered. The aptly named **Bateaux Saint-Raphaël** (T04 94 85 17 46, bateauxsaintraphael.com) runs four boats daily to St-Tropez in summer, one or two per day in winter, plus seasonal daily boats to Agay and the Iles de Lérins. Mountain bikes and scooters are available to hire in most towns.

Bus

Regional buses (transports.var.fr) are quick, efficient and cheap at €2 per ride. Only the Var region's extremities – Toulon and St-Raphaël – are connected by train. Two main bus lines, nos 7801 and 7802, run every hour or so from Toulon to St-Tropez via Hyères. At Bormes-les-Mimosas no 7801 splits and runs along the coast road via Le Lavandou, Rayol Canadel and Gassin, while the 7802 runs along the N98 via Cogolin and La Môle. Heading east, no 7601 links St-Tropez with St-Raphaël via Ste-Maxime. To the north, nos 7701 and 7202 link St-Tropez with La Garde-Freinet via Grimaud. Regular buses also run from St-Raphaël to Nice airport and from St-Tropez to Toulon-Hyères aiport. Toulon-Hyères airport is also served by buses from Toulon (30 mins) and Hyères (10 mins) five times daily.

Contents

Haute-Provence

An aqueduct in the Haute Var.

Introduction

The least visited area of Provence defines the country at its most raw. Its snow-capped Alpine peaks melt into several lush valleys and flow in part into the Gorges du Verdon, Europe's very own Grand Canyon.

Pages of history have been written in the wilds of the Merveilles National Park near Tende, where cavemen scrawled birds, tools and human figures on rocky canvases. Several millennia later, Bonaparte carved the Route Napoléon through Digne and Barrême on his way up to Paris in 1815. A succession of train routes vied for supremacy at the turn of the 20th century and tamed the interior – to an extent, at least. The blocky stations of the fabulously green Haute Var region now lie dormant, but a superannuated line, the Train des Pignes, still creeks through the Var Valley past several fairytale hilltop retreats including Entrevaux and Peillon. Another picturesque line pushes up the Italianate Roya Valley – which only became part of France in 1947 – past the adventure sports centres of Breil-sur-Roya and Gorges de Saorge.

The Gorges du Verdon, despite only having been 'discovered' a century ago, have been firmly put on the map by thrill seekers – bungee jumpers, hill walkers and kayakers included. Plus, just 90 minutes north of the Riviera lies a host of family-friendly ski resorts. This being France, all are linked by an efficient public transport system, with buses between the slopes and the coast costing just €1 each way.

Fountain in hilltop Fayence.

What to see in...

...one day
Wherever your base, a day discovering a hill village like tranquil **Seillans** or towering **Entrevaux**, a big lunch and walk in the surrounding countryside is on the cards. The more adventurous are spoilt for choice for activities: try canoeing in the **Gorges du Verdon**, gliding above **Fayence** or summertime hiking in the ski resorts of **Auron** and **Isola 2000**.

...a weekend or more
Travel the entire **Roya Valley** or **Var Valley** by train, or plan a serious trek in the **Mercantour** or **Merveilles National Parks**. A cosy weekend using pretty **Bargemon**, **Moustiers-Ste-Marie** or **St-Martin-Vésubie** as a base for local exploration is an equally attractive alternative.

The Haute Var

Locals in this clean, green area of Provence grew up fearful of invasion from the coast. The legacy is a string of impregnable fairytale towns that stretches all the way from Aups and Entrecasteaux along the D562 to Seillans and Fayence on the edge of the Alpes-Maritimes border. Even Draguignan, the region's uninspiring commercial centre, owes its modern prosperity to armaments, firing ranges and military barracks. The entire Haute Var is carved by lonely hill-winding roads, and dotted with vineyards, vast forests, rocky outcrops and countless stumble-upon *chambres d'hôtes*, most of which are cheap and charming.

Abbaye du Thoronet

Le Thoronet, T04 94 60 43 90, thoronet. monuments-nationaux.fr. Daily Apr-Sep 1000-1830 (Sun closed 1200-1400), Oct-Mar 1000-1300, 1400-1700. €7, €4.50 concessions, under 18s free.

Cistercian monks established this vast pink and grey stone abbey in the 12th century. Fed up with the crooked riches of their overlords in Burgundy, they championed the simple life at this retreat, hidden away from temptation in a woody glen. Beside the peaceful Romanesque church are attractive yet austere cloisters, set on different levels to accommodate the sloping ground.

Aups, Contignac, Entrecasteaux & Salernes

Lovely, lofty **Aups** may date from Roman times but now it's mostly medieval turrets, towers and tiles that emanate out from place Martin-Bidrouré. Olives and vines surround unhurried, upmarket **Cotignac** further west, the fruit of which find their way into the oil and wine sold along its medieval streets. The highlight amid a swathe of refined architecture is the Romanesque 12th-century Eglise St-Pierre.

To the south, tiny gem **Entrecasteaux** is visited for its commanding **château** (T04 94 04 43 95, chateau-entrecasteaux.com, Easter-Oct Sun-Fri guided tour at 1600, additional tour Aug only 1130, €7, €4 concessions), a knights of yore experience with suits of armour and dark, imposing portraits. The **gardens** (daylight hours, free) are the fervent creations of André Le Nôtre, who dreamt up the gardens of Versailles and the Jardin des Tuileries in Paris. The centre of this archaic clutch of villages, sleepy **Salernes**, is famed for its ceramics and is dominated by a ruined medieval castle. The River Bresque, which brushes past the town, can be dived into at La Muie, a sublime swimming spot.

Essentials

❶ Getting around Autocars Blanc, T04 94 69 08 28, runs between Brignoles and Aups passing Contignac, Entrecasteaux and Salernes. Transport Gagnard, T04 93 36 27 97, links all points between Draguignan and Fayence including Seillans and Bargemon.

❷ ATMs Can be found in every town and village.

⊕ Hospital Centre Hospitalier, route Montferrat, Draguignan, T04 94 60 50 00, ch-dracenie.com.

⊕ Pharmacy Pharmacie Centrale, 2 place du Marché, Draguignan, T04 94 68 02 26; Pharmacie du Village, place Eglise St-Jean-Baptiste, Fayence, T04 94 76 00 61.

❶ Tourist information office Place Léon Roux, Fayence, T04 94 76 20 08, mid June-mid September Monday-Saturday 0900-1230 & 1400-1830, mid September-mid April Monday-Saturday 0900-1200 & 1400-1730, mid April-mid June Monday-Saturday 0900-1230 & 1400-1800, Sunday 1000-1200.

Above and opposite page: Thoronet Abbey from outside and in.

Around the region

Bargemon, Clavier & Callas

The fountains, al fresco restaurants and lazy beech-dappled squares of **Bargemon** were on the map before the Beckhams bought a villa near here in 2003. The town has fine views both of the valleys below and across to the perched one-restaurant-village of **Clavier**, which can be hiked to along the valley floor. A few kilometres further south, the stone houses of colourful **Callas** spread up the hill. From Bargemon, the D19 offers a heady link direct to Seillans and Fayence.

Seillans

Nestled in raggedy-jaggedy hills, stone-built Seillans is romantically strewn with ivy and window boxes. Home to a summer **opera festival** (see page 49), its colour and flamboyant outlook welcomed surrealist artist Max Ernst, who resided here and left a legacy of lithographs in the **Maison Waldberg** (mid Jun-mid Sep Tue-Fri 1000-1230 & 1430-1700, Sat 1430-1700, mid Sep-mid June Tue-Sat 1430-1730, €2) by the Tourist Office.

Fayence & around

Defensively positioned on a hilltop redoubt, the best view from Fayence is from the top, where a 5-m-long viewing tablet highlights every hill and hamlet in the bucolic surrounding area. A market is held (Mon, Thu & Sat mornings) under the swaying beech trees of **place St-Jean-Baptiste** with its commanding **18th-century church**.

South of the town, **Lac de St-Cassien** offers pedalos and outdoor lakeside dining for those who can't make the Gorges du Verdon (see page 162).

Autumn in Seillans.

Gorges du Verdon

t took millions of years for the topaz-coloured River Verdon to carve out the Gorges du Verdon, Europe's largest canyon. Over 20 km long and 700 m deep, it's one of the most arresting sights on the continent. It first came to national attention when Edouard Martel, who was surveying the area for the Southeast Electricity Company, stumbled upon it in 1905. Given that it's drawn visitors for less than a century, the valley is carpeted with orchids, sweet peas and other wild flowers, and it's possible to spot the odd golden eagle or Egyptian vulture circling overhead. The entire area was given National Park status in 1977 (parcduverdon.fr).

Famous for whitewater rafting and hardcore rock-climbing – with scary sounding routes like 'La Demande' and 'Dingomaniaque' – the Verdon spills into the gentler jade-green Lac de Ste-Croix. This watery theatre is great for sailing, kayaking, swimming and fishing, or simply tooling around on an electric boat.

Driving around the Gorges

Many visitors approach the Gorges from **Castellane**, a soaring hill village with commanding views over the raw countryside below, all crowned with the Notre Dame du Roc chapel, a 30-minute hike above the *vieille ville*. A self-styled Gateway to the Gorges with heaps of hotels and restaurants, Castellane serves as an excellent base.

Some 12 km south, the D952 road splits into northern and southern circuits of the Gorge. Here, the D555 runs past arty **Trigance** to the tortuous southern edge of the Gorge, the true-to-its-name **Corniche Sublime** (D71). Heading 10 km southeast of Trigance, park up at the **Balcons de la Mescla**, a skin-crawling viewing platform which lends a gross sense of scale to proceedings. Further west is the 650-m-high **Pont d'Artuby**, a bungee-jumping Mecca guaranteed to turn the tummy of anyone who drives it.

Towering **Aiguines** marks the western end of the Corniche Sublime. A climbing and rafting centre, it's also a great base for more placid water

Gorges du Verdon, Europe's largest canyon.

sports on nearby Lac de Ste-Croix. Some 17 km to the north is ludicrously pretty **Moustiers-Ste-Marie**, the classiest spot for exploring the Gorge, and the centre of the region's fine *faïence* pottery. Conversely **Riez**, 15 km further east, is a lavender industry town, almost untouched by tourism.

Heading west from Castellane past the Point Sublime viewing deck, the Gorges' heady northern edge is ringed by the **Route des Crêtes**. This road forms a breathtaking circle dotted with viewing platforms, its cliffhanging tarmac not for the faint-hearted. The route begins by functional **La-Palud-sur-Verdon**: a hiking, climbing and accommodation centre.

The Gorges on foot

Several footpaths cross the Gorges' monumental valley floor, including sections of the GR4 and GR49. Any walk requires forward planning in terms of weather, sustenance and the raging River Verdon's water level. Most arduous of these treks is the **Sentier Martel**, named after the Gorges' 'discoverer',

panning for seven or so hours from the Chalet de Maline to the Point Sublime (walkers will need to be picked up at the other end). Easier, shorter and better-marked routes are centred round the **Sentier du Lézard** trail, near the Point Sublime.

Essentials

❶ Getting around Be aware: distances around the Gorges and lake are massive, and public transport is not a viable option. Allow an entire day to tour around the area by car, and be sure to make an early start in high summer to avoid the inevitable traffic. Restaurants, post offices, pharmacies and shops for a picnic lunch are found in all the major Gorges villages.

❶ Tourist information office Place de l'Eglise, Moustiers-Ste-Marie, T04 92 74 67 84, moustiers.fr; avenue Tilleuls, Aiguines, T04 94 70 21 64, aiguines.com; rue Nationale, Castellane, T04 92 83 61 14, castellane. org; Le Château, La-Palud-sur-Verdon, T04 92 77 32 02, lapaludsurverdon.com.

Digne-les-Bains & Trains des Pignes

In terms of raw physical beauty, this most northerly area of Provence trumps the southern French coast. The only mountain rail line to breach the Provençal Alps, the Train des Pignes (so called as pine cones were originally used to ignite the engine) is a single-gauge railway that still serves the mountain communities, and is the best way of seeing the rivers, mountains and lakes of the Var valley and beyond. The network of helpful tourist offices along the route are stacked full of outdoor activities: Digne's has further information about 130 km of bikeways, the canyoning trails and climbing routes in the surrounding area, and can also book mountain accommodation on your behalf.

Dignes-les-Bains.

Digne-les-Bains

Ringed by green Alpine mountains, Digne-les-Bains is the northern railhead of the Train des Pignes and capital of the 'Alpes-de-Haute-Provence' department, hosting both the museums and bureaucratic trappings associated with such a position. Digne is also an excellent place to bed down on the cheap, and has a country cuisine beefy enough to fill the hungriest hiker, mountain-biker, kayaker or hill-walker. The 'les-Bains' suffix refers to the healing **thermal waters** (see page 172) in use since Roman times, which spring forth from the earth in avenue des Thermes.

Place du Général de Gaulle is Digne's café-lined main square. Just north, the **Musée Gassendi** (64 bd Gassendi, T04 92 31 45 29, musee-gassendi.org, Apr-Sep Wed-Mon 1100-1900, Oct-Mar Wed-Mon 1330-1730, €4, €2 concessions, under 21s free) offers everything from science to contemporary art. Heading 1 km south past the *vielle ville* and the gothic Cathédrale St-Jerome is the **Maison Alexandra David-Néel** (27 av Maréchal Juin, T04 92 31 32 38, alexandra-david-neel.org, obligatory 2-hr guided visit daily at 1400 and 1530, additional tour at 1000 from Apr-Dec, free). This fascinating former home of the French explorer charts her tour of Tibet in the 1950s by way of postcards, photographs and letters. She died in Digne in 1969, aged 101.

Train des Pignes

The Train des Pignes (trainprovence.com) opened up Haute Provence when the first steam train rattled down to Nice in 1911. A century later, now using a zippy Diesel engine, the three-hour journey to Nice is an experience in itself. Passengers can hop on and off at any of the chunky mountain stations using the same ticket. For the best view, sit by the big windows next to the drivers' seat at the very front, or very rear, of the carriage.

The four-times daily departure from Digne starts at a trundle through Alpine pastures, crags and cliffs to Mézel. The route then picks up speed through the dense primary forest – a patchwork of beech, oak, gorse, pine and heather – before running alongside the N85 by **Barrême**, a noted paragliding

Essentials

◎ **Train station** Train des Pignes (trainprovence.com): avenue Sémard, Digne-les-Bains, T04 92 31 01 58; 4 rue Alfred Binet, Nice, T04 97 03 80 80.

⊖ **Bus station** Digne-les-Bains, T04 92 31 50 00. Digne Taxi T04 92 31 26 22.

⊖ **ATMs** Stock up with cash at ATMs in Digne or Nice.

⊕ **Hospital** Quartier St Christophe, Digne-les-Bains, T04 92 30 15 15.

✛ **Pharmacy** Gilly, 14 place du Marché, Digne-les-Bains, T04 92 32 32 47.

↷ **Post office** 4 rue Honnorat, Digne-les-Bains, T04 94 30 80 52.

❶ **Tourist information office** Place du Tampinet, Digne-les-Bains, T04 92 36 62 62, ot-dignelesbains.fr, Monday-Saturday 0900-1200 & 1400-1800 (July & Aug daily).

Via Ferrata

Via Ferrata, meaning Iron Road in Italian, is the sport of traversing Alpine areas using zip lines, aerial walkways and iron stairs built into the rock. Digne's **Rocher de Neuf Heures** (T04 92 68 40 39, viaferrata-alpes.com, mid Jun-Sep daily, Oct-mid June Mon-Sat), a 500-m beginners' trail, opened in 2009, and is just one of many in the region. The location is a stiff, well-signed 30-minute hike up from place du Gaulle. Guides and full equipment (€12, €10 concessions) can be hired from the Tourist Office.

centre (see page 172). **St-André-les-Alpes**, the base for swimming and boating excursions on Lac de Castillon, is next up and makes a worthy stop.

Half an hour past the precipitous viaduct crossing at **Méaille** is the mountain stronghold of **Entrevaux**. Entrance to the remarkably pretty walled town is via a creaky drawbridge over the raging River Var. A menacing 17th-century castle (€3, open at all times) casts a shadow from above; it's worth a trip up the 156 m of stairs to the 360° observation panel at the top. Some 15 km further on, **Puget-Théniers** has a pretty old town and is ringed by walking routes. The perched village of **Villars-sur-Var**, an hour north of Nice, is a further 20 minutes down the track.

The Vésubie & Roya valleys

These two Alpine valleys are magically animated and eminently accessible. Both are crammed with activities that range from whitewater rafting to thermal relaxation; the Provençal accent and flavour of the austere Vésubie valley neatly contrasts with the colourful Italianate nature of the Roya. Both valleys meet in the Parc National du Mercantour, an unaffected sanctuary of soaring eagles and bronze-age cave paintings, criss-crossed with 600 km of footpaths that would take a lifetime to fully explore.

Parc National du Mercantour.

St-Martin-Vésubie & around

The 'Suisse Niçoise', as St-Martin-Vésubie is known, becomes a haven of cool respite for Riviera residents each summer. A network of narrow lanes, squares, churches and mini-canals lead off from the principal commercial artery, rue Cagnoli, which has its own little stream tumbling through it.

Come autumn and spring, the surrounding mountains burst with colour. They can be traversed along one of several **walking routes**. St-Martin's tourist office has information about several of these including the 10-km route to **Berthemont-les-Bains** (see page 172), a sulphurous regenerative spa in use since Roman times. Nearby **Venanson** (venanson.fr) is an easier, albeit uphill, walk. A silent, austere place, its highlight is the Chapelle Ste-Claire, decorated with dark frescoes depicting the life of Saint Sebastian. Outside on place St Jean is a water fountain rich in healthy minerals. For a longer jaunt, head up to **Colmiane** (colmiane.com), an Alpine ski and summer resort: it's a three-hour hike over cloud-obscured cliff edges and through dense pine forest.

Parc National du Mercantour

St-Martin-Vésubie sits on the edge of the 685 sq km **Mercantour National Park** (T04 93 16 78 88, parc-mercantour.eu). Designated as a National Park in 1979, 100 walking routes are available on the park's website as printable maps with descriptions in English, or are written-up in the Randoxygene guides (randoxygene.org) available from most tourist offices (free). Almost a million people come to enjoy the scenery each year, which takes in several 3000-m-plus peaks and a vibrant flora, and is home to reclusive chamois, stags, eagles, ermine, marmots, ibex and the odd deer.

The Roya valley train into Italy

This unruly, little-explored valley (royabevera.com) is linked by a railway line, which squeezes through the Alps four times daily all the way to Italy. Gifted to the new Kingdom of Italy in 1860 – the Roya valley was a favourite hunting ground of Turin-based King Vittorio

Essentials

⊖ **Bus station** Place de la Gare, St-Martin-Vésubie, T04 93 03 20 23.

⊛ **ATMs** Several in St-Martin and Tende; it's best to withdraw money for trips to nearby villages.

⊕ **Pharmacy** 50 rue Cagnoli, St-Martin-Vésubie, T04 93 03 20 02.

⌕ **Post office** Alongside tourist office in both St-Martin and Tende.

❶ **Tourist information office** Place Félix Faure, St-Martin-Vésubie, T04 93 03 21 28, saintmartinvesubie.fr, daily July-August 0900-1200 & 1400-1900, September-June 0900-1200 & 1400-1800 (closed Sunday afternoon); 103 avenue 16 septembre 1947, Tende, T04 93 04 73 71, tendemerveilles.com, daily 0900-1200 & 1400-1700 (closed Sun afternoon).

Emanuele II – they voted overwhelmingly to become part of France right after the Second World War.

The first stops of interest are the perched villages of **Peille** and **Peillon** (both a few kilometres from the train tracks) in the so-called *l'arrière pays*, the wild hiking country 30 minutes north of Nice by car. Next up is **Sospel**, a little gem of a town blessed with stunning views, several bridges, restaurants and country craft shops around place du Marché. Ten minutes further is **Breil-sur-Roya**, fast becoming an outdoor exploration centre, with River Roya walks and canoeing in the Gorges de Saorge (see page 172). **Saorge** and **La Brigue** are another 15 and 30 minutes along respectively, both unpolished yet all-too-beautiful retreats crammed with fresco-filled churches.

The highest point on the track is **Tende**. This busy market town boasts an atmospheric *vieille ville*, several Italian eateries and the **Musée des Merveilles** (av du 16 septembre 1947, T04 93 04 32 50, museedes merveilles.com, May-mid Oct daily 1000-1830, mid Oct-Apr Wed-Mon 1000-1700, free). The latter highlights the pre-Christian engravings and wacky geography found in the Vallée des Merveilles, just inside the Mercantour National Park, for which Tende serves as an excellent exploration base. Bustling **Cuneo**, an hour north, is the first major town over the Italian border.

Ski Provence

Provence isn't all sun, sand and sea. The lucky locals not only bask in year-round sun, but are also blessed with a handful of family-friendly ski resorts right on their doorstep, clustered an hour or so north of the coast. Remarkably, getting to most of them by public transport is a cinch. Most bus routes to the slopes cost just €1 each way, but must be reserved in advance.

The area's four major resorts are also keen to promote themselves as summer destinations. A mixture of mountain hiking, biking, horse riding, fishing, tennis, spa treatment and archery are available at each one. Their official websites flip from summer sports to winter snow mode each October in anticipation of the mid December to late March ski season.

Come snow or sun, all roads lead up from Nice's bus station, with a stop to pick up more passengers at the airport. The resorts, especially Isola 2000 and Auron, are set up for day-skiing, while there are plenty of hotels to rent for a single night should you prefer to squeeze in two full days on the slopes. Ski lessons at each resort are run by L'Ecole du Ski Français (esf.net), and are great value for groups. A final tip: the resorts get packed out on sunny winter weekends, so visit midweek if possible.

Auron

Tourist Office: Grange Cossa, T04 93 23 02 66, auron.com.
Day ski pass: €28.80, €24.40 students/over 65, €20.70 child.
Santa Azur (T08 00 06 01 06, santa-azur.com) line no 740 each morning, €1 each way. Ski Bus (T04 93 85 92 60) from Cannes and Antibes, weekends and school holidays, €35 return including ski pass.

Some 42 runs (nine black) over 135 km of pistes lead off this classy 1930s resort. There's a half-pipe and snowboard club for boarders, and the cute cross-country ski resort of **St-Dalmas le Selvage** (T04 93 02 46 40, saintdalmasleselvage.com) is 20 minutes away.

Isola 2000

Tourist Office: Immeuble Le Pélevos,
T04 93 23 15 15, isola2000.com.
Day ski pass: €28.80, €24.40 students/over 65,
€20.70 child.
Santa Azur (T08 00 06 01 06, santa-azur.com)
line no 750 each morning, €1 each way.
Ski Bus (T04 93 85 92 60) from Cannes and
Antibes, weekends and school holidays, €35
return including ski pass.

The closest resort to Nice (the journey can be done
in just over an hour by car from Nice airport) and
consequently busy at weekends. Around 120 km of
runs (three black) plus superb snowpark for boarders.
Curling, ice-karting and snowmobiling also possible.

La Foux d'Allos

Tourist Office: Centre Ville, La Foux,
T04 92 83 80 70, valdallos.com.
Day ski pass: €29, €24.80 students/under 24s,
€23.40 child (6-12)/over 65.
Haut Verdon Voyages (T04 92 83 95 81, haut-
verdon-voyages.com) runs a daily direct ski bus
from Digne-les-Bains (2 hrs) and from Thorame
on the Train des Pignes (1 hr, see page 165) line.
It also runs Saturday-only ski buses from Nice
airport (3 hrs, €45 return) and Aix-en-Provence
TGV station (3 hrs 45 mins, €30 return).

Climbing up from this massive timber-built resort
at a height of 1800 m are around 180 km of pistes.
The hundred lifts, chairs, gondolas and cable cars,
plus a reputation for persistent winter snow, makes
this a delight for serious skiers. Boarders can use
the snowpark areas, non-skiing kids the luge,
trampoline and snow gardens.

Valberg

Tourist Office: place Ginesy, T04 93 23 24 25,
valberg.com.
Day ski pass: €27.20, €22.90 students/over 60,
€20.20 child.
The Nice-Valberg line no 770 departs several
times daily from Nice bus station and airport
Terminal 1 each morning, €1 each way.

Valberg's 90 km of pistes (with six black runs) stretch
up to 2000 m and offer heaps of choice, especially
for blue and green runs. The usual snowy activities
from quad safari to ice-climbing are available too.
Kids will like the resort: there's a new crèche,
inexpensive children's ski lessons and a luge

Sleeping

Salernes

Le Mas des Oliviers €
Route de Sillans la Cascade, T04 94 70 75 20, masdesoliviers-salernes.com.
Cheerful *chambre d'hôtes* with pool, parking and simple dining *en famille*. The handful of bedrooms is a blue and yellow vision of Provence, with tiled floors, antique beds and big old furniture: rooms for couples as well as families of up to four.

Fayence

Moulin de la Camandoule €€-€€€
Chemin Notre Dame, T04 94 76 00 84, camandoule.com.
Polished former olive oil mill, now a hotel in 11 acres of orchards, parks and riverside lawns, 2 km downhill from Fayence. A dozen rustically chic bedrooms brim with antique charm. On-site Restaurant l'Escourtin (€€€) is a playful delight; the €30 lunch menu grants access to the hotel pool.

Aiguines

Altitude 823 €-€€
Grand Rue, T04 98 10 22 17, altitude823-verdon.com.
In haughty Aiguines, looking out over Lac de Ste-Croix. Nine simple rooms with a great restaurant attached (€€-€€€ for half-board). Free parking.

Moustiers-Ste-Marie

La Bouscatière €€€
Chemin Marcel Provence, T04 92 74 67 67, labouscatiere.com.
A five-room medley of Victorian rolltop baths, exposed beams, high-grade linen, double sinks and fireplaces, laid upon traditional Provençal tiles. In a converted mill in Moustiers' pleasant village centre.

Digne-les-Bains

Hôtel Central €
28 bd Gassendi, T04 92 31 31 91, lhotel-central.com.
A cosy hotel, well run by a husband and wife duo in downtown Digne. The bedrooms wouldn't make it into Elle Décor, but are clean, comfy and can accommodate from one to three people. Cheaper rooms without en suite are also available. Free Wi-Fi. Open year round.

St-André-les-Alpes

Hôtel Lac et Forêt €
Route de Nice, T04 92 89 07 38, lacforet.com.
A solid 1930s former 'Grand Hôtel' with views out on to Lac de Ste-Croix. The sheer number of rooms does justice to its elegant former incarnation; TV salon, restaurant, meeting room, plus 30 bedrooms for two, three or four persons. Mountain bike hire and free Wi-Fi available.

St-Martin-Vésubie

La Bonne Auberge €
98 allée de Verdun, T04 93 03 20 49, labonneauberge06.fr.
A solid, homely inn with a dozen standard rooms, midway between the bus station and St-Martin's sleepy town centre. The bar-restaurant reception area, which serves up three set menus of top country fare, is jam-packed with mountain guidebooks, an open fire and bottles of local firewater.

Auron

Le Chalet d'Auron €€€
Centre Village, T04 93 23 00 21, chaletdauron.com.
Very chilled out set-up of 17 Alpine-style rooms, all with free access to the jacuzzi, Turkish bath and pool. Hearty dishes in the restaurant; half-board available. Outdoor bar for winter sun; log fire and library inside for snowy nights.

Isola 2000

Hôtel du Soleil Chastillon €€
Centre Village, T04 93 23 26 00.
Like most of Isola's buildings, the Chastillon is a blocky concrete affair, but if you intend to just ski in and ski out – it's right by the lifts – there are few places better. Decent hot breakfasts and tasty dinners for those on half-board. Great midweek deals available.

Eating & drinking

Seillans

La Gloire de Mon Père €€€
Place Thouron, T04 94 76 98 68.
Fri-Tue 1200-1430 & 1930-2200.
Towering sycamores shade La
Gloire's idyllic outdoor terrace and
fountain on Seillans' prettiest
square. Culinary treats include
monkfish stew, sea bass with
champagne *coulis* and *filet mignon*
of wild boar. Understated elegance.

Fayence

Restaurant Le Provençal €€
*8 place Eglise St-Jean-Baptiste,
T04 94 76 24 91.*
Tue-Sun 1200-1500 & 1900-
2300, closed Nov.
Rustic hole-in-the-wall eatery,
which spreads over the square
during summertime. The menu
features regional wines,
home-baked breads (garlic or
tapenade) and hearty cuisine:
shepherd's salads, local cheeses,
beef stew and lasagne.

Moustiers-Ste-Marie

Bastide Moustiers €€€€
*Chemin de Quinson, T04 92 70 47
47, bastide-moustiers.com.*
Thu-Mon 1230-1400 &
1930-2130, closed Jan-Feb.
Sexy, modern Provençal
guesthouse (€€€€) and
restaurant from Alain Ducasse.
Chef Wilfrid Hocquet serves two
set menus of southern French
country cooking: mushrooms,
pigeon, local lamb et al.

Digne-les-Bains

La Chauvinière €-€€
56 rue de l'Hubac, T04 92 31 40 03.
Tue-Sat 1200-1400 & 1900-2230,
Sun 1200-1430.
Aside from some well-prepared
grilled sea bass and salmon
dishes, La Chauvinière turns out
unashamedly local meaty
cuisine. Its tried and tested menu
includes *faux-filet grillé*, frogs' legs
and *pavé de rumsteck*. Giant
salads brim with cheese, eggs,
sausage, *lardons*, chicken and
tomatoes.

La Taverne €
36 bd Gassendi, T04 92 31 30 82.
Daily 1130-1500 & 1830-2400.
Digne's coolest spot boasts black
chairs on the terrace and
lunchtime *plat du jour* bargains.
Pizza and salads sit with meat
and duck options, plus a trio
of two-person sharing plates:
a giant *côte de bœuf*, grilled
seafood platter or a mixed grill.

Entrevaux

Restaurant du Pont Levis €€
*Opposite the drawbridge,
T04 93 05 40 12.*
Sat-Thu 1230-2200.
Refined restaurant with a pretty
terrace overlooking Entrevaux's
drawbridge. Try *confit de lapin*
with rosemary, fresh fish from
the coast, or *secca d'Entrevaux*,
a local dried salt-beef dish.

St-Martin-Vésubie

Le Vieux Four €€
*3 rue Jacques Barraja,
T04 93 03 36 06.*
Tue-Sun 1900-2230.
Pizzas and grills based around a
massive wood-fired oven at the
end of a cavernous cellar. Salads
heaped with local cheeses, plus
cheap wine by the jug.
Unaffected and hearty.

Peillon

L'Auberge de la Madone €€€€
*Centre Village, T04 93 79 91 17,
auberge-madone-peillon.com.*
Thu-Tue 1200-1400 & 1930-
2200, closed Dec-Jan.
Michelin-starred French country
cooking in a fairytale 'perched
village'. Three set menus of
gastronomic creations, including
a stunning lamb with thyme
confit. Provence and Bellet wines
on offer. Sumptuous rooms with
half-board (€€€) are also available.

Sospel

Bel-Aqua €€
*7 bd de Verdun, T04 93 04 00 09,
sospel.net.*
Wed, Fri-Mon 1200-1400 &
1930-2100, closed Nov-Mar.
The Hotel des Etrangers' (€€)
cheap but classy restaurant. The
speciality is local trout, dished up
from tank to *assiette* in a matter
of minutes. Outdoor summer
terrace and great selection of
local Bellet wines.

Shopping

Food & drink
Pain d'Epicerie
Rue de Marché, Entrevaux,
T04 93 05 49 89.
Home-made chutneys,
herb-laden *pastis* and local
honey sold from a vat.

Outdoor gear
Decathlon
5 route de Marseille, Digne-les-Bains, T04 92 36 67 50.
Big branch of the outdoor chain:
stock up on camping gas,
torches and hiking boots.

Le Perroquet Vert
La-Palud-sur-Verdon village, T04 92 77 33 39, leperroquetvert.com.
Climbing shop *par excellence*;
doubles as an inexpensive
chambre d'hôtes.

Souvenirs
Sylviane Leibovitz
9 rue de l'Eglise, Seillans, T04 94 76 98 99, impression-maison-leibovitz.com.
Locally sourced linen, canvas
handbags and screen-printed
tablecloths.

Activities & tours

Adventure sports
Aboard Rafting
Place de l'Eglise, Castellane, T04 92 83 76 11, aboard-rafting.com.
Canyoning, kayaking, rafting and
hiking from established outfit.

Base Sport Nature
Entrevaux village, T04 93 05 41 18, basesportnature.com.
Local canyoning, Via Ferrata,
canoeing, plus rafting in the
Gorges du Verdon.

Ecole de Parapente
Barrême village, T04 92 34 34 00, haut-les-mains.fr.
First-time paragliding, tandem
gliding and equipment for hire.

Escapade
Place du Marché, St-Martin-Vésubie, T04 93 03 31 32, guidescapade.com.
Guided canyoning, Via Ferrata
and adventure sports in the
Mercantour National Park.

Fayence Gliding Club
Aérodrome de Fayence-Tourrettes, T04 94 76 00 68, aapca.net.
Day glides at Provence's biggest
gliding centre. Courses and cheap
accommodation also available.

Loisirs Mercantour
394 route St Pierre, Breil-sur-Roya, T04 93 04 92 05, loisirs-mercantour.com.
Central reservation point for
4WD drives, canoeing and hiking
in the Roya valley.

Ranch de l'Aubarède
Mons, T04 94 85 35 36.
Hour-long (€25) to two-day
(€185) horse riding expeditions.

Wellbeing
Thermes de Digne-les-Bains
Route des Thermes, Digne T04 92 32 58 46, eurothermes.com.
Thermal pool access from €4 a
day to zen and aromatherapy
treatments.

Thermes de Berthemont-les-Bains
Roquebillière village, T04 93 03 47 00, vesubian.com/sites/cure.htm.
Thermal baths and gloriously
cheap half-day massage
packages.

Transport

Using both the **Train des Pignes** (trainprovence.com) for
points up to Digne or the **line to Tende** (ter-sncf.com/paca) is
straightforward, as is hopping
aboard a dedicated ski bus. A
twice-daily bus links Nice with
St-Martin-Vésubie (€1 each way).
Be warned, however, that trying
to use public transport to visit
anywhere north of Fayence can
be a complete nightmare.
▸**Transports Gagnard** (T04 94 76 02 29) run buses between
Claviers, Fayence, Seillans and
Bargemon, while **SCAL** run lines
around Digne (T04 92 51 79 36,
scal-amv-voyages.com).

Entrevaux train station.

Contents

Marseille & the Calanques

Backstreets of Cassis Old Town.

Introduction

F rance's second biggest city and the country's busiest port, Marseille is the region's buzzing, boisterous capital. Saddled with a sorry reputation in the 1970s – *The French Connection* police drama did it no favours – the city has changed beyond recognition in the past decade, with a vibrancy not seen in any other city in Provence.

Marseille has always been a place of dynamic arrivals. Original Ligurian residents mixed with the Greeks who arrived in 600 BC, giving birth to the city-state of Massalia. Roman traders and Christian crusaders were thrown into the mix, and the arrival of 19th-century trains and ships would eventually put Marseille on course to become the most ethnically varied city in France. Home to large North African, Jewish and Italian populations, Marseille wears its diversity proudly. Huge swathes of the city continue to evolve, as the Euroméditerranée urban regeneration project sweeps positive transformation through the city.

The towns that surround Marseille make for a striking contrast. Assuredly more homogeneous, don't be surprised to meet five generations of wine-producers in Bandol, fishermen in Sanary-sur-Mer or restaurateurs in Cassis. These are all extremely welcoming places, with residents happy to share their history, local tips or even their favourite recipes. Time balanced between Marseille's metropolis and the nearby rural idyll makes for a delightful trip.

...one day
Spend the day in Marseille: stroll around Le Panier, take your pick of museums, watch the sun go down with a *pastis* in the Vieux Port, then top it all off by dining on the city's most famous dish, *bouillabaisse*.

...a weekend or more
Start by exploring Marseille's highlights, including the Château d'If (of *Count of Monte-Cristo* fame), then get out of town. Head to the fishing village of Cassis, hike your way into the natural beauty of the Massif des Calanques or drive through Bandol's cascades of vineyards.

Daily fish market at Marseille's Vieux Port.

Marseille

A teeming mix of international influences, city chaos and a thriving counter-culture, much of Marseille is exactly what the rest of Provence is not: no snoozy afternoons, ambling retirees or seafront promenades here. But for many visitors, this contrast is exactly what makes the city so appealing. Annual urban festivals crowd the city's calendar. There are art galleries and theatre performances by the dozen, a strong music – particularly hip-hop – scene and an innovative culinary tradition: the city claims both *bouillabaisse* (see box, page 182) and *pastis*, the *anis*-flavoured aperitif, as its own.

Dawn over Marseille's Vieux Port.

Marseille revels in its appointment as Europe's 2013 Capital of Culture (marseille-provence2013.fr). A driving factor behind the council's unanimous vote is the city's ongoing **Euroméditerranée project** (see box, page 188). A master plan for Marseille's urban regeneration, it includes the long-awaited **Musée des Civilisations de l'Europe et de la Méditerranée** (MuCEM, see page 185), now partially complete and holding temporary exhibitions in Fort St-Jean, plus a new 3-km seafront esplanade and many other developments.

The non-stop action is not just downtown: during summer, locals hit the city beach, **Plage des Catalans**. True sun-worshippers would do better to head to the stunning western Calanques (see page 192) or south to the **Plage du Prado** seaside park. Near the latter, pretty **Parc Borély**, with its rowing lake, and the **Musée d'Art Contemporain** (MAC, 9 av de Haïfa, T04 91 25 01 07, marseille.fr, Tue-Sun Jun-Sep 1100-1800, Oct-May 1000-1700, €3, €1.50 students/child (10-16), under 10s/over 65 free) make for great days out.

Vieux Port

M1 to 'Vieux Port'.
Map: Marseille, p180.

It was here (or near enough) that Greeks are said to have dropped anchor and founded the ancient metropolis of Massalia. Today, Marseille's old port remains the city's hub. To the north lies Le Panier, the true Old Town, while La Canebière, Marseille's central but slightly scruffy main drag, runs from the port eastwards to Palais Longchamp. The newly restored rue de la République also radiates out from here, its first few blocks lined with High Street chains, its buildings Parisian-sparkly and uplit as the wide road makes straight for place de la Joliette. Bars and restaurants crowd the pedestrian streets that wind their way through the neighbourhood south of the Vieux Port.

The harbour itself is flanked by 17th-century Fort St-Nicolas and Fort St-Jean, and packed with pleasure boats. Frequent ferries (see page 210) run to the Château d'If, Frioul islands – visible on the

Essentials

❶ Getting around Marseille is a hilly town, although the energetic will have no problem navigating the downtown area on foot. Marseille has two relatively new tram lines. The most useful for tourists is T2, which runs along La Canebière and northwards to place de la Joliette. There are two metro lines, linking Gare St-Charles with the Vieux Port (M1) or place Castellane, the Stade Vélodrome and points south (M2). The city is also home to an extensive network of buses, which will get you anywhere else you need to go. The same ticket is valid for travel on buses, trams or on the metro; a single ride on any of these costs €1.50. If you plan to use a fair amount of public transport, or are in town for a few days, it's worth buying a *carte journée* (day pass, €5) or carnet of tickets (5 rides €6.30, 10 rides €12.60). You can buy tickets in metro stations, on the bus or from automatic kiosks at each tram stop. Note that tickets are not sold on trams, and you must validate your ticket at one of the small, freestanding machines before boarding. For further information about public transport in Marseille, see rtm.fr. Taxi stands are dotted around town, including one in the northeast corner of the Vieux Port (across from Bar de la Samaritaine); you can also arrange a pick-up by contacting Taxi Radio Marseille (T04 91 02 20 20). Although plenty of ferries run trips to the nearby Calanques, they're always return excursions, rather than an actual means of transport. For links to and from Marseille Provence Airport, see the Transport section at the end of this chapter.

❷ Train station Gare St-Charles, square Narvik.

❸ Bus station Gare St-Charles, rue Honnorat.

❹ Ferry station Place de la Joliette & boulevard des Dames.

❺ ATMs Throughout the city.

❻ Hospital Hôpital de la Timone, 264 rue St-Pierre, T04 91 38 60 00, ap-hm.fr.

❼ Pharmacy Pharmacie Tran Nghi, 10 cours Belsunce, T04 91 90 14 58.

❽ Post office 1 cours Jean Ballard, T04 96 11 23 63.

❾ Tourist information office 4 la Canebière (Vieux Port), T04 91 13 89 00, marseille-tourisme.com, Monday-Saturday 0900-1900, Sunday & holidays 1000-1700.

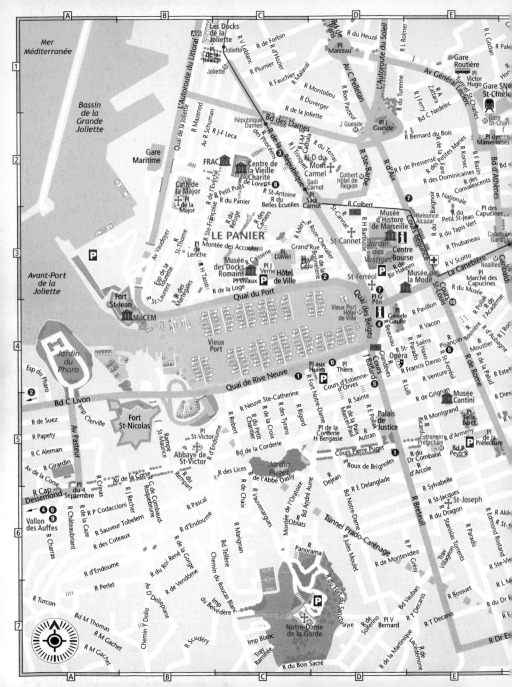

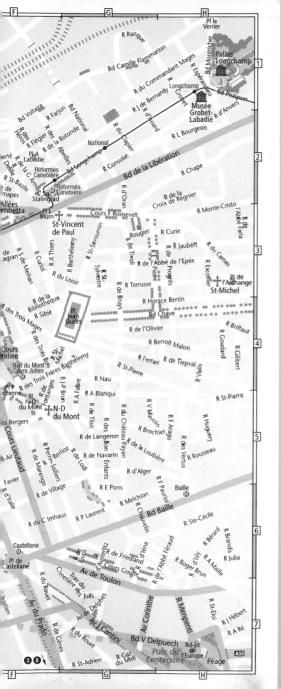

Marseille listings

Sleeping

1 Hôtel du Palais *26 rue Breteuil* D5
2 Hôtel Hermes *2 rue de la Bonneterie* D3
3 Hôtel Le Corbusier *280 boulevard Michelet* F7
4 Hôtel Péron *119 Corniche de Président John Fitzgerald* A6
5 Hôtel St-Ferréol *19 rue Pisançon* E4
6 Le Petit Nice Passédat *17 rue des Braves* A6
7 New Hôtel Vieux Port *rue de la Reine Elisabeth* D3
8 Villa Massalia *place Louis Bonnefon* F7

Eating & drinking

1 Bar de la Marine *15 quai Rive Neuve* C4
2 Chez Michel *6 rue des Catalans* A5
3 Heng-Heng *65 rue de la République* C2
4 OM Café *quai des Belges* D4
5 Orange Basilic *11 cours d'Estienne d'Orves* D4
6 Oscar's *24 quai du Port* D3
7 Pâtisserie d'Aix *2 rue d'Aix* E2
8 Pizzeria Etienne *43 rue de Lorette* C2
9 Restaurant Le Rhul *269 Corniche J F Kennedy* A6
10 Toinou *3 cours St-Louis* E4

Jardin des Vestiges, Marseille.

Tip...

If you plan to buckle down for some heavy sightseeing, pick up a **City Pass** (one day €20, two days €27) from the Tourist Office. The Pass gives the holder free entrance to 15 museums and monuments, return boat trips to Château d'If and all public transport for its duration.

Souped up

Plenty of restaurants include Marseille's most famous dish on their menus. But how do you know if the fish stew on offer is the genuine stuff? Traditional *bouillabaisse* should include at least four different fish (take your pick of red mullet, John Dory, conger eel, skate or scorpion fish); monkfish and spiny lobster are optional. The fish should be cooked in a tomato and rockfish stock, along with potatoes. *Bouillabaisse* is eaten as two courses – first the soup, then the fish, which must be deboned and prepared in front of the diner. *Rouille*, a saffron and paprika mayonnaise, is served alongside. If you want to be really sure you're dining on *la vraie bouillabaisse*, check if the restaurant is a member of **La Charte de la Bouillabaisse Marseillaise**. This local stamp of approval guarantees authenticity; of the mere eleven restaurants the charter recognises, seven are in Marseille. And finally, remember other restaurants do dish up excellent renditions of *bouillabaisse*, even if they bend the authentic guidelines laid out here.

horizon from the mouth of the port – and the nearby Calanques. As day breaks fishermen drag their catch on to the quai des Belges, setting up stalls for the daily fish market; chefs and locals soon arrive, shopping for local red mullet, rockfish and the makings of *bouillabaisse* (see box, page below).

Musée de l'Histoire de Marseille & Jardin des Vestiges (Port Antique)

Square Belsunce, Centre Bourse, T04 91 90 42 22.
Mon-Sat 1200-1900. €2, €1 students/child (10-16), under 10s/over 65 free.
M1 to 'Vieux Port'.
Map: Marseille, D3, p180.

Accessed via the ground level of the Centre Bourse, traces of the city's ancient Roman port and Greek city walls are contained within the open-air Jardin des Vestiges. Discovered during the shopping centre's construction in 1967, the ruins are complemented by the adjacent Marseille History Museum. Exhibits cover finds from the port, including an ancient merchant vessel discovered in 1974, models of the Greek city and late 19th-century advertisements. There's also a temporary exhibition space dedicated to other aspects of local culture and history, including early 20th-century photographs.

Musée de la Mode

11 La Canebière, T04 96 17 06 00,
espacemodemediterranee.com.
Tue-Sun Jun-Sep 1100-1800, Oct-May 1000-1700.
€3, €1.50 students/child (10-16), under 10s/over 65 free.
M1 to 'Vieux Port'.
Map: Marseille, E3, p180.

Since 1988, this niche Fashion Museum has been drawing crowds with both its permanent collection (over 6000 articles of 20th-century clothing and accessories, on rotating display) and interesting range of temporary exhibits – a recent show covered Armenian cobblers in the south of France. **Café de la Mode**, downstairs, makes for a pleasant pit stop.

Tip...

Musée Cantini, Musée Grobet-Labadié and the Musée des Docks Romains are open Tuesday-Sunday June-September 1100-1800, October-May 1000-1700. Entry fees are €2, €1 students/child (10-16), under 10s/over 65 free.

Musée Cantini

19 rue Grignan, T04 91 54 77 75, marseille.fr.
M1 to 'Estrangin-Préfecture'.
Map: Marseille, E5, p180.

Located within a beautiful 17th-century former private home, the Cantini Museum was donated to the city by marble artisan (and creator of the ornate carved statue in place Castellane) Jules Cantini in 1917. Its permanent collection covers the 20th-century masters comprehensively, including works by Paul Signac, Vassily Kandinsky, Fernand Léger, Picasso, Jean Dubuffet and Francis Bacon. Additional major artists of the era are represented in the museum's temporary exhibitions, such as Gustav Klimt in 2009.

Rue Paradis & rue St-Ferréol

Map: Marseille, p180.

The heart of Marseille's shopping district, rue Paradis and rue St-Ferréol as well as their many cross streets, are lined with boutiques: high-end brands (Montblanc, Lacoste, Chopard) flank the former, French chain staples (Naf-Naf, Kookai) the latter. There are plenty of one-off shops too. Expect elbow room only on Saturday afternoons.

For more shopping in Marseille, see page 208.

Palais Longchamp

Bd Montricher/bd de Longchamp.
M1 to 'Cinq-Avenues-Longchamp', bus 81, T2.
Map: Marseille, H1, p180.

An imposing, colonnaded building, Palais Longchamp peers down the long boulevard out front from its perch atop Parc de Longchamp. It took over three decades to construct the ornate Palais; its completion in 1869 marked a glorious celebration of the city's new aqueduct, bringing torrents of drinking water from the Durance River, 80 km inland.

Within one wing of the building, the **Musée d'Histoire Naturelle** (T04 91 14 59 50, marseille.fr, Tue-Sun 1000-1700, €4, €2 students/child (10-16), over 65/under 10s free) charts the area's indigenous flora, fauna and fossils, while the other wing is home to the **Musée des Beaux-Arts**, closed since 2005 for an indeterminate period of renovations. It's possible to see some of the Beaux-Arts' highlights in other temporary locations around the city, particularly at the **Musée d'Arts Africains, Océaniens et Amérindiens** (see page 184).

Just south of the Palais, the quirky former home **Musée Grobet-Labadié** (bd Longchamp, T04 91 62 21 82, marseille.fr) shows how well-heeled locals of the previous century lived.

Le Panier

Map: Marseille, C3, p180.

A warren of steeply inclined alleys wind their way over Le Panier, Marseille's original Old Town, located on the north side of the Vieux Port.

Meaning 'the breadbasket' – although the reason behind the name has been attributed to anything from its original market to a popular local restaurant – Le Panier was first settled by Greeks. Over the centuries, these trendsetters have been generally emulated by every wave of immigrants to arrive – from Algerians and Tunisians to Italians and Poles – each group digging in their heels here first, before earning a little cash and moving on to bigger and better neighbourhoods.

An association with poverty plus incoming immigrants awarded Le Panier an edgy reputation.

Tip...

Head to the perched Jardin de Pharo for fabulous shots of the city: the bird's eye angle takes in the Vieux Port, Fort St-Jean, Cathédrale de la Major and Le Panier.

Around the region

In 1943, occupying Nazis believed the neighbourhood to be a bastion of Resistance fighters. They gave a 24 hours' notice before bombing half of the district to rubble, parcelling off many of the fleeing residents to labour camps, and the heavy Jewish population to concentration camps. The legacy of this destruction can be seen in the imposing 1950s architecture that swamps the southern side of Le Panier.

Le Panier is still home to a sprinkling of historical sights, including 18th-century **Hôtel Dieu** and **Vieille Charité** (see opposite). At its western end stands tiny **Eglise St-Laurent**. Around the corner the design for 19th-century **Cathédrale de la Major's** (Tue-Sat 1000-1800) massive edifice was based on that of Istanbul's Hagia Sophia. At the heart of the district, the **Musée des Docks Romains** (place Vivaux, T04 91 91 24 62, marseille.fr) details the city's old Roman dockyards. Atop Le Panier's highest – and windiest – point, pretty **place des Moulins** is now home to just three stone bases of its fifteen 16th-century windmills.

Normally held during the third weekend in June, the annual **Fête du Panier** (fetedupanier.org) sees the neighbourhood fill with concerts, artisan workshops and late-night revellers.

Centre de la Vieille Charité

2 rue de la Charité, T04 91 14 58 80,
vieille-charite-marseille.org.
Tue-Sun Jun-Sep 1100-1800, Oct-May 1000-1700.
€4, €3 students/child (10-16), under 10s/over 65 free.
M2 to 'Joliette', bus 55, T2.
Map: Marseille, C2, p180.

Designed by Pierre Puget as a poorhouse during the 17th century, la Vieille Charité came close to condemnation during the mid 20th century. It was only through the ambitious efforts of architect Le Corbusier that the magnificent structure – four pale, arcaded wings around a freestanding chapel – still exists. Today, the centre houses the **Musée d'Archéologie Méditerranéenne**, home to a large ancient Egyptian collection, and the **Musée d'Arts**

Eglise St-Laurent, Le Panier, Marseille.

Below: Les Docks de la Joliette, Marseille.
Bottom: Interior courtyard of La Vieille Charité, Marseille.

Tip...

A free ferry runs across the Vieux Port from place aux Huiles to Hôtel de Ville. Long the speediest way to circumnavigate the harbour, the old boat was replaced with an eco-friendly, electro-solar model in early 2010.

Africains, Océaniens et Amérindiens, as well as the art house cinema **Le Miroir** and **Regards** bookstore. Note that entry times and prices for temporary exhibitions can vary; entry to the courtyard is free.

Fonds Régional d'Art Contemporain de Marseille (FRAC)

1 place Francis Chirat, T04 91 91 27 55, fracpaca.org.
Tue-Sat 1400-1800. Free.
M2 to 'Joliette', T2.
Map: Marseille, C2, p180.

One of Marseille's finest contemporary art venues, showcasing three to four annual exhibitions within its petite Panier premises. In 2012, the FRAC will make the leap to a new cutting-edge space, designed by Japanese architect Kengo Kuma, at 10 boulevard de Dunkerque behind place de la Joliette.

Musée des Civilisations de l'Europe et de la Méditerranée (MuCEM)

Fort St-Jean, entrance for L'Espace Georges Henri Rivière at Esplanade St-Jean, entrance for La Tour du Roy René at quai du Port, T04 96 13 80 90, musee-europemediterranee.org.
Opening hours vary, many exhibitions free.
Buses 55 & 83.
Map: Marseille, B4, p180.

Housed within the refreshed 17th-century Fort St-Jean, MuCEM currently organises temporary exhibitions dedicated to folk art, culture and traditions of the Mediterranean. Construction of a secondary edifice that will house MuCEM's permanent collection, a contemporary cube-shaped building designed by architects Rudy Riciotti and Roland Carta, has started to the Fort's west; it's due to be completed in 2012.

Les Docks de la Joliette

10 place de la Joliette.
M2 to 'Joliette' & T2.
Map: Marseille, C1, p180.

Constructed over the decade between 1856 and 1866, the Joliette Docks originally served as Marseille's primary warehouse, storing the bulk cargoes that flooded into France's biggest commercial port. Reflecting the structure's historic importance, renovations of the building were the first project undertaken under the city's Euroméditerranée project (see page 188). Work was led by architect Eric Castaldi and completed in 2002. The 80,000 sq m edifice is now part of the economic fabric of Marseille and houses 250 businesses, plus several restaurants and shops.

What the locals say

When my friends come to visit we like to go to **La Bastide des Bains** (19 rue Sainte, T04 91 33 39 13). It is a beautiful big Moroccan hamman in the centre of the city. My favourite treatment is the body bluff, essential oil massage and Moroccan clay mask.

Then we might go to **Pain et Compagnie** (18 place aux Huiles, T04 91 33 55 00) for brunch. Long rustic wooden tables are laced with unlimited baskets of fresh organic bread and home-made jams, conserves and chocolate spreads, plus individual portions of cheeses, salmon, hams, scrambled eggs, yoghurt, fruit, coffee, tea, fresh orange juice. It's a feast.

While there I'd have to pop next door to **Rive Neuve** (20 place aux Huiles), which has original fashion from local designers.

For the afternoon, there's nothing like a leisurely paddle around the Calanques, stopping at some of the hidden beaches that can only be reached by sea. Kayaks can be hired from **Yakaramer** (yakaramer.com, T06 23 06 90 17) or at various points around Marseille and Cassis.

In the evening I'd recommend heading to **La Tosca** (102 rue Ferrari, T04 91 42 26 02) in La Plaine district. It's a tapas bar with a cute garden courtyard filled with fairy lights and statues lost beneath layers of dripping wax. The mojitos are great.

For more live music we might head to **La Paradox** (127 rue d'Aubagne, T04 91 63 14 65) for local funk, rock, soul, blues or reggae bands. Unlike a lot of the bars in Vieux Port the drinks are really well priced.

Marseillaise Mairi McCallum, Freelance web marketing and English communications.

Marseille's Vieux Port and Basilique de Notre-Dame-de-la-Garde.

Basilique de Notre-Dame-de-la-Garde

Place Colonel Edon, T04 91 13 40 80, notredamedelagarde.com.
Daily 0700-1815. Free.
Bus 60.
Map: Marseille, C7, p180.

Also referred to as 'La Bonne Mère' ('the Good Mother'). The cathedral's 10-m gilded Madonna has been casting a protective eye over the city's fishermen since its consecration in 1864. Built on the site of a 13th-century chapel, the Romanesque-Byzantine basilica was designed by Henri Espérandieu and completed by his student, Henri Révoil; the interior is a tapestry of colours, shimmering with mosaics and golden statues. The cathedral is positioned on Marseille's highest natural point, and is visible everywhere from the Vieux Port to the Prado beaches, making for fantastic views from outside the church itself.

Cours Julien

M2 to Notre-Dame-du-Mont (Cours Julien), buses 41 & 81.
Map: Marseille, F4, p180.

A network of one-off boutiques, galleries, bars and terraced restaurants, the neighbourhood around pedestrianised cours Julien makes for a pleasant wander, night or day. Nearby, **Le Palais des Arts** (1 place Carli, T04 91 42 51 50, regards-de-provence.org, daily 1000-1800, €4.50, €2.30 16-18s, €1.50 students/12-15s, under 11s free) hosts celebrated exhibitions, including the recent 'Jean Cocteau et la Méditerranée', as well as concerts.

Abbaye de St-Victor

3 rue de l'Abbaye, T04 96 11 22 60, saintvictor.net. Daily 0900-1900. Basilica free, crypts €2, €1 child. Map: Marseille, B5, p180.

On the southern side of the Vieux Port, this imposing abbey was built during the 13th century to replace an original fifth-century church, destroyed by Saracen invaders 200 years earlier. Its crypts house a creepy necropolis (second century BC to the early Christian era), as well as the Abbey's famous 'Black Madonna' statue.

For over four decades, the Abbey has been hosting **Le Festival de Musique** (T04 91 05 84 48, saintvictor.chez.com) during October and November, although its most popular festival is its **Candlemas** celebrations (Feb).

Vallon des Auffes

Bus 83.
Map: Marseille, A6, p180.

Petite, pastel and a striking contrast to Marseille's often-gritty streets, Vallon des Auffes is a half-hour stroll from the Vieux Port. Equal parts fishing boats and charming cottages, it's also a restaurant Mecca. For a treat, **Chez Fonfon** (chez-fonfon.com) and **L'Epuisette** (l-epuisette.com) are both exquisite dining options.

Back on the main corniche stands Sartorio's World War I memorial, **Monument aux Morts des Armées d'Orient**, while further south is César's propeller-like **Monument aux Repatriés d'Afrique du Nord**.

Marseillaise Markets

All of the following markets run from 0800-1300, except where indicated. For the biggest bargains, it's best to arrive very early or very late.

❶❷ **Vieux Port Fish Market** Quai des Belges (daily) & **Flower Market** (Tue & Thu). One of the few city markets where fishermen still pitch up to ply their own catch.

❸ **Marché des Capucins** Place des Capucins (daily 0800-1900). Cheap wholesale fruit and veg, plus North African nibbles.

❹ **Cours Julien Organic Market** (Wed). Sheep's cheese, an organic butcher, honey and wine; look out for Sisteron-based bakery La Paline's famous *fougasse à l'anchois*.

❺ **Marché aux Puces** Avenue du Cap Pinède (Sun 0900-1900). Massive flea market north of the city centre.

Artichokes for sale at the Marché des Capucins.

Euroméditerranée project

CGM Tower.

A huge-scale project to regenerate the city's downtown neighbourhoods, the Euroméditerranée project has been slowly changing the face of Marseille since 1995. All undertaken projects are now finished or works in progress, with the bulk of unfinished tasks due for completion in 2012, well in advance of the city's 2013 European Capital of Culture celebrations.

The redevelopment is taking place in five main areas, which are spread over 480 urban hectares:

Joliette-Arenc The city's docklands and ferry terminal area. Projects include the **Joliette Docks** (see page 185); the **Cœur Méditerranée** (bd de Dunkerque) on the south side of new **place de la Méditerranée**, which includes two hotels (Suite and Ibis); the new **FRAC** (see page 185); and **M3 Euromed Station-Urban Square**, comprising shops, offices and a retirement home.

St-Charles & Porte d'Aix Focusing on cleaning up the area around the city's main bus and train stations. Installation of open green expanses and student housing.

Belle de Mai Centred around the beloved **La Friche la Belle de Mai** (lafriche.org), a renovated former tobacco factory in the city's northeast. The sprawling edifice now includes an audiovisual centre, studios (where Marseille's ultra-popular answer to Eastenders, *Plus belle la vie*, is shot), performance spaces and artists' workshops. The **MuCEM Archives** are also located near here.

Rue de la République Sweeping from the back of the port to place de la Joliette, this grand *rue* marks the core of the **Opération Programmée d'Amélioration de l'Habitat (OPAH)**. The project aims to clean and restore the down-at-heel Haussmann buildings that line the street; the first phase of the project, covering the blocks south of place Sadi Carnot, was completed in 2007.

Cité de la Méditerranée Spanning 3 km of waterfront from the Vieux Port in the south to Arenc in the north. Projects include the creation of **Esplanade du J4**, a pedestrian promenade outside of Fort St-Jean, which will eventually include a panoramic elevated walkway; the C-shaped, semi-submerged **Centre Régional de la Méditerranée**, to house exhibition spaces, boutiques, cafés and private residences; the wide **Esplanade de la Major**, in front of the Cathédrale de la Major, will be home to a 53-m fountain and the expanded ferry terminal; the **Euromed Center**, Italian architect Massimiliano Fuksas's futuristic new cultural complex housing a Marriott hotel, convention centre and film director Luc Besson's multiplex cinema; the redeveloped **Quais d'Arenc**, which will include international shipping group CMA CGM's 33-floor skyscraper designed by award-winning architect Zaha Hadid, Le Silo, Arenc's former silos transformed into a performance centre, and four office and apartment blocks, designed by Jean Nouvel, Yves Lion, Jean Baptiste Pietri and Roland Carta (lesquaisdarenc.fr); and the new **MuCEM** (see page 185).

For a peek at the city skyline upon completion of the various projects, check out the interactive maps and artists' interpretations on the Euroméditerranée website.

Essential information

Office: 10 place de la Joliette, Atrium 10.3, T04 91 14 45 00, euromediterranee.fr.
Mon-Fri 1130-1830.
M2 to 'Joliette' & T2.
Map: Marseille, p180.

The Frioul Islands & north of Marseille

Close enough to be considered suburbs, the Frioul Islands, around 20 minutes off Marseille's coast, and L'Estaque and the Côte Bleue Calanques, just northwest of the city, are all ideal escapes when the urban jungle becomes a little too oppressive. Further north, Martigues is a charming mini-Venice, rarely visited by tourists.

Below: One of Martigues' tiny ports. Opposite page: Ferrières Old Town, Martigues

Château d'If

T04 91 59 02 30, if.monuments-nationaux.fr.
May-1st week Oct 0930-1830, 2nd week Oct-Apr
0900-1730, closed Mon mid Sep-Mar. €5, €3.50
18-25s, under 18s free, EU citizens under 26 free.

On the smallest island in the Frioul Archipelago
and clearly visible from Marseille's shoreline, the
Château d'If was built under François I in 1524.
The sandy stone structure served as both a fortress
and a prison, but it's perhaps best known as the
fictional setting for Alexandre Dumas' *Le Comte
de Monte-Cristo*.

To clamber over the Château and its island, hop
aboard the **Frioul If Express** (1 quai des Belges, T04
96 11 03 50, frioul.cityway.fr, €10 return), a frequent
ferry service that runs from the Vieux Port and on
to the Frioul Islands. For more information about
the Frioul and Riou Archipelagos, see
ilesdemarseille.fr (French only).

L'Estaque

Bus 35 from place de la Joliette.

Formerly a stand-alone fishing village, l'Estaque
became a popular destination for artists after Paul
Cézanne set up his easel here in 1870; painters
Raoul Dufy, André Derain, Georges Braque and
Renoir quickly shadowed his footsteps. Today,
you too can make like the modern masters:
the Marseille Tourist Office hands out maps of
l'Estaque printed with two walking routes, the
Grand and **Petit Chemins de Peintres**.

The Côte Bleue Calanques

Limestone cliffs, or *calanques*, surround Marseille,
making both for jaw-dropping landscapes and a
range of outdoor activities. To the west of
l'Estaque, turquoise coves are tucked among the
pines and the rugged shoreline, including the
Calanques du Jonquier and **de l'Everine**, west of
Niolon, **Calanque de Méjean** and **Calanque de la
Redonne**. All are peppered with much-coveted
weekend homes belonging mainly to wealthy
Marseillaise. Pack a picnic lunch and take your pick.
Further along are the buzzy beach resorts of **Carry-
le-Rouet** and **Sausset-les-Pins**.

For information about the more frequently
visited Calanques near Cassis, to the southeast of
Marseille, see page 192.

Martigues

On the edge of the vast Etang de Berre, Martigues
is made up of three distinct areas, all formerly
villages in their own right. The Martigues Tourist
Office (av Louis Sammut, T04 42 42 31 10,
mairie-martigues.fr) is located near the Hôtel de
Ville, west along the northern shore in Ferrières.
Pleasantly unpretentious, the latter's open squares
are lined with yellow and pink buildings. Nearby,
the **Musée Ziem** (bd du 14 Juillet, T04 42 41 39 60,
Wed-Sun Jul-Aug 1000-1200 & 1430-1830, Sep-Jun
1430-1830, free) celebrates turn-of-the-century
artist Félix Ziem, who painted landscapes of the
local spot known as *Miroir aux Oiseaux*. The
museum also includes pieces by other great artists
of the period, such as Paul Signac and François
Picabia. To the south, a residential island laced with
waterways sits in the middle of the Canal de
Caronte, while across another bridge is the more
affluent Jonquières neighbourhood.

Tip...

L'Estaque, the Côte Bleue and Martigues are all
accessible via the local train to Miramas.

Cassis &
the Calanques

Southeast of Marseille, the Massif des Calanques comprises close to 20 km of rocky limestone cliffs, deep inlets and translucent waters. Trails tangle through the wilderness, making the 4000-ha protected area best explored on foot or by boat.

It was here in 1985 that local boy Henri Cosquer discovered a stunning Ice Age cave, its walls decorated with hundreds of animal paintings (approximately 18,000 years old) and hand tracings, dating from around 27,000 years ago. Inaccessible to the public after three divers died trying to reach the cave in 1992, the entrance to the Grotte Cosquer lies at 37 m below sea level, between the Calanques of Sormiou and Morgiou.

Sandwiched between the Massif des Calanques and Cap Canaille, the latter boasting Europe's highest seaside cliff (Grande Tête, 394 m), the fishing village of Cassis has always been one of the southern French coast's most enchanting. Paul Signac painted the bay and headlands in 1899; Winston Churchill took art lessons here in 1920, bedding down at the Hotel Panorama (now the Camargo Foundation cultural centre, camargofoundation.org); and Virginia Woolf and friends spent long periods in Cassis during the 1930s, staying with her sister, Vanessa Bell.

Cassis, although certainly a lot busier, retains its appeal today. A medieval castle overlooks the town's harbour, which in turn is packed with traditional wooden fishing boats and pleasure craft. Kiosks selling sea urchins line the quays, opposite terraced restaurants and pavement cafés. North of town there are inland valleys of vineyards, renowned for their production of crisp white wine. Just a small percentage of this hand-harvested nectar is exported abroad, making the AOC area (just 196 ha) still the best place to sample it.

GIE des Bateliers Cassidains

Cassis port, cassis-calanques.com; a full list of boats and contact telephone numbers can be downloaded from the website.
Tours: three Calanques (Port Miou, Port Pin & En Vau): Feb-Oct daily 0930-1700 every half hour, Jan-Feb from 1030 by reservation only, 45-min boat ride. €13, €7 under 10s. Five Calanques (as above, plus L'Oule & Devenson): Feb-Oct daily 1130, 1200, 1500, 1530, 1630, 65-min boat ride. €15, €10 under 10s. Eight Calanques (as above, plus L'Oeil de Verre, Sugiton & Morgiou): Feb-Oct daily 1030, 1100, 1330, 1400, 1430, 1600, 90-min boat ride. €19, €13 under 10s.
Tickets go on sale at the port's yellow kiosk 30 mins before tour departures.

During the summer months, setting out to see the Calanques from the water can be one of the region's most relaxing activities. As these organised tours chug westwards, it's increasingly difficult to believe you're less than half an hour from Marseille's urban mass.

Essentials

Note that shops and services (as listed below) are all concentrated in Cassis: make sure you've stocked up on food, drink and any essentials before exploring the surrounding Calanques.

❶ Getting around Cassis is tiny, and its village roads and pedestrian port are best explored on foot. Buses run to and from the train station. There's a taxi stand (T04 42 01 78 96, cassis.taxis.free.fr) next to the yellow boat kiosk in Cassis's harbour. A car can be useful for getting around the coastal region, particularly out of season; car parks are placed around town and are well signposted.

❷ Train station Place de la Gare, 3.5 km outside of Cassis's town centre.

❸ Pharmacy Pharmacie Trossero, 11 avenue Victor Hugo, T04 42 01 70 03.

❹ ATMs Various ATMs in Cassis, including one on quai Jean-Jacques Barthélemy.

❺ Post office Avenue de l'Arène, T04 42 01 98 30.

❻ Tourist information office Quai des Moulins, T08 92 25 98 92, ot-cassis.fr, daily June-September 0900-1900, October-May Monday-Friday 0930-1230 & 1430-1800, Saturday 1000-1230 & 1430-1830, Sunday 1000-1230.

Picnicking on Cassis' seafront.

Above: An old hand-painted sign in Cassis. Opposite page: View over Morgiou Calanques.

Note that you're rarely allowed to hop off the Calanques tour boats before they arrive back in Cassis. However, occasional summer morning tours will allow you to descend at En Vau: inquire at the yellow boat kiosk in Cassis's port. From here you can swim, snorkel and then hike back to town (see below).

If you'd rather captain your own ship, **JCF Boat Services** (jcf-boat-services.com) rents large and small motorboats (half days from €135, excluding petrol). For a more physical experience, paddle around the inlets in one of **Cassis Sports Loisirs Nautiques**' one- or two-person kayaks; prices start at €10/hr (mid Apr-Oct).

Visiting the Calanques from Marseille

To access the Massif from Marseille, take bus no 21 from La Canebière to Luminy. From here you can hike into the Calanques. Bus 23 departs from Rond-Point du Prado; its two destinations allow access to the Calanques Sormiou and Morgiou respectively. Marseille's Tourist Office also organises group walks every Friday from mid September to mid June (T04 91 13 89 00). Alternatively, **Bleu Evasion** (bleu-evasion.com) runs boat tours from Marseille's Vieux Port or the more southerly Port de la Pointe Rouge.

Exploring Cassis & the Calanques on foot

All of Cassis's town maps are marked with a variety of hiking trails. Easiest is the two-hour **Vin et Terroir** walk, looping past all twelve of the town's vineyards, plus olive groves and traditional stone *bastides*.

For limestone cliffs, turquoise waters and isolated beaches, head west out of town, through residential neighbourhoods, following **La Presqu'île** to Calanque de Port-Miou (45 mins). Keep on along the new **Découverte entre Terre et**

Mer (Land & Sea Discovery, 1 hr) trail; the more ambitious can continue hiking **Les 3 Calanques** (4-6 hrs), a difficult path that explores the Calanques de Port Pin and d'En Vau, plus the valley behind the two. Kids will enjoy **Le Sentier du Petit Prince** (1½ hrs): leave your wheels at the Presqu'île car park, then head off to explore Cap Cable.

Cap Canaille and the **Route des Crêtes**, covering the 12 km between Cassis and La Ciotat, offer some of the coast's most breathtaking panoramas. The two long circuits over this headland involve lengthy, steep climbs: be sure you're prepared in terms of appropriate footwear, drinking water and level of physical fitness.

Tip...

During the dry summer months, access to the Calanques is often restricted due to high risk of forest fires or strong winds. Check with the Tourist Office in Cassis or Marseille, or call T08 11 20 13 13, before setting off.

Five of the best

Calanques

❶ **Sormiou** The largest, sheltered by cliffs to the east and west. The wide sandy beach is easily accessed, and there's a restaurant and car park.

❷ **Morgiou** Crowded with fishing boats and home to one restaurant. Follow the trail skirting the shore eastwards for isolated beaches, and on to the hard-to-reach Calanque de Sugiton.

❸ **Devenson** Rugged, windy cliffs and sheer sea drops that will appeal to hardcore rock-climbers. Arrive on foot, or park up at the La Gardiole car park (closed Jun-Sep).

❹ **En Vau** Possibly the prettiest. Access is steep and difficult (unless you arrive by boat) but the clear waters, white sand and shingle beach are well worth the effort. No nearby spots to pick up snacks, so pack a picnic lunch.

❺ **Port Pin** The smallest, with a petite beach ringed by Aleppo pines. Moderately difficult access via 'Les 3 Calanques' trail from Cassis.

Bandol & around

The seaside resort of Bandol is this area's most famous, drawing visitors with its unaffected attitude and luscious wines. But the surrounding hilltop villages and coastal towns – plus the offshore islands of Ile de Bendor, Ile Verte and Ile des Embiez – each hold their own unique appeal.

Poseidon, Ile de Bendor, Bandol.

Mention 'Bandol' to any French person, and the first association is likely to be one of the south of France's finest appellations. While the Bandol region is known to produce a tasty vintage, the town itself is a popular coastal resort: more sand castles, chips and kids than elegant old quaffers.

But it wasn't always so. During the late 19th and early 20th centuries, Bandol provided creative inspiration to German writer Thomas Mann, who stayed at the beachfront Grand Hôtel, and New Zealand-born author Katherine Mansfield. French celebrities flocked to the town, from popular cabaret performer Mistinguett to singer Henri Salvador, and Bandol's renown slowly grew.

Nowadays, a pretty, palm-lined promenade separates the compact town centre from the deep marina, while looping around past the remains of a château, **Plage de Rènecros** is a perfect crescent of a beach. An easy, yellow-marked *sentier littoral* continues 12 km westward along the seafront from Rènecros to Les Lecques, passing **Plage de Barry** where Jacques-Yves Cousteau, Philippe Tailliez and Frédéric Dumas are said to have invented the first aqua-lung in 1943. On the other side of town, beach after beach creates a smooth succession of sun, sea and sand from the Casino most of the way to Sanary-sur-Mer.

Ile de Bendor

1.5 km off Bandol's coast, bendor.com.
Daily ferries: Jul-Aug 0700-0210 (every 30 mins-1 hr), Apr-Jun & Sep 0700-1900 (every 30 mins) & 1920-2400 (by advance reservation), Oct-Mar 0745-1700 (hourly); 7-min crossing. Apr-Sep €10, €8 child (2-12), under 2s free; Oct-Mar €8, €6 child (2-12), under 2s free.

A tiny, 7-ha island just off Bandol's coast, the Ile de Bendor was purchased during the 1950s by Paul Ricard, founder of Ricard pastis. It was here that Ricard created his own unconventional world, hosting rollicking parties and entertaining the era's most sought-after socialites and celebrities,

Essentials

❶ Getting around Towns listed in this section are all small enough to explore on foot. They are connected by buses and trains (see Transport, page 210). In Bandol, there are six private Taxis Bandolais (T04 94 32 46 46; Taxi rank T04 94 29 43 67; other numbers available from the Tourist Office).

🚊 Train station Avenue de la Gare.

🚌 Bus station Buses depart from the bus stop in the port.

➕ Pharmacy 1 boulevard Victor Hugo, T04 94 29 41 06.

💲 ATMs Along Bandol's avenue du 11 Novembre.

✆ Post office Avenue du 11 Novembre, T04 94 29 31 40, Mon-Wed & Fri-Sat 0830-1200, Thu 0830-1100, Mon-Fri 1400-1700.

❶ Tourist information office Allée Vivien, T04 94 29 41 35, tourisme.bandol.fr, July-August daily 0930-1900, April-June & September Monday-Saturday 0900-1200 & 1400-1800, October-March Monday-Saturday 0900-1200 & 1400-1700.

For more information about the towns dotted around Bandol, visit their Tourist Office websites:
Le Castellet ville-lecastellet.fr
La Cadière d'Azur lacadieredazur.com
St-Cyr-sur-Mer & Les Lecques saintcyrsurmer.com
La Ciotat tourisme-laciotat.com
Sanary-sur-Mer sanarysurmer.com

including Salvador Dali. As an amateur artist, Ricard eventually opted to transform the island into a public *île des arts*; local artisans opened ateliers, hotels and restaurants set up camp, and holidaymakers were welcomed to the island.

Today, visitors can hop on one of the frequent seven-minute ferries from Bandol's port and spend an afternoon exploring Bendor. An easy, 20-minute footpath rings the island, taking in one small sandy beach, various bathing terraces and, especially on its south side, plenty of russet rocky outcrops. The island is home to six bars and restaurants, three hotels, a helipad and the quirky **Exposition Universelle des Vins et Spiritueux** (T04 94 05 15 61, euvs.org, Jul-Aug daily 1100-1400 & 1540-1940, Apr-Jun & Sep Wed-Sun 1100-1400 & 1540-1940,

lords of Les Baux to Angevin rule (15th century), and eventually on to the Lombards, who ruled the walled stronghold until the French Revolution.

More recently, Le Castellet is most famous as the setting for Marcel Pagnol's 1938 film, *La Femme du Boulanger*. Wander within Le Castellet's ramparts, shop for unique artisan-made gifts at the town's many gallery-shops or head to *Le trou de Madame* (signposted), a balcony-like opening in the city walls, affording views all the way to the sea.

Nearby, the **Circuit Paul Ricard** (circuitpaulricard.com) hosted Formula 1 races through the 1970s and 80s, although its current competitions are more low-key.

La Cadière d'Azur

A peaceful hilltop town, La Cadière remains elegantly laid-back, even during summer's peak. Visit for the picturesque pavement cafés, shady cobbled streets and panoramic vineyard views.

St-Cyr-sur-Mer & Les Lecques

Directly west of La Cadière d'Azur and Le Castellet, Les Lecques has a magnetic appeal for families, both due to its long, sandy beach and nearby **Aqualand** (T04 94 32 08 32, aqualand.fr, early Jul-Aug 1000-1900, mid Jun-early Jul & 1st week Sep 1000-1800, €24.50, €18 child (3-12)/over 65, under 1 m free).

Inland, St-Cyr's main claim to fame is its small, gold leaf-covered version of sculptor Frédéric Auguste Bartholdi's **Statue of Liberty**, which sits in place Portalis; wealthy resident Anatole Ducros donated it to the town in 1913.

La Ciotat

The bay curves westwards, Les Lecques' beach eventually merging with a strip of seafront hotels on the edge of La Ciotat. A working town, long associated with its now-defunct dockyards, La Ciotat had a brief encounter with international fame when it featured in brothers Auguste and Louis Lumière's 1898 film, *L'arrivée d'un train en gare de La Ciotat*, although viewers of the silent movie leapt out of

free). Set up by Ricard in 1958, this museum is frescoed with ceiling scenes of joyful alcoholic consumption; beneath is a neat collection of more than 8000 bottles of wines and spirits, as well as old wine lists, cocktail-making instruments and other drinking paraphernalia.

During July and August, ferries also run from Sanary-sur-Mer to the island, departing from Général de Gaulle wharf (15-20 min crossing). Note that most shops and all but two of the restaurants shut down from October to March.

Around Bandol

Le Castellet

It's mostly French visitors who flock to this medieval perched village. Built during the 12th century, control of the town bounced from the

the silent movie theatre to avoid the 'oncoming train'. The small **Espace Lumière** (20 rue Maréchal Foch, T04 42 08 69 60, Jul-Sep Tue & Sat 1000-1900, Wed & Fri 1500-1800, Oct-Jun Tue-Wed & Fri-Sat 1500-1800, free) has photos and posters that document the era.

La Ciotat is home to two alluring spots of natural beauty: the **Anse de Figuerolles** and the **Ile Verte**. The former is a cool, pebbly Calanque to the west of the town, while the latter is a small island, less than 500 m by 250 m, located just off La Ciotat's coast. Frequent ferries run visitors to the island from April to September, including a special early-bird run for fishermen, departing at 0700 on weekends (laciotat-ileverte.com, €9 return, €6 under 10s return).

Sanary-sur-Mer

A rosy-hued fishing village to Bandol's east, Sanary served as a safe harbour for German Jews during World War II: Bertolt Brecht and Thomas Mann both settled here, joining Aldous Huxley, also a short-term resident of the town.

Today, Sanary is a relaxed spot to be based. Its cute harbour is lined with fish restaurants, and there's a lively market here on Wednesday mornings. In the hills above the town, the child-friendly **exotic zoo** (Le Jardin Exotique, T04 94 29 40 38, zoosanary.com, Jul-Aug Mon-Sat 0800-1200 & 1400-1900, Sun & hols 1000-1200 & 1400-1900, Sep-Jun Mon-Sat 0800-1200 & 1400-1800, €8.50, €6 child (3-10), under 3s free) is packed with parrots, peacocks, monkeys and a botanical garden.

South of here at Le Brusc, ferries zip along the 12-minute route to **Ile des Embiez** (les-embiez. com), another island snapped up by Paul Ricard during the 1950s. The island is home to three hotels, eight restaurants, various beaches, an Oceanographic Institute (institut-paul-ricard.org) and Domaine des Embiez, its own 10-ha vineyard. During July and August, ferries also run to and from Sanary-sur-Mer directly.

Driving the Bandol Vineyards

Close to 60 vineyards ripple through the countryside north of Bandol, producing red and rosé wines based on a majority percentage of Mourvèdre grapes. If your days sunning on the beach have begun to lose their lustre, a drive around these hilltop towns, valleys and vineyards may make for the perfect antidote.

Leave Bandol along the D559b. This northbound route heads in the direction of Le Beausset, crossing the A50 motorway along the way. To your west are the perched **Château de Pibarnon** (T04 94 90 12 73, pibarnon.com) vineyards. Or opt to head east, following the signs for **Château Ste-Anne** (T04 94 90 35 40). Both are family-run and welcoming, although it's best to call ahead for a (free) tour, particularly out of season. If you'd rather just cruise around, taking in the scenery, stop by **La Cadierenne** (off the A50 at junction 11, Quartier Le Vallon, La Cadière d'Azur, T04 94 90 11 06, cadierenne.net, daily 0900-1200 & 1400-1730), a cooperative selling a variety of nearby producers.

Don't have your own wheels? Time a visit to Bandol to coincide with the annual **Fête du Millésime**. Local wine producers line the port on the first Sunday in December, offering lip-smacking samples of their latest vintage.

For more information about Bandol wine and its vineyards, see vinsdebandol.com.

Toulon

Toulon moves to its own rhythm. Billboards advertise €25-a-night hotel rooms, the local fashion is for discount bling and there's hardly a retail chain in sight. In terms of tourism, this port city, home to France's Mediterranean navy and its megalith aircraft carrier, the *Charles de Gaulle*, is a town that time forgot. But what it does have is something lacking in its beachy neighbours: an authentic offbeat culture and a history shaped by its bustling port.

Below and opposite page: Toulon harbour.

Essentials

❶ Getting around Although Toulon is a large city, it's easy to walk to most sights of tourist interest from the train station. Radios Taxis Toulonnais can be reached on T04 94 93 51 51, taxi-toulon.com.

❷ Train station Place de l'Europe, T36 35; the city's bus station (T04 94 24 60 00) is next door.

⊕ Hospital Hôpital de Toulon Font-Pré, T04 04 94 61 61 61, ch-toulon.fr.

❸ Pharmacy Pharmacie du Palais, Palais Liberté, 249 boulevard du Maréchal Leclerc, T04 94 91 33 74.

❾ ATMs There are plenty of ATMs, particularly along boulevard du Maréchal Leclerc.

❓ Post office Rue Prosper Ferréro.

❶ Tourist information office 334 avenue de la République, T04 94 18 53 00, toulontourisme.com, Monday-Saturday 0900-1800 (Jul & Aug until 2000), Sunday & holidays 1000-1200.

A young Napoleon Bonaparte made his name by taking charge of Toulon harbour's guns and turning them against the occupying British in 1793, a passage relived in all its nationalistic detail inside the excellent **Musée National de la Marine** (place Monsenergue, T04 94 02 02 01, musee-marine.fr, Jul & Aug daily 1000-1800, Sep-Jun Wed-Mon 1000-1800. €5, €4 concessions, under 25s free). Almost the entire French fleet was scuttled to avoid being captured by the surrounding Germans in 1942 and the city was consequently battered by Axis artillery, although the job was roundly finished off by Allied bombs a year later. The damaged city was clunkily redrawn with strangely alluring Stalin-meets-Le Corbusier blocks of flats.

Nowadays, tours run around the huge **Naval docks** from bistro-lined **quai de Cronstadt**, while *navettes* run to chilled seaside suburb of **St-Mandrier** and the beach resort of **Les Sablettes**. A few streets back, the neighbourhood known as *le Petit Chicago* is still a den of sailor bars and sexy shops, although the **Maison de la Photographie** (T04 94 93 07 59, Tue-Sat 1200-1800, free) is more in keeping with 21st century Toulon, and boutiques and bookshops are springing up around nearby place du Globe. Further west the **Hôtel des Arts** (236 bd Maréchal Leclerc, T04 94 91 69 18, free) is an excellent contemporary art space, freshly reopened after renovations in early 2010.

Pétanque in Toulon.

Sleeping

Le Petit Nice Passédat €€€€
Anse de Maldormé, corniche JF Kennedy, T04 91 59 25 92, passedat.fr.
Map: Marseille, A6, p180.
Managed by three generations of the Passédat family since it opened in 1917, this petite enclave of exclusivity draws luxury-seekers and a celebrity clientele. Rooms are sea-facing,

La Petit Nice Passedat Hotel, Marseille.

Tip...
Unlike most places along the Côte d'Azur, Marseille's high season doesn't include July and August: during these hot summer months, many residents flee to hilltop towns or along the nearby coast for a breath of fresh air. Be sure to ask hotels about their summer discounts and reduced rate packages.

and there's a stunning garden terrace and heated outdoor pool, plus renowned gastronomic restaurant. Worth the splurge.

Villa Massalia €€€€
17 place Louis Bonnefon, T04 91 72 90 27, concorde-hotels.com.
Map: Marseille, F7, p180.
In a smart residential district near the Stade Vélodrome and a favourite with visiting footballers, Villa Massalia is modern luxury all the way: Nespresso machine in each spacious room, hammam, fitness area, sauna and outdoor pool (non-guests welcome, €45). Local fishermen provide daily fresh fish for the Yin Yang Chinese restaurant, on site.

New Hôtel Vieux Port €€€
3bis rue Reine Elisabeth, T04 91 99 23 23, new-hotel.com.
Map: Marseille, D3, p180.
Spacious, subtly themed rooms (African, Land of the Rising Sun, Arabian Nights) steps from the port and La Canebière. Flat-screen TVs, and some rooms boast private balconies. Discount packages, particularly on weekends.

Hôtel Le Corbusier €€-€€€
280 bd Michelet, T04 91 16 78 00, hotellecorbusier.com.
Map: Marseille, F7, p180.
A site of architectural pilgrimage, also referred to as 'Unité d'Habitation' and 'la Cité Radieuse'. Designed by Swiss architect Le Corbusier and

constructed during the late 1940s, this structure was originally intended to help stem the period's drastic housing shortage. The hotel's cabin rooms and studios are spread over two of the building's floors.

Hôtel du Palais €€-€€€
26 rue Breteuil, T04 91 37 78 86, hoteldupalaismarseille.com.
Map: Marseille, D5, p180.
A few blocks south of the Vieux Port in a semi-residential neighbourhood, this affable spot makes a good base for sightseeing. Rooms are small but modern, staff are welcoming and there's free Wi-Fi. Recommended.

Hôtel St Ferréol €€-€€€
19 rue Pisançon (corner rue St Ferréol), T04 91 33 12 21, hotel-stferreol.com.
Map: Marseille, E4, p180.
Friendly bargain spot in the heart of Marseille's shopping district. The 19 rooms – some standard, some superior – are small but neat, and have a/c and free Wi-Fi. Bargain rates available out of season.

Hôtel Hermes €€
2 rue Bonneterie, T04 96 11 63 63, hotelmarseille.com.
Map: Marseille, D3, p180.
Twenty-eight basic rooms, some with views over the port, at the foot of the Panier district. There's a fantastic roof terrace, and kitsch but appealing murals of

ancient Greece adorning the breakfast room walls downstairs.

Hôtel Péron €€
119 corniche JF Kennedy, T04 91 31 01 41, hotel-peron.com.
Map: Marseille, A6, p180.
Friendly, family-run spot between downtown Marseille and Vallon des Auffes. Funky, 1960s decor dotted throughout; best are the corner rooms, which look out over Château d'If and the Frioul islands.

Cassis

Maison°9 €€€-€€€€
Quartier Les Janots, 9 av du Docteur Yves Bourde, T04 42 08 35 86, maison9.net.
Luxury B&B set just out of town among Cassis's vineyards. The four suites have private terraces and mini-kitchenettes. Breakfasts feature home-made and locally sourced ingredients. There's also an outdoor pool, fruit garden and *pétanque* area.

Hôtel de la Plage Mahogany €€€
19 av de l'Amiral Ganteaume, T04 42 01 05 70, hotelmahogany.com.
A beach-lover's dream, just over the road from the Plage de Bestouan. The 30 rooms are a mix of bright colours and modern decor (sea-facing) and subdued Provençal hues (overlooking the garden). A short walk into town.

Camping
Camping les Cigales
Av Marne, T04 42 01 07 34, campingcassis.com.
Mid Mar-mid Nov, €5.85 per person, €2.60 under 7s, €4.80 per pitch.
Pleasant campsite 1.5 km out of Cassis, with pitches for tents, trailers and campervans. No reservations accepted.

See also **Nino** (page 205) and **Le Clos des Arômes** (page 205) for additional accommodation options in Cassis.

Bandol & Ile de Bendor

Le Delos €€€-€€€€
Ile de Bendor, T04 94 05 90 90, bendor.com.
Designed by Paul Ricard at the island's eastern end, Le Delos has 19 bright, unique rooms, an outdoor pool and on-site restaurant, the latter overseen by truffle expert Bruno Clément. The hotel also manages the 36-room **Le Palais**, Ricard's take on a Venetian Palace, and eight one- and two-bedroom maisonettes (all same contact details). Breakfast and return ferry trip included in rates.

Hôtel Key Largo €€-€€€
19 corniche Bonaparte, T04 94 29 46 93, hotel-key-largo.com.
A gorgeous 18th-century former private home, midway between the Rènecros beach and Bandol's port. Rooms are decked out with

bright contemporary accents or artwork; the seafront ones (eight of the 18) look out over the Ile de Bendor. There's a large ground floor terrace, and breakfast (buffet or in bed) included. No internet access to date.

Hôtel Plein Large €€-€€€
Plage de Rènecros, T04 94 32 23 32, hotelpleinlarge.com.
At the eastern tip of Rènecros bay, Hôtel Plein Large offers seven simple, motel-type rooms with terraces, which face directly on to the sea. Also on site are the restaurant Chez Julie and friendly snack bar/sunlounger terrace Chez Maeva. Three triples (no balconies) available too.

St-Cyr-sur-Mer

Dolce Frégate €€€-€€€€
Lieu-dit Frégate, Route de Bandol, T04 94 29 39 39, dolce-fregate-hotel.com.
Paradise for golf fiends, sporting two courses (9- and 18-hole, dolcefregate-golf-provence. com) plus a golf academy between Cassis and Bandol. Provençal-style rooms are airy, and there's also a spa complex, indoor and outdoor pools.

La Ciotat

Hôtel Les Lavandes €-€€
38 bd de la République, T04 42 08 42 81, hotel-les-lavandes.com.
This family-run, budget spot is located in downtown La Ciotat,

Eating & drinking

within an easy stroll of the town's beaches. The 14 rooms are basic but clean and bright, the breakfast spread is tasty (€6.50) and there's free Wi-Fi.

Sanary-sur-Mer

Hôtel de la Tour €€-€€€
24 quai Général de Gaulle,
T04 94 74 10 10,
sanary-hoteldelatour.com.
Sitting directly on Sanary's port, many of Hôtel de la Tour's modern, French-style rooms have harbour views. Old photos of the village line the common areas, and there's an exceptional seafood restaurant downstairs. A/C and free Wi-Fi to boot.

Toulon

Grand Hôtel du Dauphiné €-€€
10 rue Berthelot, T04 94 62 16 69,
grandhoteldauphine.com.
Super-central classic hotel with blanket Wi-Fi, equidistant from the train station and port. Rooms have fine linen, desks, a/c and satellite on the flatscreen TVs.

Marseille

Chez Michel €€€€
6 rue des Catalans, T04 91 52 30
63, restaurant-michel.com.
Daily 1200-1400 & 2000-2200.
Map: Marseille, A5, p180.
Across from the pretty Plage des Catalans and with views out to Château d'If, this spot is recommended by locals time and again for their choice *bouillabaisse* (€60 per person); the *bourride* (a fish stew variation, blended with garlicky aïoli, €53 per person) is also delectable. Under family management since 1946.

Restaurant Le Rhul €€€€
269 promenade Corniche J F
Kennedy, T04 91 52 54 54.
Daily 1200-1400 & 1900-2200.
Map: Marseille, A6, p180.
One of the city's finest spots to dine on traditional *bouillabaisse*; the menu also features a range of excellent fish and seafood dishes. As favoured by Jacques Chirac and French celebrities.

Toinou €€-€€€
3 cours St-Louis, T04 91 33 14 94,
toinou.com.
Daily 1100-2300.
Map: Marseille, E4, p180.
Oysters, urchins, crab and plenty more at this relaxed seafood specialist, a Marseillaise favourite for over four decades. Self-catering? Pick up your own spread from the restaurant's kiosk outside.

Bar de la Marine €€
15 quai de Rive Neuve,
T04 91 54 95 42.
Daily 0700-0200.
Map: Marseille, C4, p180.
The easygoing port-side bar featured in Marcel Pagnol's novels and films, *Marius, Fanny,* and *César;* it was also a Portuguese stand-in for a scene in the film *Love Actually.* Good salads ('La Marine' features red mullet, sardines and salmon, €11) and *steak haché* (€12).

Heng-Heng €
65 rue de la République,
T04 91 91 29 94.
Wed-Mon, 1230-1430 & 1930-2300.
Map: Marseille, C2, p180.
The furnishings may be basic, but Heng-Heng is one of the city's finest Vietnamese eateries. Roast duck (*canard laqué*, their speciality) is succulent, as are the noodle dishes, particularly the shrimp ravioli, served in a roasted garlic broth. An author's favourite.

Pizzeria Etienne €
43 rue de Lorette, T04 91 54 76 33.
Mon-Sat 1800-2300.
Map: Marseille, C2, p180.
Tucked away in Le Panier's back streets, Etienne's decor is pleasantly dated and the delectable menu brief: half-anchovy, half-cheese pizza (for one-four diners), *côte de bœuf* (rib steak, for one-three diners) and a smattering of starters. Well worth seeking out.

See **Vallon des Auffes** (page 187) for more Marseille dining options.

Cafés & bars

OM Café
25 quai des Belges, T04 91 33 80 33.
Daily 0900-2300.
Map: Marseille, D4, p180.
Join supporters of local football team Olympique Marseille (OM) for this spot's tasty bistro fare: *entrecôte*, or *marmite du pêcheur*. There are plenty of big screens dotted around on match nights.

Orange Basilic
11a cours d'Estienne d'Orves, T06 03 80 06 94.
Mon-Sat 0900-1830.
Map: Marseille, D4, p180.
Freshly squeezed juices, smoothies, salads and light meals, just off the Vieux Port.

Oscar's
8 quai Rive Neuve, T04 91 33 28 86.
Daily 0900-1900.
Map: Marseille, D3, p180.
The Vieux Port's newest addition, serving up New York-style bagels, doughnuts and big cups of coffee. Best is the Classic Bagel Sandwich (€5.50), stuffed with smoked salmon, cream cheese, red onions or capers.

Pâtisserie d'Aix
2 rue d'Aix, T04 91 90 12 50.
Tue-Sun 0900-1800.
Map: Marseille, E2, p180.
Cosy North African pastry shop near the city's Bibliothèque de l'Alcazar, serving glasses of tasty mint tea among their heavenly pyramids of sticky sweets.

Niolon

Auberge du Mérou €€-€€€
Calanque de Niolon, T04 91 46 98 69, aubergedumerou.fr.
Mon-Sat 1200-1400, Tue-Sat 1930-2130.
Dine on seafood, just metres above the turquoise sea. Best is their ultra-fresh fish, simply grilled or cooked in a salt crust. The Auberge also has five basic bedrooms (€), half-board optional.

Martigues

Le Bouchon à la Mer €€-€€€
19 quai Lucien Toulmond, T04 42 49 41 41, lebouchonalamer.fr.
Tue-Sat 1230-1400 & 1900-2200, Sun 1230-1400.
Contemporary French cuisine, from local chef Christophe Perrin. Go for the rabbit terrine, served with a coriander salad, or treat yourself to the decadent foie gras and poached oysters in truffle sauce.

Cassis

Le Clos des Arômes €€€
10 rue Abbé Paul Mouton, T04 42 01 71 84, le-clos-des-aromes.com.
Tue-Sun 1200-1500 & 1930-2300.
Provençal dining within a lovely walled garden, under the canopy of a giant fig tree. Set menus (€26 or €38) feature *daube* ravioli, *moules farcis gratinées* and veggie lasagne. Fourteen simple double rooms (€€) also on site.

Fleurs de Thym €€€
5 rue La Martime, T04 42 01 23 03, fleursdethym.com.
Daily 1930-2300, closed Nov-Jan.
Creative Mediterranean cooking. Unusual dishes include a trio of filet mignon (beef, veal and pork), or an asparagus, smoked duck, Parmesan and vanilla-infused olive oil salad. During warmer months, white wooden tables spill on to the quiet road out front. Menus from €28.

Restaurant Nino €€€
1 quai Jean-Jacques Barthélemy, T04 42 01 74 32, nino-cassis.com.
Tue-Sun 1230-1400 & 1900-2230.
Elegant yet unpretentious. Garlic wafts from the open kitchen; choose between the three-course set menu (€32) or specialities like *rascasse au basilic* (basil-drenched scorpion fish). Nino also offers

Tip...
Be sure to arrive in L'Estaque hungry: it would be a shame to miss out on the local speciality, *chichi fregi*. These spiral-shaped doughnuts, subtly flavoured with orange blossom and deep fried, are sold from the kiosks that line the port. Beware: slimming they are not!

stylish accommodation (one double, two duplex suites, breakfast included €€€) overlooking Cassis's port.

Poissonnerie Laurent €€-€€€
6 quai Jean-Jacques Barthélemy, T04 42 01 71 56.
Fri-Wed 1200-1430.
Half fish shop, half restaurant, port-side Poissonnerie Laurent has been running under the same family management since 1880. Dishes of the day include *petit bourride* (€16), and the menu is littered with fabulous fish *tartares*, scallops and rockfish included. No credit cards.

La Bonaparte €€
14 rue du Général Bonaparte, T04 42 01 80 84.
Tue-Sun 1200-1400 & 1930-2230.
Friendly budget spot on Cassis's back streets, owned by the gregarious Jean-Marie. Go for the very good *soupe de poissons* or daily fish specials; be sure to book in advance, particularly on summer evenings.

Bandol & Ile de Bendor

Les Oliviers €€€€
Hôtel Ile Rousse, 25 bd Louis Lumière, T04 94 29 33 12, ile-rousse.com.
Daily 1200-1400 & 1900-2200.
Overlooking the sheltered Rènecros bay, Les Oliviers serves up some of Bandol's most refined cuisine. Menus from

Jean-Paul Lanyou (€36-62) are likely to mix Mediterranean influences, such as basil *pistou* soup with Corsican sheep's cheese dumplings.

KV&B €€€-€€€€
5 rue de la Paroisse, T04 94 74 85 77.
Tue-Sun 1200-1430 & 1930-2230 (Sep-May closed Thu lunch).
Little sister to the well-established Le Clocher (1 rue de la Paroisse) down the road, KV&B is part trendy restaurant (crystals shimmer against the black ceiling), part very good wine bar. Menus (€28/35) are modern French; mixed plates of *charcuterie* and cheeses are also available.

Le Grand Large €€-€€€
Ile de Bendor, T04 94 29 81 94, restaurantgrandlarge.com.
Daily 0900-1400, closed mid Nov-mid Dec.
Boasting a terrace with sea views over the Ile des Embiez (plus unusual wines from Embiez on the menu), Le Grand Large is pleasantly laid-back. Top dishes include *escargots flambés* in Ricard pastis. One of the island's few spots to remain open (almost) all year round.

Pizzeria le Pinocchio €€
5 rue Docteur Louis Marçon, T04 94 29 41 16.
Daily 1200-1400 & 1900-2215.
Le Pinocchio's personal pizzas may weigh in around €14 each, but they're worth it. Dough is

made according to a secret family recipe; pizzas are crisped in their roaring wood-fired oven. The restaurant also offers a two-course menu (€20.50, with coffee), featuring picks like Texan pork ribs or gratinéed mussels.

La Cadière d'Azur

Hostellerie Bérard €€€€
6 rue Gabriel Péri, T04 94 90 11 43, hotel-berard.com.
Mid May-Oct daily 1930-2200, Wed-Sun 1200-1400, Nov-mid May Wed-Sun 1200-1400 & 1930-2200.
Exceptional cuisine by chefs Réne and his son Jean-François Bérard. Dinner menus range from a delectable three courses (€43) to an eight-course gourmet bonanza (€146); well-executed dishes include wild duck with caramelised beets and deconstructed *tarte tatin*. Learn how to recreate your meal at the cookery school (see page 210).

Toulon

Sidi Bou Saïd €€
43 rue Jean Jaurès, T04 94 91 21 23.
Tue-Sat 1200-1430 & 1900-2300.
Great North African specialist with chic interior, complete with wacky central water feature. Tunisian specials include *brick au thon*, a deep-fried tuna and egg pocket, and spicy *salade mechouia*, along with couscous and *tajines*. Tunisian, Algerian and Moroccan wines available.

Entertainment

Clubs & bars

La Caravelle
34 quai du Port, T04 91 90 36 64.
Daily 0800-0200.
Aperitifs from 1800 with amazing tapas, overlooking the Vieux Port. Live music Friday evenings.

Tip...

In Marseille, get the lowdown on what's going down (club nights, new shops, current exhibitions) with one of these free newspapers:

L'Hebdo French, marseillelhebdo.com

COTE French/English, cotemagazine.com

Ventilo French, journalventilo.fr

César French

Le Cri du Port
8 rue du Pasteur Heuzé, T04 91 50 51 41, criduport.fr.
International jazz acts, most evenings Thu-Sun 2030.

The New Cancan
2 rue Sénac, T04 91 47 05 26, newcancan.com.
Thu-Sun 2300-dawn.
The city's best gay club pulls in a mixed crowd.

Le Pelle-Mêle
8 place aux Hulles, T04 91 54 85 26.
Mon-Sat 1800-0200, live shows usually Fri & Sat 2230.
Local and international jazz concerts from €6; also a great place for a late night drink.

Le Polikarpov
24 cours Honoré d'Estienne d'Orves, T04 91 52 70 30, lepolikarpov.com.
Daily 0900-0200.
Tiny vodka bar, with temporary art installations and live DJs most weekends.

Trolleybus
24 quai Rive Neuve, T04 91 54 30 45, letrolley.com.
Wed-Sat, from 2300.
Enduringly popular port-side club since its opening in 1989, playing 80s, house and disco. For both club nights and theatre performances, see also **La Friche la Belle de Mai** (page 189).

La Caravelle's petite balcony, Marseille.

Shopping

Tip...

Pick up tickets for exhibitions, concerts and theatre performances at Marseille's **Espace Culture** (42 La Canebière, T04 96 11 04 60, espaceculture. net, Mon-Sat 1000-1845).

Sports
Stade Vélodrome
1 bd Michelet, om.net.
Sixty-thousand-seat Olympique de Marseille stadium; football matches and other sporting events.

Theatre
Opéra Municipal de Marseille
2 rue Molière, T04 91 55 11 10, marseille.fr.
Opera and ballet performances from September-June.

Théâtre National de la Criée
30 quai Rive Neuve, T04 91 54 70 54, theatre-lacriee.com.
Closed Aug.
Premier theatre, located within the city's former fish market.

Bandol

Casino
Le Grand Casino de Bandol
2 place Lucien Artaud, Bandol, T04 94 29 31 31, casinobandol.com.
Daily 1300-0400.

Marseille

Art & antiques
d+ design
52 rue de Lorette, T06 89 13 49 77.
Tue-Sat 1100-1900.
Lamps, furnishings and kitchenware from the 1950s-70s.

Books
Librairie-Galerie Imbernon
280 bd Michelet, Le Corbusier no357, T04 91 22 56 84, editionsimbernon.com.
Tue-Sat 0930-1300 & 1500-1930.
Architecture book specialist.

Clothes & shoes
Antoine & Lili
38 rue Montgrand, T04 91 52 73 70, antoineetlili.com.
Mon, Wed-Thu 1030-1330 & 1430-1930, Tue & Fri-Sat 1000-2000.
Paris-based brand, selling dashing Asian-inspired clothes and shoes for women.

La Compagnie de Provence Marseille
18 rue Francis Davso, T04 91 33 04 17, compagniedeprovence.com.
Mon-Sat 1000-1900.
Natural soaps and creams, locally produced.

Esprit-Raphia
5 cours Julien, T04 91 94 03 86, esprit-raphia.com.
Handmade leather and canvas espadrilles: pick up a pair (each one is unique) or ask Annie to make the shoes of your dreams.

La Sardine à Paillettes
9 rue de la Tour, T06 18 31 46 04, lasardineapaillettes.com.
Mon 1400-1900, Tue-Sat 1030-1330 & 1430-1900.
Fabulous kids' clothes from Danish designer Louise Hjorth, plus Japanese lunchboxes, tights and bags.

Repetto
24 rue Francis Davso, T04 91 91 53 09, repetto.fr.
Mon-Sat 1000-1900.
Soft leather ballerina shoes, created for French dancers, now internationally coveted.

Food & drink
Four des Navettes
136 rue Ste-Anne, T04 91 33 32 12, fourdesnavettes.com.
Sep-Jul Mon-Sat 0700-2000, Sun & Aug 0900-1300 & 1500-1930.
Marseille's oldest bakery (founded in 1781) and purveyors of *navettes*, the city's famous orange-blossom, cakey biscuits. From €8 per dozen.

Maison de Pastis
108 quai du Port, T04 91 90 86 77.
Mon-Fri 1030-1900, Sat 1000-1900, Sun 1030-1700.
For all things pastis: pick up big brands or herby artisan specials.

See also box Five of the best Marseillaise Markets, page 187.

Good luck shells, known as 'œil de Ste-Lucie', or Saint Lucy's eye.

Activities & tours

Transport

Souvenirs
L'Eau de Cassis
2 place Barganon, T04 42 01 25 21,
leaudecassis.com.
Mon-Sat 1000-1300 &
1500-1900.
Creating natural perfumes
since 1851.

Ile de Bendor

Art & antiques
La Tintounette
T04 94 29 78 52.
Daily in season.
Blown glass jewellery and
sculptures by Antoine Ithamar.

Toulon

Souvenirs
Billie Brindille
26 rue de Pomet, T04 94 62 99 15,
billiebrindille.com.
Tue-Fri 1000-1300 & 1400-1900,
Sat 1000-1900.
Wacky Ekobo homeware and
ladies' luggage from La Vie
Devant Soie.

Cultural
Idées Seniors
Available at the Marseille Tourist
Office.
Seasonal magazine listing
quality activities and excursions
aimed at the city's older visitors.
In French.

Food & wine
Bouillabaisse Cooking
Lesson
T04 91 13 89 00, marseille-
tourisme.com.
Once a month, the Marseille
Tourist Office organises a
bouillabaisse lesson in
collaboration with Restaurant
Miramar. €120 per person.

Hostellerie Bérard
Cookery School
6 rue Gabriel Péri, La Cadière
d'Azur, T04 94 90 11 43,
hotel-berard.com.
Four days of market shopping,
vineyard visits and cooking
classes. Prices start at €1388 per
person, including food and
accommodation. Wine-tasting
classes also available.

Wellbeing
Thalazur Bandol
Thalassothérapie & Spa
Hôtel Ile Rousse, 25 bd Louis
Lumière, Bandol, T04 94 29 33 00,
bandol.thalazur.fr.
Thalassotherapy, massage and
skincare treatments, steps from
Bandol's plage de Rènecros.

Additional information about
buses around the region can
be found at lepilote.com.

Marseille Provence Airport
(mrsairport.com) is around 25 km
west of the city centre. **Shuttle
buses** (navettemarseilleaeroport.
com) run between the airport
and Marseille's bus station at
Gare St-Charles every 20 minutes
(25 mins); there are also shuttles
to Aix-en-Provence (30 mins,
departures every half hour).
  Various companies run **ferries**
from Marseille to Corsica, Sardinia,
Tunisia and Algeria. See the
following websites for prices
and schedules: SNCM (sncm.fr),
Compagnie Tunisienne de
Navigation (ctn.com.tn) and
Algérie Ferries (algerieferries.com).
  There are frequent trains from
Marseille to Cassis (25 mins),
La Ciotat (35 mins), Bandol (45
mins), Sanary-sur-Mer (50 mins)
and Toulon (40 mins-1 hr). Trains
every one to two hours along the
Côte Bleue to Martigues (45 mins).

Trains every one to two hours
along the Côte Bleue to Marseille
(45 mins).

Frequent trains west to Marseille
(25 mins); east to La Ciotat
(10 mins), Bandol (20 mins),

Sanary-sur-Mer (25 mins) and Toulon (35 mins). Four to five daily buses to La Ciotat (15 mins).

Bandol

Six to ten buses per day to Sanary-sur-Mer (15 mins) and Toulon (50 mins). Frequent trains east to Sanary-sur-Mer (5 mins) and Toulon (15 mins); west to La Ciotat (10 mins), Cassis (20 mins) and Marseille (45 mins). Three to nine daily buses to Le Castellet (10 mins) and La Cadière d'Azur (15 mins).

Le Castellet

Three to nine daily buses to La Cadière d'Azur (5 mins) and Bandol (10 mins).

La Cadière d'Azur

Three to nine daily buses to Le Castellet (5 mins) and Bandol (15 mins).

La Ciotat

Frequent trains east to Bandol (10 mins), Sanary-sur-Mer (15 mins) and Toulon (25 mins); west to Cassis (10 mins) and Marseille (35 mins). Four daily buses to Cassis (15 mins).

Sanary-sur-Mer

Hourly buses to Toulon (35 mins). Seven to ten daily buses to Bandol (15 mins). Frequent trains east to Toulon (10 mins); west to

Bandol (5 mins), La Ciotat (15 mins), Cassis (15 mins) and Marseille (50 mins).

Toulon

Seven to ten daily buses to Bandol (50 mins). Hourly buses to Sanary-sur-Mer (35 mins). Frequent trains Bandol (15 mins), Sanary-sur-Mer (10 mins), La Ciotat (25 mins), Cassis (35 mins) and Marseille (40 mins-1 hr).

Ferry crossing Vieux Port, Marseille.

Contents

Aix-en-Provence & the Lubéron

The hilltop village of Gordes, in the Lubéron.

Introduction

Aix-en-Provence and the Lubéron encompass all the charms of Provence. The former is a contented, attractive city, blessed with leafy, bourgeois boulevards and pretty open *places*, easily navigated on foot. Centuries of stability and wealth have allowed Aix to cultivate a prolific artistic community: it's no surprise that the city's most famous son, Paul Cézanne, worked and resided here all his life. Aix's museums, boutiques, morning market (place Richelme, daily) and pavement cafés promise to keep any visitor seriously captivated; the city is also an excellent base for exploring the surrounding region.

Just north of Aix, the bucolic Lubéron countryside is peppered with isolated hilltop villages. Its rich earth is bountiful year round, yielding Cavaillon melons, figs, honey, truffles and tomatoes, and of course, plenty of wonderful wines. A foil for Aix's more cosmopolitan pastimes, the landscape here is spliced with trails and cycle routes, snaking through fields of sweet-smelling lavender, past flaming ochre peaks.

Both Aix-en-Provence and the Lubéron attract thousands of tourists every year. Visiting in late spring or early autumn will allow you to examine their allure on a more intimate basis, although their vibrant appeal is obvious in any season.

Shadow Cézanne's footsteps in Aix-en-Provence by following the 'C' brass studs in the city's pavement .

What to see in…

…one day
Spend the morning at **Cézanne's Atelier**, followed by lunch on Aix's **cours Mirabeau**. In the afternoon, visit the perched village of **Gordes**, stopping at the **Pont Julien** on the way; or head to **Roussillon** and hike the gentle **Sentier des Ocres**.

…a weekend or more
Devote a day to **Aix's** main sights, before making your way into the heart of the **Lubéron**. Base yourself in **Lourmarin** or near **Gordes**, hiking, cycling or visiting the **Abbaye de Sénanque**; follow up with a lingering meal, sampling the local cuisine and wines.

Aix-en-Provence

Aix-en-Provence (originally 'Aquae Sextiae') was founded in 122 BC when Roman troops discovered underground thermal springs. Wooed by the region's mild climate they settled down into permanent camps. A precious gem, ripe for conquest, the town bounced between ruling powers over the centuries, until reaching its 15th-century zenith under Louis II of Anjou, and his son, 'Good René'. The former established Aix's renowned university in 1409; the latter was the beloved final king of independent Provence, before the region was absorbed into the Kingdom of France.

Aix went on to grow in affluence. Archbishop Mazarin established the elegant Quartier Mazarin, and scholars and aristocrats arrived by the dozen. During the 19th century, the town nurtured the talents of one of the world's most influential artists, Paul Cézanne, as well as those of his prominent friend, novelist Emile Zola.

Today, the city remains a bastion of cultural development. Thousands of foreign students – particularly Americans – flood into Aix annually, to perfect their French or study at one of the city's many universities. The contemporary Pavillion Noir (see page 234), an award-winning glass and iron cube designed by architect Rudy Ricciotti, is home to the internationally renowned Ballet Preljocaj. Young and thriving, yet revelling in its rich history, Aix is invariably appealing.

Tip...

Follow the trail of 'C' brass studs embedded in the city's pavements: these will take you around town to the spots where Cézanne used to live and work.

Cours Mirabeau

Running from place du Général de Gaulle (also called La Rotonde), outside the Tourist Office, to the 18th-century Hôtel du Poète at its eastern end, cours Mirabeau bisects Aix's city centre. The affluent, residential Mazarin neighbourhood sits to its south, while the heart of the Old Town, criss-crossed by winding alleys and narrow roads, lies to its north. The cours' towering trees shelter pavement cafés, including **Les Deux Garçons** (see page 232), evening craft markets and ambling tourists by the dozen. It's also home to three of the city's famed fountains: Fontaine des Neuf Canons, formerly a livestock watering hole; Fontaine Moussue, a mossy fountain bubbling warm water; and Fontaine du Roi René, marked with an imposing sculpture of 'Good René'. Throughout Cézanne's childhood, the future artist lived with his family at number 55, upstairs from his father's successful *chapellerie* (hat shop). Further west on the same side of the cours, **Galerie d'Art du Conseil Général** (21 cours Mirabeau, T04 42 93 03 67, Tue afternoon-Sun, summer 1030-1300 & 1400-1800, winter 0930-1300 & 1400-1800, free) hosts four contemporary art shows every year, highlighting works by artists from the Bouches-du-Rhône region.

Musée Granet

Place St Jean de Malte, T04 42 52 88 32, museegranet-aixenprovence.fr.
Tue-Sun Jun-Sep 1100-1900, Oct-May 1200-1800 (ticket desks close 1 hr earlier). €4, €2 students/ under 26, under 18s free, free 1st Sun of month, temporary exhibitions additional fee.
Map: Aix-en-Provence, p218.

Housed in the Eglise St-Jean-de-Malte's former priory, Musée Granet hosts an excellent range of

Essentials

❶ Getting around Walking is the easiest way to get around the city, as the Old Town is compact, with most points of interest no more than 20 minutes apart by foot. Buses (aixenbus.com) for Aix sights outside the centre depart from La Rotonde (place du Général de Gaulle), near the Tourist Office. Tickets (€1.10) can be purchased on board. There are taxi stands at the bus and train stations; alternatively contact the Association Taxis Radio Aixois (T04 42 27 71 11, taxisradioaixois.com) for pick-up.

❷ Train station TGV: RD 9, plateau de l'Arbois, T08 36 35 35 35, tgv.com; SNCF: rue Gustave Desplaces, T36 35, voyages-sncf.com.

❸ Bus station Avenue de l'Europe, T08 91 02 40 25, infotelo.com. Frequent shuttles (*navettes*) operate between the TGV and bus stations (20 mins, €3.70, tickets can be purchased on board).

❹ ATMs There are plenty of ATMs dotted throughout the city, including seven along cours Mirabeau.

❺ Hospital Centre Hospitalier du Pays d'Aix, avenue des Tamaris, T04 42 33 50 00, ch-alx.fr.

❻ Pharmacy 17bis cours Mirabeau, T04 42 93 63 60.

❼ Post office Place de l'Hôtel de Ville, T04 42 17 10 41, Monday & Wednesday-Friday 0800-1830, Tuesday 0800-1215 & 1330-1830, Saturday 0800-1200.

❽ Tourist information office 2 place du Général de Gaulle, T04 42 16 11 61, aixenprovencetourism.com, Monday-Saturday 0830-1900, Sunday 1000-1300 & 1400-1800, July-August extended hours. Buy an **Aix City Pass** (€15, available from the Tourist Office, valid for five days) for free entry to four major sights, tours of the Atelier Cézanne and Jas de Bouffan, a **city tour** (see page 237) and a free loop around the city on **Le Petit Tourist Train** (cpts.fr).

La Rotonde, Aix en Provence.

Aix-en-Provence listings

❶ Sleeping

1 28 à Aix *28 rue du 4 Septembre*
2 Hôtel Cézanne *40 avenue Victor Hugo*
3 Hôtel des 4 Dauphins *54 rue Roux-Alpheran*
4 Hôtel des Augustins *3 rue de la Masse*
5 Hôtel Le Pigonnet *5 avenue St-Michel du Pigonnet*
6 Hôtel Paul *10 avenue Pasteur*

❶ Eating & drinking

1 Bar Brigand *17 place Richelme*
2 Brasserie Léopold *2 avenue Victor Hugo*
3 Le Clos de la Violette *10 avenue de la Violette*
4 Le Passage *10 rue Villars*
5 Le Zinc d'Hugo *22 rue Lieutaud*
6 Les Deux Garçons *53 cours Mirabeau*
7 Restaurant Pierre Reboul *11 petite rue St-Jean*
8 Toute une Histoire *place des Tanneurs*
9 Simply Food *67 rue Espariat*

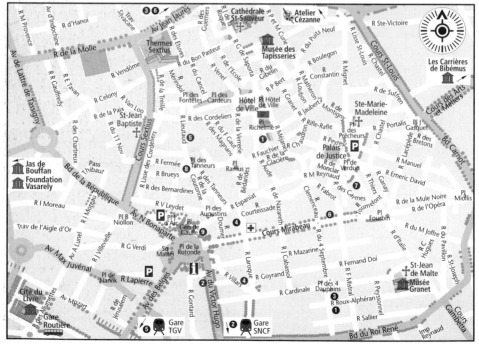

temporary exhibitions (2009's Picasso-Cézanne show was a recent highlight) as well as a permanent collection comprised of modern art, 18th- and 19th-century sculpture displayed in a pale olive-toned gallery, and archaeological finds. Petite but pithy, the first floor's 'De Cézanne à Giacometti' collection includes works by Fernand Léger, Paul Klee, Giorgio Morandi and Nicolas de Staël. The museum also owns a selection of Cézanne watercolours and drawings, although these are only exhibited for three months of every year due to the artworks' fragility.

Les Thermes Sextius

55 av des Thermes, T04 42 23 81 82, thermes-sextius.com.
Treatments Mon-Fri 0830-1930, Sat 0830-1930, Sun & hols 1030-1630; Fitness & Relaxation Area Mon-Fri 0830-2030, Sat 0930-1930, Sun & hols 1030-1730. Day entrance to Fitness & Relaxation Area (pool, saunas, hammam and gym) €42, treatment packages start around €89.
Map: Aix-en-Provence, p218.

During the second century BC, Roman leader Sextius Calvinus stumbled across thermal waters bubbling up from under the earth at a balmy 34°C. Baths installed, the town of Aix was founded. The tradition continues over two millennia later. Although a small line of Roman pools are still visible outside the entrance, the bulk of the Sextius Thermal Baths are built into a mix of 18th-century mansion and a more modern complex. Drop in for a soak in the therapeutic baths, opt for 'Operation New Skin' (scrub with Camargue salt) or book a facial (Nuxe products are used). Les Thermes also run package deals with **Hôtel Aquabella** (aquabella.fr) next door.

Cathédrale St-Sauveur

Rue Jacques de La Roque, cathedrale-aix.net.
Daily 0730-1200 & 1400-1800. Free.
Map: Aix-en-Provence, p218.

Sitting at the heart of Aix's Old Town, the Cathédrale St-Sauveur was built over a period of

Tip...

The **Aix et le Pays d'Aix** pass (Pass for Aix and Aix Countryside, aixenprovencetourism.com, €2, available from the Tourist Office) will entitle the holder to free or discounted entry to museums (including **Musée Granet** and **Fondation Vasarely**), vineyards, concerts, tours and transport in and around Aix.

Above: Cathedrale Saint Sauveur, Aix-en-Provence.
Opposite page: One of the city's numerous fountains.

Around the region

close to 1300 years. The cathedral's history is neatly reflected in its mix of architectural styles: Roman and Gothic gates, and its three naves (Roman, Gothic and Baroque). Head inside for a peek at both the 18th-century organ and Nicolas Froment's recently restored masterpiece, *The Burning Bush*. Adjacent are the cathedral's cloisters, its courtyard lined with ornately carved columns.

Musée des Tapisseries

Ancien Palais de l'Archevêché, 28 place des Martyrs de la Résistance, T04 42 23 09 91.
Wed-Mon mid Apr-mid Oct 1000-1800, mid Oct-mid Apr 1330-1700. €3.
Map: Aix-en-Provence, p218.

The Archbishop's former palace is the unique setting for this collection of 17th- and 18th-century tapestries. The museum opened in 1909, but it was only in 1979 that contemporary textiles were included; it now also organises temporary exhibitions of modern art, and has a wing dedicated to the history of the annual **Festival International d'Art Lyrique** (festival-aix.com).

Cité du Livre

Bibliothèque Méjanes, 8-10 rue des Allumettes, T04 42 91 98 88, citedulivre-aix.com.
Tue, Thu & Fri 1200-1800, Wed & Sat 1000-1800.
Map: Aix-en-Provence, p218.

A cultural centre located in an old match factory, with the Méjanes Library at its core. The Cité du Livre offers a lively monthly programme of art house films in original language, lyric art and filmed opera showings (usually free), plus children's workshops.

Ancient Roman fountains outside Termes Sextius, Aix-en-Provence.

Atelier Cézanne

*9 av Paul Cézanne, T04 42 21 06 53,
atelier-cezanne.com.*
Jul-Aug 1000-1800, tour (English) 1700, Apr-Jun &
Sep 1000-1200 & 1400-1800, tour (English) 1700,
Oct-Mar 1000-1200 & 1400-1700, tour (English)
1600. €5.50, €2 under 25s, under 12s free. Bus no
1 to 'Paul Cézanne'.
Map: Aix-en-Provence, p218.

A brisk 10-minute hike out of town, Cézanne's final
atelier, and the rambling gardens that surround it,
are well worth the (uphill) effort needed to arrive
as the artist did every day, on foot.

Two years after his mother's death, Cézanne
was forced to sell the family home, Jas de Bouffan
(see page 223). With the proceeds, he purchased

this plot of land on Les Lauves hill in 1901, designed
his own studio and had it purpose-built. He came
here daily, following a strict painting schedule
(0600-1030, lunch in Aix, straight back to the
studio until 1700) until his death in 1906.

The northern side of the 50-sq-m studio is one
massive wall of glass, while the southern has two
large windows, in order to allow as much natural
light into the room as possible. As the 19th century
petered to a close, painting nude models al fresco
was still a social no-no; the studio's swathes of
natural light allowed Cézanne to create the perfect
conditions to complete his unfinished *Grandes
Baigneuses* and other masterpieces.

Post Cézanne's death, the studio remained
closed for 15 years. Marcel Provence, who
purchased the building and its land in 1921, kept
everything just how he found it. And happily so:
today, it's possible to see the very wine bottles,
chairs, pitchers, fruit stands, skulls and an armless
statue of a toddler that feature in some of Cézanne's

Tip...

To see Mont Ste-Victoire through the artist's eyes,
continue another 2 km past Cézanne's Atelier to the
crest of Les Lauves hill: the **Terrain des Peintres**, from
where Cézanne painted, still offers a clear view of
stunning natural beauty.

Top: Atelier Cézanne. Above: Mont Ste-Victorie.

most famous artworks, as well as the artist's coat, hat and personal photos. French- and English-speaking staff are on hand to answer questions.

Jas de Bouffan

Route de Galice, T04 42 16 10 91.
Jun-Sep 1030-1730, hourly tours (45 mins), 1330 English tour, Apr-May & Oct Tue, Thu & Sat 1030-1730, hourly tours, 1330 English tour, Jan-Mar Wed & Sat 1000-1045 (one tour only). €5.50, €2 under 25s, under 12s free. Bus no 6 to 'Corsy'. Map: Aix-en-Provence, p218.

This sprawling 18th-century mansion was the Cézanne family home from 1870 to 1899. Cézanne used one of the spacious ground floor rooms as his studio, and it was here that he painted 12 of his masterpieces directly on to the walls (since removed and transferred to various museums). From his outdoor easel, Cézanne turned his attention to the house and grounds, depicting it in over 50 artworks. Note that Jas de Bouffan can only be visited on one of the scheduled tours; it is also due to undergo general renovations, so it's best to check with the Tourist Office before visiting.

Les carrières de Bibémus (Bibémus quarries)

Chemin de Bibémus, T04 42 16 10 91.
English tours: Sat 1000; French tours: Jun-Sep 0945-1045 (one tour only, 1 hr), Apr-May & Oct Mon, Wed, Fri & Sun 1030-1730, hourly tours, Jan-Mar Wed & Sat 1500-1600 (one tour only). €6.60, €3.10 under 25s, under 12s €1.10, entrance includes return ticket for the shuttle bus (obligatory transport to quarries from 3 Bons Dieux car park).
Bus no 4 to '3 Bons Dieux'. Map: Aix-en-Provence, p218.

During the 1890s, Cézanne rented a tiny house in the abandoned Bibémus stone quarries. The orange, blocky paintings he created here during this period are generally heralded as precursors to the Cubist movement of the early 20th century. Note that a trip to the Bibémus quarries may be

most appealing to those who enjoy an out-of-town ramble, as opposed to art enthusiasts. Visits can only be undertaken on one of the scheduled tours; comfortable walking shoes are advised.

Fondation Vasarely

1 av Marcel Pagnol, Jas de Bouffan, T04 42 20 01 09, fondationvasarely.fr.
Tue-Sat 1000-1300 & 1400-1800. €7, €4 students/ child (7-18), under 7s free, free audioguide. Bus nos 4 or 6 to 'Fondation Vasarely'. Map: Aix-en-Provence, p218.

Through the 1940s and '50s, Hungarian-born artist Victor Vasarely's spiral swirls and geometrical patterns of black, white and solid colours helped establish the optical art, or op art, movement.

Provence had long been a favourite region for Vasarely. Although he lived near Paris, his summer holidays were spent in Gordes; the artist even established his first museum (now closed) in the hilltop town's 16th-century castle. From 1971, Vasarely designed and planned the construction and layout of his Fondation; in 1973 the Aix-en-Provence municipality donated land to the artist for its creation, and construction began. The Fondation was finally inaugurated in 1976.

Over the 30 years since its opening, the museum has been fraught with drama, from leaky roofs to artworks siphoned on to the black market by the Fondation's previous director. Still a treat, on the ground floor seven rooms ('hexagonal cells') display Vasarely's 42 giant 'architectural integrations' beneath their 11-m ceilings. The museum also stages temporary exhibitions.

Tip...

If you plan to visit **Cézanne's Atelier, Jas de Bouffan** and the **Bibémus Quarries**, purchase the discounted **Cézanne Pass** (€13.10), which allows one entry into each of the three sites, and is valid for the calendar year. Note that the return ticket for the Bibémus quarries shuttle bus (€1.10, obligatory transport to quarries from 3 Bons Dieux car park) is not included in the pass.

The Lubéron

Perhaps best known for its starring role in the film and novel, *A Good Year* (see page 228), the region rolling north of Aix-en-Provence barely breaks a metaphorical sweat, so effortlessly does it attract visitors by the busload. The *villages perchés* (hilltop villages), enchanting ochre cliffs, vineyards, sunflowers and especially the lavender – come July and August it's purple as far as the eye can see – are trumpeted by their supporters as an antithesis to glitzier towns dotted along the Mediterranean coast.

Yet the Lubéron and its environs have long been favoured by escaping expats and famous French: Samuel Beckett, Albert Camus, Picasso and Dora Maar, John Malkovich, Ridley Scott and Pierre Cardin, among so many others, all chose to make this area their (sometimes second) home. The region isn't 'undiscovered', but that doesn't negate that there is indeed something magical about the postcard-perfect countryside around here: get off the main tourist trails and you'll soon find it.

Note that the Lubéron is poorly connected by public transport. If you choose to bed down out of town, it's wise to ensure your hotel has an on-site restaurant (and that it's open). After a busy day sightseeing, all you may be up for is tucking into a rack of local Sisteron lamb, then tucking yourself up into bed.

The archetypical Provençal perched village of Gordes soars above the undulating vineyards and fields of lavender that gather at its base. Buildings of the palest golden stone clamber perilously atop each other: the town is almost more scenic from afar than within, not least because you're still a peaceful distance from its (often) tourist-clogged streets.

At the heart of Gordes' town centre sits its 16th-century **château**, which has been used alternatively as a prison, barracks, post office and boys' school. Between 1970 and 1996, the castle housed a museum dedicated to Victor Vasarely. This same space is now home to the **Musée Pol Mara** (entrance place Genty Pantaly, T04 90 72 02 75, daily 1000-1200 & 1400-1800, €4, €3 child (10-17), under 10s free) – the Belgian contemporary artist was a former resident of the village – and the **Tourist Office** (T04 90 72 02 75, gordes-village. com). The pretty square out front, place Genty Pantaly, featured in Ridley Scott's 2006 film *A Good Year* (based on Mayle's book), as did the hotel and restaurant **La Renaissance** (see page 233).

Heading downhill, peek inside the richly painted Eglise de St-Firmin, before continuing on to the **Caves du Palais St Firmin** (rue du Belvédère, Jul-Aug daily 1030-1900, mid Apr-Jun & Sep-mid Oct Wed-Mon 1100-1800, €5, €4 students/under 17s), stone cellars that burrow beneath a former noble home and demonstrate old-style manual agricultural tasks, such as making olive oil. Near the cellars' entrance, there are stunning panoramic views over the Théâtre des Terrasses (occasional site of the town's annual Les Soirées d'Eté de Gordes) and the valley below.

Space allowing, it's best to park at the car park above place du Château (direction Murs); the lower car park (nearest the turn off for the Abbaye de Sénanque, direction Venasque) requires a steep hike uphill to the town centre.

Essentials

➊ Getting around It's easiest to explore the heart of Provence using your own vehicle. For car rental agencies, see page 237. Buses run between most of the Lubéron's towns (see page 237). Taxi Lubéron (T06 86 74 52 74, taxi-luberon.com) operates in the region, and can also arrange personalised tours.

➌ ATMs Most Lubéron towns have an ATM in the main square. It's best to travel with some cash, as smaller shops and restaurants often don't accept cards.

⊕ Hospital Centre Hospitalier du Pays d'Apt, 225 avenue Philippe de Girard, Apt, T04 90 04 33 00.

✚ Pharmacy 3 rue Raspail, Bonnieux, T04 90 75 82 35; route d'Apt, Lourmarin, T04 90 68 20 25.

➋ Post office Place du Jeu de Boules, Gordes; avenue Victor Hugo, Apt; place de la Poste, Roussillon.

➊ Tourist information office Le Château, Gordes, T04 90 72 02 75, gordes-village.com; 20 avenue Philippe de Girard, Apt, T04 90 74 03 18, ot-apt.fr; place de la Poste, Roussillon, T04 90 05 60 25, roussillon-provence. com; avenue Philippe de Girard, Lourmarin, T04 90 68 10 77, lourmarin.com; 16 place du Docteur Joubert, Manosque, T04 92 72 16 00, manosque-tourisme.com.

Vineyards ripple through the valley below Gordes.

Abbaye Notre-Dame de Sénanque

RD 177, route de Venasque, T04 90 72 05 72, senanque.fr (abbey), abbayedesenanque.com (boutique).
Grounds always open, access to interior by guided visit only (in French, 50 visitors max per tour, 1 hr). Tours: Jul-Aug Mon-Sat 0950, 1010 & 1030, daily 1430, 1450, 1510, 1530, 1545, 1600, 1615 & 1630; Jun & Sep Mon-Sat 1010 & 1030, daily 1430, 1510, 1530, 1610 & 1630; Apr-May Mon-Sat 1010 & 1030, daily 1430, 1530 & 1630; Feb-Mar & Oct-mid Nov Mon-Sat 1030, daily 1430, 1530 & 1630; mid Nov-Jan daily 1450 & 1620; Boutique: Feb-mid Nov Mon-Sat 1000-1800, Sun 1400-1800; mid Nov-Jan 1400-1800. €7, €5 students/under 25s, €3 child (6-18), under 6s free.

Set in a bucolic valley 4 km from Gordes, this Cistercian abbey was built in 1148 and has been religiously active ever since. The grounds are always open to the public: wander through the lavender fields or circle around the back for a peek at the resident monks' vegetable gardens. Join one of the abbey's guided tours in order to visit the monks' former dormitory, the Abbey church, cloisters and 'scriptorium' (where manuscripts were transcribed). The Abbaye also welcomes individuals for spiritual retreats (max 8 days, approx €30/day, frere.hotelier@senanque.fr for further information).

Note that clothing and behaviour should be appropriate to the strict religious setting. The on-site boutique sells the abbey's own honey and lavender products.

Village des Bories

West of Gordes, direction Cavaillon, T04 90 72 03 48.
Daily 0900-sunset. €5.50, €3 child (10-17), under 10s free.

Bories – unusual, often conical drystone dwellings – can be found all over Provence. Rather than primary residences, *bories* were enclosed, functional spaces: storerooms for agricultural tools, shelter for a shepherd's flock, outdoor kitchens or even houses for silkworm farms.

This cluster of 30 or so huts is the largest grouping in the region. Abandoned over a hundred years ago, these *bories* were built any time between the seventh and 19th centuries; they were heavily restored between 1969 and 1976, then declared a protected site in 1977. Visitors can also stop in at the small museum dedicated to dry-stone architecture at the entrance to the village.

Musée de la Lavande

Route de Gordes, Coustellet, T04 90 76 91 23, museedelalavande.com.
Daily May-Sep 0900-1900, Apr & Oct 0900-1300 & 1400-1800, Feb-Mar & Nov-Dec 0900-1215 & 1400-1800, ticket desks close 30 mins earlier. €6, €5 students, under 15s free if accompanied by paying adult, free audioguide.

A shrine to the fragrant purple blossom for which the Lubéron is so famous. Owned by **Le Château**

Above: Abbaye Notre-Dame de Sénanque.
Opposite page: The ochre façades of village homes in Roussillon.

du Bois (espritlavande.eu), an 80-ha estate producing 10% of France's lavender, the museum charts the history and current production methods used for harvesting the plant's essential oil. It also houses a huge collection of copper stills (used for distilling lavender oil), as well as antique perfume bottles and traditional local costumes. On your way out, stock up on all things lavender – soap, candles, tea and honey – at the on-site boutique.

Roussillon

Long renowned for its ochre deposits, deep red and yellow-based pigments found in the clay of the immediate area, Roussillon remains a vision of glowing sunset hues. The village's hilltop houses range from amber to russet, the colours intensified against a backdrop of dark oak forests and rolling vineyards.

Ochre can be used to dye anything from textiles to cosmetics, and mining for the local pigments peaked in the 1920s. Less than three decades later, the town's foundations were in danger of collapsing due to the avid mining, and activity soon ground to a halt.

Explore the former quarries along **Le Sentier des Ocres de Roussillon** (Ochre Footpath, entrance signposted a 5-min walk from the town centre, daily 0900-1730, €2.40, joint ticket Usine Mathieu & Sentier des Ocres €6.80, under 10s free; short walk 35 mins; long walk 50 mins). Or head 1.5 km out of town to the **Ancienne Usine Mathieu** (RD104, T04 90 05 66 69, okhra.com, Jul-Aug daily 0900-1300 & 1400-1800, Sep-Jun Tue-Sun 0900-1300 & 1400-1800, €6, joint ticket as above, under 10s free), a former ochre factory, where visitors can see how the pigments were washed, processed and transformed from earthen clay to dye.

Bonnieux

A hilltop village crowded with cobblestone streets, antique stores and pavement cafés, Bonnieux's panoramic vistas (best seen from near the old church) are 'a terrace overlooking the world' according to one overheard visitor. Bonnieux also boasts the quirky **Musée de la Boulangerie** (12 rue de la République, T04 90 75 88 34, Wed-Mon Jul-Aug 1000-1300 & 1400-1800, Apr-Jun & Sep-Oct 1000-1230 & 1430-1800, €3.50, €1.50 students/child (12-16)/over 60, under 12s free), which traces the cultivation of wheat, the process of refining flour and various methods of baking.

North of the town, heading towards Apt, don't miss the 2000-year-old **Pont Julien** spanning the Calavon River. The dry-stone bridge is part of the old Via Domitia, the principal Roman trade route between Italy and the Iberian Peninsula. The bridge is accessible by bike and on foot; it's also visible from the D108 that runs parallel past it.

Lacoste

In 2001, fashion tycoon Pierre Cardin purchased Lacoste's medieval castle, formerly the residence of the infamous Marquis de Sade. The castle, under slow restoration, is used in part for the town's

Tip...

The **Couleur Pass Lubéron** (€5, valid for 1-4 persons, available from Tourist Offices throughout the Lubéron) gives discounts of up to 50% on 16 activities throughout the region, including the **Ancienne Usine Mathieu** (see page 227), the **Village des Bories** (see page 226) and **Montgolfière Vol-Terre** (see page 236).

Provence for copycats

In 1989, Peter Mayle, former copywriter and children's author, published his expat-abroad memoir, *A Year in Provence*. Moving to Ménerbes, Mayle and his wife attempted to fulfil the rural idyll. Assimilating into the local culture turned out to be an obstacle course of (very funny and ultimately positive) trials and tribulations. Little did anyone foresee the ripple-turned-tsunami effect Mayle's witty autobiography would cause. It turns out that every one of us harbours a romantic 'ditch it all' dream, and Provençal pilgrims have been filing through the Lubéron ever since. Places mentioned in Mayle's book (Café de la Poste, Goult) continue to bask in everlasting fame, despite changes over the past two decades (Café du Progrès, Ménerbes; La Petite Maison, Cucuron). Fans hungry for more Mayle on Provence can dip into the author's follow-ups: *Toujours Provence, Encore Provence, Bon Appetit! A Good Year* and *Provence A-Z*.

annual **Festival d'Art Lyrique et de Théâtre de Lacoste** (Jul-Aug, festivaldelacoste.com), and its views, to Bonnieux and beyond, are well worth the hike. However, Cardin's long-term plans for the town have proved controversial: he intends to create a 'cultural St-Tropez', snapping up (in some estimates) close to 40 village homes for his project, paying around twice their market value. His critics accuse Cardin of stifling the community, transforming the town into a cluster of desolate streets. Visit out of season and their comments ring painfully true.

The town is also home to a branch of the Savannah College of Art and Design (scad.edu); temporary installations of artwork are frequently dotted around the village.

Lourmarin

Oh-so-pretty Lourmarin ticks all the boxes: pretty winding alleys, Provençal shops stocked with local wine and linens, and plenty of terraces, perfect for lingering over a glass of rosé. The town boasts one of the region's best weekly **markets** (see box opposite), although its main cultural draw is the Renaissance **Château de Lourmarin** (T04 90 68 15 23, chateau-de-lourmarin.com, Jun-Aug daily 1000-1800, May & Sep daily 1000-1130 & 1430-1730, Mar-Apr & Oct daily 1000-1130 & 1430-1630, Feb & Nov-Dec 1000-1130 & 1430-1600, Jan Sat & Sun 1430-1600, €5.50, €3 students, €2.50 child (10-16), under 10s free), located a five-minute walk west of the village and surrounded by olive trees. The Château houses a collection of antique furniture, musical instruments and prints.

Lourmarin's most famous resident was Algerian-born author Albert Camus, who lived in the town during the last years of his life; his remains are buried in the town cemetery.

Five of the best

Provençal markets

Any of the following are an excellent source of local fruits and vegetables, cheese, *charcuterie*, olives, honey, nougat, organic essential oils, soaps and pottery; in addition, look out for Cavaillon's famous melons (Jul) and truffles from the hills around Apt (Nov-Mar).

❶ **Cavaillon** Place du Clos, Monday mornings.

❷ **Vaison-la-Romaine** throughout the town centre, Tuesday mornings. Lying in the Vaucluse's northern region, the market town of Vaison-la-Romaine (vaison-la-romaine.com) makes an appealing day out for those with their own transport. Visit Vaison's Roman sites, Puymin and Villasse, its ampltheatre or cross the Ouvèze River by a bridge from the same period. Head up to the medieval Huate-Ville for fabulous views over Mont Ventoux and the valleys below.

❸ **Lourmarin** Place Henri Barthélémy, Friday mornings.

❹ **Manosque** Place Marcel Pagnol, Saturday mornings.

❺ **Apt** Place de la Bouquerie and around, Saturday mornings.

Right: Belltower, Lacoste.
Opposite page: A sculpture of the Marquis de Sade, former resident of Lacoste's Chateau

Sleeping

28 à Aix €€€€
*28 rue du 4 Septembre,
T04 42 54 82 01, 28-a-aix.com.*
Map: Aix-en-Provence, p218.
Modern and elegant, 28 à Aix,
a 17th-century townhouse
opened in 2008 by the founders
of Villa Gallici (a luxury hotel just
outside Aix's centre, T04 42 23 29
23). All four suites are sumptuous:
Suite 1 features a four-poster bed
draped in luxury linens, Suite 3 a
private terrace overlooking Aix's
rooftops. Two nights minimum.

Hôtel Le Pigonnet €€-€€€€
*5 av du Pigonnet, T04 42 59 02 90,
hotelpigonnet.com.*
Map: Aix-en-Provence, p218.
Less than a kilometre from
downtown Aix, Le Pigonnet's
position allows guests to relax
far from the crowds, yet easily
explore the city sights by foot.
Gardens, including a pool, are
rambling and lush; Cézanne
reputedly painted Mount
Ste-Victoire from here. Rates
can range from bargain to steep,
depending on the season and
room category.

Hôtel Cézanne €€€
*40 av Victor Hugo, T04 42 91 11 11,
cezanne.hotelaix.com.*
Map: Aix-en-Provence, p218.
Hip Hôtel Cézanne touts itself as
the city's only boutique option.
Bright colours and animal prints
grace the ground floor common
areas, while bedrooms are more

neutral, but just as funky. There's
a small honesty bar, plus a free
guest car park around the corner.

Hôtel des Augustins €€-€€€
*3 rue de la Masse, T04 42 27 28 59,
hotel-augustins.com.*
Map: Aix-en-Provence, p218.
Formerly a 12th-century convent,
Hôtel des Augustins claims
Martin Luther as its most famous
guest: the father of Protestantism
temporarily resided here in 1521,
post excommunication by Pope
Leo X. The 29 atmospheric rooms
mix monastic decor with
Provençal prints and more
luxurious trimmings.

Hôtel des 4 Dauphins €€
*54 rue Roux Alphéran, T04 42 38
16 39, lesquatredauphins.fr.*
Map: Aix-en-Provence, p218.
Thirteen petite rooms, down the
street from the Quatre Dauphins
fountain. Decor has been chosen

with attention to detail, keeping
an authentic Provençal theme
throughout. Although only a
five-minute walk from the town's
bustling centre, the hotel's
position in residential Quartier
Mazarin means evenings are
quiet year round.

Hôtel Paul €
*10 av Pasteur, T04 42 23 23 89,
aix-en-provence.com/hotelpaul.*
Map: Aix-en-Provence, p218.
Hôtel Paul lies north of the Old
Town, just beyond Cathédrale
St-Sauveur. Tiny, basic and very
friendly, the hotel is decorated
with giant Cézanne prints (the
artist's Atelier, see page 222, is up
the road). Rooms are all en suite,
and there's a shady garden for
breakfast (€5).

Clocktower in place de l'Hôtel de Ville, Aix-en-Provence.

Gordes

Hôtel Les Bories €€€€
*Route de l'Abbaye de Sénanque,
T04 90 72 00 51,
hotellesbories.com.*
Craving physical immersion in all
that fragrant lavender? Guests at
this sumptuous spot can take
advantage of La Maison d'Ennea
(see page 237), the on-site spa,
as well as indoor and outdoor
pools, tennis court and chef
Pascal Ginoux's fine dining.
Although the 27 rooms and two
suites are pricey, the hotel often
offers packages; check online.

La Ferme de la Huppe €€-€€€
*RD 156, Les Pourquiers, T04 90 72
12 25, lafermedelahuppe.com.*
Ten airy, pale-stone bedrooms are
dotted around this 18th-century
bastide; each one retains the
name of its former function, such
as L'Ecurie (stables) or La Cuisine
(kitchen). A few kilometres
outside the tourist haven of
Gordes, the hotel also has pool
and restaurant on site. New
management (in place since mid
2009) promises to meet the
established high standards.

Les Gros

Le Moulin des Sources €€-€€€
*Les Gros, T04 90 72 11 69,
le-moulin-des-sources.com.*
Closed mid Nov-mid Feb.
More a cushy stay with friends
than a standard B&B. Peeking out

over the pool and olive trees,
Geneviève and Gérard's five en
suite rooms are decked out in
sophisticated grey. A couple of
nights per week, Gérard cooks
up a communal feast (€35 per
person, including aperitif, wine
and coffee), served in the garden
or alongside the kitchen's open
fire. No TV; limited English.

Les Beaumettes

Au Ralenti du Lierre €€
*Village des Beaumettes, T04 90
72 39 22, auralentidulierre.com.*
A lovely B&B between Ménerbes
and Gordes, managed by the
gregarious Thierry. High-
ceilinged bedrooms blend
Provençal greens, blues and reds
with wooden *armoires* and
wrought iron chairs. Breakfast
breads, pastries and jams are
home-made, and there's a
fabulous pool and garden out
back. Guests benefit from both
Au Ralenti's intimacy and its
superb village location.

Bonnieux

Auberge de l'Aiguebrun
€€€-€€€€
*Domaine de la Tour, T04 90 04 47
00, aubergedelaiguebrun.fr.*
Closed early Jan-mid Mar.
Four kilometres outside
Bonnieux's town centre, Auberge
de l'Aiguebrun is a perfect
hideaway. Dip into the pool, dine
at the divine restaurant (closed
Mon-Wed out of season) or

simply sprawl on one of the
canopied garden beds. More
private are the two-person
wooden chalets (€€€), built
alongside a woodland stream.

Lourmarin

Le Moulin du Lourmarin
€€-€€€
*Rue de Temple, T04 90 68 06 69,
moulindelourmarin.com.*
Le Moulin's previous incarnation
– as an 18th-century olive oil mill
– is easily envisioned within the
hotel's cavernous foyer. Airy and
open, a contemporary glass lift
whizzes guests up to the 19
pretty rooms, while an open fire
blazes downstairs in winter. The
hotel also houses the gastro-
restaurant Le Comptoir
(half-board available, see
page 234), a bakery and a small
boutique. Breakfast included.

Les Olivettes
*Av Henri Bosco, T04 90 68 03 52,
olivettes.com.*
Six studio and one-bedroom
apartments, individually
decorated and comfortably
stocked, within a large Provençal
farmhouse. Friendly owners
Elisabeth and Joe are on hand
to help guests plan outings and
pick restaurants. Rentals available
by the week during high season
(€890-1860, sleeping 2-4), and
by the week or month (heavily
discounted) from Nov-Feb;
pets welcome.

Eating & drinking

Manosque

Le Pré Saint Michel €€
Route de Dauphin, Montée de la Mort d'Imbert, T04 92 72 14 27, presaintmichel.com.
Delightfully off the tourist track, Le Pré's tasteful rooms (superior ones with private terraces) have views over the countryside and very welcome swimming pool. Breakfast (€10) is on the sundeck; bathrooms are stocked with L'Occitane products, fresh from the factory down the road (see page 237). La Table du Pré Saint Michel (see page 234) next door offers half-board options.

Saignon

Chambre de Séjour avec Vue – Demeure d'art et d'hôtes €€
Les sablières, T04 90 04 85 01, chambreavecvue.com.
Part B&B, part art gallery, Chambre de Séjour avec Vue (room with a view) is a bright, eclectic mix of colours and contemporary creations. The three intimate rooms share access to a communal living room, dining room (both with open fireplaces) and garden. Owners Pierre and Kamila are welcoming, helpful and very knowledgeable, both about local art and the region.

Aix-en-Provence

Le Clos de la Violette €€€€
10 av de la Violette, T04 42 23 30 71, closdelaviolette.com.
Tue-Sat 1200-1330 & 1930-2130.
Map: Aix-en-Provence, p218.
Michelin-starred cuisine in a pretty garden, just north of Aix's Old Town. Jean-Marc Banzo's market-based set menu (€50, not served Sun) changes daily; other set menus (€90 & €130) are seasonal.

Restaurant Pierre Reboul €€€€
11 petite rue St Jean, T04 42 20 58 26, restaurant-pierre-reboul.com.
Tue-Sat 1200-1330 & 1930-2130.
Map: Aix-en-Provence, p218.
Creating edible *trompe l'œil* since opening in 2007, Pierre Reboul's molecular masterpieces recently earned him a Michelin star. Nothing is what is seems, from Munster cheese profiteroles to his famous 'fried egg' (mango and biscuit) dessert. Menus €39-120.

Brasserie Léopold €€€
2 av Victor Hugo, T04 42 26 01 24, hotel-saintchristophe.com.
Daily 1200-1500 & 1900-2400.
Map: Aix-en-Provence, p218.
Waiters in waistcoats bustle past red leather banquettes at this unpretentious brasserie. Although you'll find classics like steak tartare, dishes are

innovative: *magret de canard* is minced with honey and figs, artichokes are paired with sweet broad beans.

Les Deux Garçons €€-€€€
53 cours Mirabeau, T04 42 26 00 51.
Daily 1200-2300.
Map: Aix-en-Provence, p218.
An 18th-century institution, favoured by Cézanne and Zola. The menu focuses mostly on seafood, although plenty of locals pop in for a sandwich and a *pression*. Service can be patchy.

Le Passage €€-€€€
10 rue Villars, T04 42 37 09 00, le-passage.fr.
Daily 1000-2400, restaurant 1130-1430 & 1930-2330.
Map: Aix-en-Provence, p218.
Housed in an old factory, Le Passage includes a restaurant, deli, seafood specialist, wine shop and cooking school. Expect excellent value set menus (a two-course lunch plus glass of wine is €13) and jazz with your evening aperitif. Fun and young.

Tip...
If you need a break from sightseeing, drop into Les Deux Garçons for their excellent value *café gourmand* (€6): an espresso, served with four small pastries. People-watch from the cours Mirabeau terrace while indulging.

Le Zinc d'Hugo €€-€€€
22 rue Lieutaud, T04 42 27 69 69, zinc-hugo.com.
Tue-Sat 1200-1430 & 1900-2230.
Map: Aix-en-Provence, p218.
Chef Christophe Formeau trained as a *charcutier* (pork butcher) in Paris; it's no surprise Le Zinc's menu is littered with homemade terrines, pâté and sausages. The rustic ambiance lends itself well to the wood-fired meats, duck, beef, lamb and pork included.

Toute une histoire €
Place des Tanneurs, T06 63 30 13 75.
Mon-Sat 1130-1500.
Map: Aix-en-Provence, p218.
Owner and chef Vanessa Laraque launched Aix's only exclusively veggie restaurant in summer 2009. For €12, diners dig into a hot and cold buffet; add €1.50 and you can pile on dessert.

Cafés & bars
Bar Brigand
17 place Richelme, T04 42 12 46 81.
Mon-Sat 0900-0200,
Sun 1400-0200.
Offering an unbeatable 40-plus beers. During happy hour (1830-2030) pints are €3.50 each.

Simply Food
67 rue Esplariat, T04 42 59 52 85, simply-food.fr.
Mon-Sat 0900-1900.
Fresh, speedy and often organic meals to take away or eat on the small terrace. Salads include courgette, chicken and

Les Deux Garçons, Aix-en-Provence.

parmesan (€5.90) and there's always a soup of the day (€3.50).

Gordes

L'Encas €-€€
Place du Château, T04 90 72 29 82.
Daily 1200-1430 & 1900-2200, closed Nov.
Pick of the in-town eateries, with quality *plats du jour*, like beef *entrecôte* with homemade chips (€11), and giant salads (from €9). In the small dining room, head for the two tables at the back, which have great views.

Cafés & bars
La Renaissance
Place Genty Pantaly, T04 90 72 02 02.
Daily 1000-2200, closed Nov.
Best savoured mid-afternoon, with a scoop of divine organic sorbet (€5.90). Also a pricey restaurant, featured in the film *The Good Life*.

Roussillon

Restaurant David €€€€
Le Clos de la Glycine, place de la Poste, T04 90 05 60 13, luberon-hotel.com.
May-Oct daily 1200-1400 & 1930-2200, Nov-Apr Mon 1930-2200, Tue & Thu-Sat 1200-1400 & 1930-2200, Sun 1200-1400, closed mid Nov-mid Dec & mid Jan-mid Feb.
Sample Jean-Luc Laborie's seasonal creations on the panoramic terrace, against a backdrop of ochre cliffs. Of particular note are the grilled red mullet and fresh coco bean salad (€18) and the veal casserole with porcini mushrooms and pumpkin (€27). Menus €33 and €65.

Bonnieux

L'Arôme Restaurant €€-€€€
2 rue Lucien Blanc, T04 90 75 88 62, larome-restaurant.com.
Easter-Oct Fri-Wed 1200-1400 & 1900-2130, Thu 1900-2130, Nov-Easter Fri-Wed 1200-1400 & 1900-2130.
Southern French cuisine, served up in the 14th-century vaulted dining room or on the terrace. Owned by chef Jean-Michel and maître d' Clara, the restaurant also has an extensive *cave à vins* (wine cellar) and always offers a special wine by the glass (€5).

Entertainment

Cucuron

La Petite Maison de Cucuron
€€€€
*Place de l'Étang, T04 90 68 21 99,
lapetitemaisondecucuron.com.*
Wed-Sun 1200-1400 &
2000-2130.
Chef Eric Sapet reopened this
charming restaurant in 2007,
and now serves just two weekly
menus (€40 and €60). Flavours
are sophisticated – pork roast
with a walnut crust, or turbot
with capers, lemon and toasted
pine nuts.

Lourmarin

Le Comptoir €€€-€€€€
*Le Moulin de Lourmarin, rue du
Temple, T04 90 75 98 76,
moulindelourmarin.com.*
Daily 1900-2200, Sat-Sun
1200-1430.
Edouard Loubet serves two
set menus (€40 or €48), or à la
carte delights like foie gras on
chestnut bread with mesclun.
Less pricy than Loubet's double
Michelin-starred restaurant, La
Bastide de Capelongue, in
nearby Bonnieux.

La Récréation €€-€€€
*15 av Philippe de Girard,
T04 90 68 23 73.*
Thu-Tue 1200-1400 &
1930-2200.
Traditional Provençal rabbit or
lamb *confit* is served up on the
sunny, sheltered terrace. There's
also a selection of salads, three

set menus (from €25-34) and a
good wine list. All organic.

Manosque

La Table du Pré Saint Michel
€€-€€€
*Le Pré Saint Michel, route de
Dauphin, Montée de la Mort
d'Imbert, T04 92 72 12 79.*
Mon-Fri 1200-1400 &1900-2200,
Sat 1900-2200.
Tasty dishes, from goat's cheese
and tomato tiramisu to chunky
country-style pork terrine. Their
three-course set menu (€24) also
allows for a cheaper choice – two
courses plus a glass of wine (€18).
Chatty and charming staff really
make this spot shine.

Valensole

Hostellerie de la Fuste
€€€-€€€€
*Lieu-dit La Fuste, T04 92 72 05 95,
lafuste.com.*
Tue-Sat 1200-1400 & 1930-2130,
Sun 1200-1400.
Rustic Lubéron cooking from
Daniel Jourdan, owner and
resident chef since 1967.
Ingredients are local, and most
come straight from the chef's
garden: rabbit terrine with
juniper, violet artichokes with
aged goat's cheese. More
decadent patrons should go
for the exquisite summer truffle
menu (€90, May-Sep only).

Aix-en-Provence

Clubs
Mistral Club
*3 rue Frédéric Mistral, T06 67 46
84 78, mistralclub.fr.*
Tue-Sat 2400-late.
Resident DJs pack the house with
electro, techno and occasionally
80s tunes.

Theatre
Pavillon Noir
*530 av Mozart, T04 42 93 48 80,
preljocaj.org.*
Contemporary performances by
the excellent Ballet Preljocaj.

Traditional calissons.

Shopping

Art
Boutique des Musées
*5 rue des Chaudronniers, T04 42
23 46 44, boutiquesdemusees.fr.*
Tue-Sat 1000-1230 & 1430-1900.
Pick up small artwork replicas
– from a Degas dancer to
sparkling sculptures by Niki
de Saint Phalle – found in
French museums.

Books
Book In bar
*4 rue Joseph Cabassol, T04 42 26
60 07, bookinbar.com.*
Mon-Sat 0900-1900.
Combo English bookstore and
cosy coffee shop.

Clothes
Papa Pique et Maman Coud
*31 rue Bédarrides, T04 42 26 64 54,
papapiqueetmamancoud.com.*
Mon 1400-1900, Tue-Sat
1000-1900.
Southern outpost of this
playful Brittany-based brand,
selling bags, barrettes and
children's clothes.

Rosalie de Montmartre
*42 rue des Cordeliers, T04 86 31
92 99, rosaliedemontmartre.com.*
Tue-Sat 1200-1900.
Starry T-shirts, Japanese-
inspired tops and made-to-
order wedding dresses, created
by Rosalie in her atelier behind
the shop.

Food & drink
Calissons du Roy René
*13 rue Gaston de Saporta, T04 42
26 67 86, calisson.com.*
Mon 0930-1300 & 1430-1830,
Tue-Fri 0930-1300 & 1400-1830,
Sat 1000-1300 & 1400-1900, Sun
1600-1900.
Purveyors of Aix's famous
candied fruit *calisson*. Pop into
the basement to check out their
dedicated museum (free).

Souvenirs
Décalé
14 rue d'Italie, T04 42 53 32 65.
Tue-Sat 1000-1230 & 1400-1900.
Ultra-design teapots, mobiles,
beaded bags and cushion covers
printed with city skylines.

Food & drink
Distilleries et Domaines de Provence
*Av St-Promasse, T04 92 75 15 41,
distilleries-provence.com.*
Jul-Aug Mon-Sat 0900-1900,
Sun 0900-1300, Apr-Jun &
Sep-Dec Mon & Wed-Sat
1000-1230 & 1400-1900.
Sample award-winning (2008
gold medal, General Agricultural
Competition in Paris) Pastis Henri
Bardouin at the source.

See also 'Five of the best
Provençal Markets', page 229.

Tip...
Aix is home to three morning
markets: **place Richelme** (daily),
place de la Madeleine and **place
des Prêcheurs** (both Tue, Thu &
Sat). All are packed with seasonal
fruits, cured meats and towers
of locally produced cheeses –
perfect for picnics or souvenirs.

Souvenirs
La Méridienne
Place du Château, T04 90 72 06 99.
Daily 1000-1900.
Provençal bedspreads, ceramic
salt and pepper shakers, sets of
gardening tools and more.

Souvenirs
Lothantique
*7 espace St-Pierre, T04 92 68 60
30, boutique-lothantique.com.*
Tue-Sat 0900-1700.
Eco-friendly essential oils, soaps
and lotions, straight from Vogade
family producers.

Cycling, hiking & climbing through Provence

Provence is packed with outdoor activities to suit every age and energy level. Most of the region forms part of the **Parc Naturel Régional du Lubéron**, encompassing towns and countryside from Manosque to Cavaillon; park territory sweeps from the Durance River in the south to the Monts de Vaucluse in the north. The Lubéron is riddled with paths to cycle, trails to hike and mountains to climb: it's only a matter of picking your passion, gearing up and getting out there.

Over the past decade, **Vélo Loisir en Lubéron** (203 rue Oscar Roulet, Rubion, T04 90 76 48 05, veloloisirluberon.com) has signposted more than 450 km of **cycling routes** throughout the region. Four marked tours of varying intensity wind their way through the Lubéron's hills and vineyards, although note that you will often share space on the sleepy country roads with snap-happy carloads of tourists. **Autour du Lubéron** is a 236-km loop, passing through Cavaillon, Manosque and Lourmarin; **Les Ocres en Vélo** (51 km total, with shorter routes possible) explores the ochre quarries around Roussillon and Villars; **Le Pays de Forcalquier et de la Montagne de Lure** (78 km) covers rougher terrain in the northeast of the region, while southerly **Le Pays d'Aigues en Vélo** (91 km) is the newest route added to the group, scaling more challenging heights. Details of specific itineraries, as well as a handy list of spots to replenish drinking water en route, can be downloaded from the Vélo Loisir website.

Keen – some may say masochistic – cyclist can up the ante with a pedal up the infamous Mont Ventoux, a Tour de France favourite. Those seeking a tamer outdoor thrill can opt instead for a hike around its surrounding slopes. Booklets mapping local walks can be downloaded from provenceguide.com; alternatively, the Bédoin Tourist Office (Espace Marie Louis Gravier, T04 90 65 63 95, bedoin.org; mid Jun-Aug Mon-Fri 0900-1230 & 1400-1800, Sun 0930-1230 & 1400-1800, Sep-mid Jun Mon-Fri 0900-1230 & 1400-1800, Sat 0930-1230) sells a detailed map with 11 plotted treks. During July and August, they also organise guided night hikes up Mont Ventoux (ascent is 1400 m so participants must be in good shape), complete with overnight camping and (fingers crossed) a magnificent sunrise over the Alps.

Lusting for the summit? If you're yearning to clamber higher, head to the more mountainous northern Lubéron, where the region melts into the foothills of the Alps. British-run **Climb France** (Les Jonchiers, Beauvoisin, Buis-les-Baronnies, T04 75 26 53 20, climbfrance.com) runs rock-climbing courses that range from half-day outings for beginners (£85 for a group of maximum six) to week-long advanced trips (from £795 per person, including all equipment, accommodation and meals). Climbing takes place around Orpierre and the team's base in Buis-les-Baronnies.

Or opt instead to take in Provence's lavender-drenched landscapes from the air. **Montgolfière Vol-Terre** (Hameau des Goubauds, St-Saturnin d'Apt, T06 03 54 10 92, montgolfiere-luberon.com) organises dawn **balloon rides** for maximum four passengers, followed by a champagne lunch after touch down. Prices start around €175 per person. Solo fliers can **paraglide** with the **Ecole de Parapente de Rustrel** (rue du Stade, Rustrel, T04 90 04 96 53, parapente.biz, 0900-1300 & 1730-2200). Soaring above the 'Provençal Colorado', nicknamed for its similarity to the US state's crimson cliffs, *baptême* flights (for first-timers) cost €70 per person; more advanced gliding is priced from €100.

To pick up more ideas, maps and inspiration for a range of outdoor activities within this sprawling land, drop into the **Maison du Parc** in Apt (60 place Jean Jaurès, T04 90 04 42 00, parcduluberon.fr, Mon-Fri 0830-1200 & 1330-1800), where friendly staff will happily point you in the right direction.

Activities & tours

Cultural

Aix-en-Provence City Tours
Office de Tourisme, 2 place du Général de Gaulle, Aix-en-Provence, T04 42 16 11 61, aixenprovencetourism.com. Tue & Sat 1000. €8, €4 concessions, under 6s free. Two-hour English-language tours of Aix's Old Town.

Evadeoz
T04 86 91 26 43, evadeoz.com. Half-day tours of Aix (€38 per person) and the Lubéron (€65 per person), as well as personal itineraries.

In the steps of Cézanne
Office de Tourisme, 2 place du Général de Gaulle, Aix-en-Provence, T04 42 16 11 61, aixenprovencetourism.com. Apr-Oct Thu 1000. €8, €4 concessions, under 6s free. English-language tours charting Cézanne's life in Aix (approx 2 hrs).

Food & wine

Patricia Wells Cooking Classes
Chanteduc, Vaison-la-Romaine, patriciawells.com. US$5000 per person. Week-long lessons led by American-born Wells, guru of French cuisine and author of the excellent *Bistro Cooking*.

Reine Sammut Cooking School
Auberge La Fenière, route de Cadenet, Lourmarin, T04 90 68 11 79, reinesammut.com. Thu or Fri mornings, €145 per person. One of France's finest female chefs, Reine offers three-hour cooking lessons, followed by lunch.

Wellbeing

La Maison d'Ennea
Hôtel Les Bories, route de l'Abbaye de Sénanque, Gordes, T04 90 72 00 51, hotellesbories.com. Essential oil-based treatments, from anti-jetlag massage (€80) to five-day 'regenerating' packages (€695).

L'Occitane
Z.I. St-Maurice, Manosque, loccitane.com. **Mon-Fri, closed 3rd week Aug & 3rd week Dec.** Contact the Manosque Tourist Office (T04 92 72 16 00, accueil@ manosque-tourisme.com) to book a one-hour free tour of L'Occitane's factory. Learn how the natural bath products are made, then shop at the on-site boutique.

Transport

Aix-en-Provence

One to four buses per day to Lourmarin (1 hr), Bonnieux (1hr 25) and Apt (1hr 45). Trains to Manosque every two hours (45 mins).

Apt

Buses approximately every two hours to Pont Julien (10 mins), Bonnieux (15 mins), Cavaillon (1 hr) and Avignon (1hr 20).

Bonnieux

One to four buses per day to Lacoste (20 mins), Ménerbes (30 mins) and Cavaillon (1 hr).

Gordes

Two buses per day to Roussillon (20 mins, Sun no buses), one to three buses per day to Cavaillon (40 mins).

Roussillon

One to two buses per day to Gordes (20 mins, Sun buses only during school holidays), one to two buses per day to Cavaillon (1 hr).

Contents

Avignon, Arles & Western Provence

A building's mural off place
du Palais des Papes, Avignon.

Introduction

What to see in…

aybe it's the Camargue cowboys, the park's indigenous bulls and herds of horses; maybe it comes from a breakaway culture, Avignon's temporary stand as papal headquarters. Or maybe it's just far from the slicker urban influences felt in Marseille, Nice and along the Côte d'Azur. Whatever the origins, there's no denying that Western Provence has a wilder, untamed feel to it.

Arles and Avignon are the region's two largest cities: the former boasts a largely intact Roman amphitheatre, the latter the massive Palais des Papes. But both also offer plenty of other intriguing sights, less visited and often a thematic contrast to their headline attractions. Visit Avignon's Musée Louis Vouland, a prestigious former home stocked with quirky furniture and art, or the cutting-edge Collection Lambert. In Arles, the Cloître St-Trophime hosts contemporary exhibitions, while Musée Réattu is home to a permanent collection of early 20th-century photos.

The surrounding countryside offers a finely weighted balance of historical ruins, including Glanum in St-Rémy-de-Provence and the Château of Les Baux-de-Provence, and stunning wildlife, concentrated in the Parc Naturel Régional de Camargue. During the summer months, you can expect to share these highlights with a fair number of international visitors. But visit off season – or seek out smaller villages, markets and country trails – and you're likely to find yourself magically alone.

Ancient carved graffiti in Arles' Amphitheatre.

…one day
Spend the morning in **Avignon**, exploring the **Palais des Papes** and the **Pont St-Bénézet**, then drive north to sample the AOC wines from **Châteauneuf-du-Pape**'s vineyards. Or head south to **Les Baux-de-Provence**, where you can clamber around the town's magnificent 10th-century Château.

…a weekend or more
Start your weekend in **Arles**, visiting the city's **Roman amphitheatre**, before striking out for an afternoon of flamingo-spotting or horse riding in the **Parc Naturel Régional de Camargue**. Spend a leisurely Sunday morning at **l'Isle-Sur-La-Sorgue**'s massive antiques market, then make your way to **Avignon** to check out the city's historical highlights.

Avignon & around

Fleeing a troubled and turbulent Rome, Pope Clement V shifted Catholicism's power base to Avignon in 1309. While both he and his successor, Pope John XXII, were content to bed down in the town bishops' old Episcopal palace (now the Musée du Petit Palais), later leaders Pope Benedict XII and Pope Clement VI dedicated their time at the Church's helm to the construction of a palace worthy of the papacy: Avignon's huge Gothic Palais des Papes now acts as the city's main draw.

Impressive as the palace is, it's worth losing the crowds to explore this beautiful walled town further. Clamber up the Rocher des Doms, a tiered park with dazzling views over the River Rhône and the tiny town of Villeneuve-lez-Avignon's Fort St André. Or hop on the river's free shuttle boat and spend an afternoon on the verdant Ile de la Barthelasse.

Summer wedding celebrations in place du Palais des Papes, Avignon.

Palais des Papes

Place du Palais des Papes, T04 90 27 50 00,
palais-des-papes.com.
Daily Mar-Jun & mid Sep-Nov 0900-1900, Jul &
1st 2 weeks Sep 0900-2000, Aug 0900-2100,
Nov-Feb 0930-1745 (ticket desks close 1 hr
earlier). Mar-mid Nov €10.50, €8.50 concessions,
Palais & Pont €13, €10 concessions; mid Nov-Feb
€8.50, €7 concessions, Palais & Pont €11, €8.50
concessions; under 8s free, free audioguide.
Map: Avignon, p244.

The Palais des Papes, or Popes' Palace, looms
over Avignon's old town and is one of the
largest Gothic buildings in Europe.

Visits begin in the Cour d'Honneur (Courtyard
of Honour), before plunging into the Palais Vieux
(Old Palace), designed by papal architect Pierre
Poisson and built under the auspices of Pope
Benedict XII. The informative audioguide will direct
you through the Treasury, with recessed floors for
stockpiling some of the Church's worldly goods, to
the 46-m-high Pope's Tower and on through to the
restored Grand Tinel Hall, which looks out over the
palace gardens to the east. But it's only upon
entering the Pope's Chamber (as painted vines
clamber up the bright blue walls, the previous
Spartan rooms are quickly forgotten) that you
can begin to envision the pampered splendour to
which these religious leaders were accustomed.

When Benedict XII died in 1342, Pope Clement
VI and architect Jean de Louvres continued to
expand his predecessor's monstrous project.
The Chambre du Cerf (Stag's Room) marks your
passage into the Palais Neuf (New Palace). Formerly
the papal study, this room boasts floor-to-ceiling
frescos: hunting and fishing scenes preserved for
over 500 years under thick layers of paint,
attributed to Italian artist Matteo Giovannetti.

Visitors are directed on through the north and
south sacristies to the vast Great Chapel. Well worth
the steep stairs are the panoramas over Villeneuve-
lez-Avignon and the Rhône from atop the Palace;
follow the signs for Le Café-Terrasse. The tour winds
down with a wander through the Great Audience

Essentials

❶ Getting around Avignon's Old Town is small,
and best navigated on foot. A shuttle bus (tcra.fr, 10
mins, departures every 20 mins) runs between the TGV
station and Porte de la République. There's a taxi stand
at Porte de la République, or you can arrange a pick-up
on T04 90 82 20 20.

❷ Train stations Gare TGV Quartier de Courtine;
Gare SNCF, boulevard St Roch.

❸ Bus station 5 avenue Monclar, T04 90 82 07 35.

❹ Hospital Hôpital Général Henri Duffaut, 305 rue
Raoul Follereau, T04 32 75 33 33, ch-avignon.fr.

❺ Pharmacy Pharmacie Tarot, 29 rue Marchands,
T04 90 82 27 91.

❻ ATMs Plenty throughout the town, including along
cours Jean Jaurès.

❼ Post office Cours Président Kennedy, T04 90 27 54
10, Monday-Friday 0830-1830, Saturday 0830-1200.

❽ Tourist information office 41 cours Jean Jaurès,
T04 32 74 32 74, ot-avignon.fr, Easter-October Monday-
Saturday 0900-1800 (until 1900 during the Festival),
Sunday 0945-1700, November-Easter Monday-Friday
0900-1800, Saturday 0900-1700, Sunday 1000-1200.

Avignon's cathedral and Rocher des Doms beyond.

Avignon listings

① Sleeping
1 Hôtel Boquier *6 rue du Portail Boquier*
2 Hôtel d'Europe *place Crillon*
3 Hôtel de Garlande *20 rue Galante*
4 Hôtel Mignon *12 rue Joseph Vernet*
5 La Mirande *4 place de l'Amirande*

① Eating & drinking
1 La Compagnie des Comptoirs *83 rue Joesph-Vernet*
2 La Fourchette *17 bis rue Racine*
3 La Vache à Carreaux *14 rue Peyrolerie*
4 Le Verso *3 place Nicolas Saboly*
5 Le Grand Café *4 rue des Escaliers Ste-Anne*
6 Restaurant Christian Etienne *10 rue de Mons*

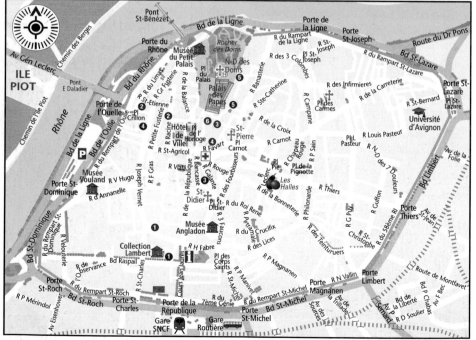

Hall, before passing through **La Bouteillerie** wine shop (tasting available from €2 a glass) and out through the Palace's well-endowed gift shop.

Pont St-Bénézet

Rue Ferruce, entrance to left of Porte du Rhône, T04 90 27 51 16, palais-des-papes.com. Daily mid Mar-mid Jun & mid Sep-Nov 0900-1900, Jul & 1st 2 weeks Sep 0900-2000, Aug 0900-2100, Nov-mid Mar 0930-1745 (ticket desks close 30 mins earlier). Mar-mid Nov €4.50, €3.50 concessions, Palais des Papes & Pont €13, €10 concessions; mid Nov-Feb €4, €3 concessions; Palais & Pont €11, €8.50 concessions; under 8s free, free audioguide. Map: Avignon, p244.

Poking halfway across the Rhône before dropping off abruptly, the Pont St-Bénézet (also called the Pont d'Avignon) is the city's public landmark, a neat contrast to the religious grandeur that is the Palais des Papes.

Not that its history is without mystique. During the 12th century, Bénézet, a shepherd from Ardèche, was ordered by God to go to Avignon and instruct the city's residents to build a bridge. After proving his divine worth by pitching an impossibly massive stone into the river, Bénézet was named a saint and the Pont St-Bénézet was constructed.

Tip...

Available at the tourist office, major sights and most hotels, the **Avignon Passion card** offers discounted visits to the city's cultural highlights. Pay full entrance to any monument or museum, making sure your pass is stamped. You and up to four other people will then be entitled to 10-50% off regular entry fees at other sights. The pass is valid for 15 days.

Above: Pont Saint-Bénezet. Opposite page: Avignon's cathedral.

Around the region

A vitally important connection between Lyon and the Mediterranean Sea, the bridge also served as an important crossing point for religious pilgrims en route to Spain. Rebuilt periodically due to frequent flooding, the bridge was eventually abandoned during the 17th century. It achieved widespread notoriety again during the 18th century, when composer Pierre Certon's 16th-century song *Sur le Pont d'Avignon* became a huge hit.

Musée du Petit Palais

Palais des Archevêques, place du Palais des Papes, T04 90 86 44 58, petit-palais.org. Wed-Mon 1000-1300 & 1400-1800. €6, €3 concessions, under 18s free, free Sun Sep-Jun. Map: Avignon, p244.

Located in the former Archbishops' Palace, the Musée du Petit Palais houses collections of medieval and Renaissance works; Sandro Botticelli's *Madonna and Child* is the highlight of pieces on permanent display. The museum also stages temporary exhibitions (separate entrance fee).

Musée Angladon

5 rue Laboureur, T04 90 82 29 03, angladon.com. Tue-Sun 1300-1800, closed Tue in winter. €6, €4 concessions, €3 students, €1.50 child (7-12), under 7s free. Map: Avignon, p244.

Owner of Parisian fashion house Doucet & Fils, Jacques Doucet assembled this small yet very personal collection of 17th- to 20th-century paintings, furniture and ceramics over the course of his lifetime. The artworks were eventually inherited by Doucet's grandnephew and his wife, Jean and Paulette Angladon-Dubrujeaud, and are now exhibited in their former home.

On the ground floor, standouts include Modigliani's *Portrait of a Woman*, Sisley's *Snow in Louveciennes*, Van Gogh's *Railroad Cars* and a bright green study for one of Degas' dancers. Upstairs, the collection ranges from French medieval to Tang sculptures. Temporary exhibitions (included in entrance fee) are often woven through the museum, such as the recent show of Robert Doisneau photos.

Musée du Petit Palais, Avignon.

Musée Louis Vouland

17 rue Victor Hugo, T04 90 86 03 79, vouland.com.
Tue-Sun Jul-Sep 1200-1800, Oct-Jun 1400-1800,
closed Feb. €6, €4 concessions, under 12s free.
Map: Avignon, p244.

Louis Vouland's home from 1927 until his death in
1973, the Hôtel de Villeneuve-Esclapon now houses
the industrial magnate's collection of primarily 18th
century decorative arts. Although not large, the
rooms themselves are cavernous; each one is
dedicated to a different region or theme, from
Vouland's luxuriant Chinese bedroom to cabinet
displays of Marseillaise porcelain. Temporary
exhibitions (included in the entrance fee) are playful
and complementary: a recent highlight dotted
antique and contemporary mirrors throughout.

Collection Lambert:
Musée d'Art Contemporain

*Hôtel de Caumont, 5 rue Violette, T04 90 16 56 20,
collectionlambert.com.*
Jul-Aug 1100-1900, Sep-Jun Tue-Sun 1100-1800.
€5.50, €4 concessions, €2 child (6-12), under 6s free.
Map: Avignon, p244.

Yvon Lambert opened this contemporary museum i
n 2000, providing Avignon with a much-needed
counterbalance to the historical and religious art on
permanent display. Each year, three exhibitions are
showcased throughout the 18th-century Hôtel de
Caumont's labyrinthine rooms. These range from
spotlighting single artists, including New York
photographer Roni Koon or Belgian video artist
Francis Alÿs, to thematic exhibitions, such as post-20th
century Japanese show, *Eijanaika, Yes Future!* The
museum also houses a very good bookshop.

Tip...

Avignon's bike-sharing scheme has put 200 sturdy
bikes on to the city streets. Buy a day (€1) or week (€3)
pass at one of the 17 stations dotted around town;
bike use is free for up to 30 minutes a pop. More info
can be found at velopop.fr.

Around Avignon

Sitting 18 and 29 km north of Avignon respectively,
Châteauneuf-du-Pape and Orange are two of the
region's most rewarding day trips. History buffs
should head to the Théâtre Antique d'Orange, one
of the best-preserved Roman theatres in existence
today; wine aficionados will revel in Châteauneuf-
du-Pape's first-class AOC vineyards. Note that
getting around the area is difficult if you don't
have your own transport.

Châteauneuf-du-Pape

Although the town's origins date to the 11th century,
the area around Châteauneuf-du-Pape rose in
importance during the 14th century, when the
region was lavished with affection from Pope
Clement V. The Avignon-based pope encouraged

Essentials

⊘ **Train station** Avenue Frédéric Mistral, Orange,
T04 90 11 88 03.

⊖ **Bus station** Parking de l'Arc de Triomphe, Orange,
T04 90 34 15 59.

⊕ **Hospital** Centre Hospitalier Louis Giorgi, avenue
de Lavoisier, Orange, T04 90 11 22 22.

⊕ **Pharmacy** Pharmacie Bertrand Cadi Couchet,
4 rue St Martin, Orange, T04 90 34 10 64.

⊖ **ATMs** Plenty in Orange, including two on rue de
la République. It's best to have cash to hand if you're
heading into the surrounding countryside.

⊃ **Post office** 679 boulevard Edouard Daladier,
Orange, T04 90 11 11 10, Monday-Friday 0830-1215 &
1330-1800, Saturday 0830-1200.

❶ **Tourist information offices** 5 cours Aristide
Briand, Orange, T04 90 34 70 88, uk.otorange.fr, July-
August Monday-Saturday 0900-1930, Sunday & holidays
1000-1300 & 1400-1900, April-June & September
Monday-Saturday 0900-1830, Sunday & holidays 1000-
1300 & 1400-1830, October-March Monday-Saturday
1000-1300 & 1400-1700; place du Portail, Châteauneuf-
du-Pape, T04 90 83 71 08, ccpro.fr, June-September
Monday-Saturday 0930-1800, October-May Monday-
Tuesday & Thursday-Saturday 0930-1230 & 1400-1800.

local wine production, and vineyards soon supplied the Papacy with year-round, top-notch *cru*. Pope John XXII took his passion a step further, overseeing the construction of Châteauneuf-du-Pape's **Château des Papes** and spending his summers there.

Today, most tourists visit the area for its sumptuous **vineyards**, which produce almost 14 million bottles of strong, Grenache noir, Syrah and Mourvèdre-based red AOC wines every year; just 6% of the AOC's annual production is white wine.

Théâtre Antique d'Orange

Rue Madeleine Roch, T04 90 51 17 60, theatre-antique.com. Jun-Aug 0900-1900, Apr-May & Sep 0900-1800, May & Oct 0930-1730, Jan-Feb & Nov-Dec 0930-1630. €7.90, €5.90 concessions, Théâtre & Château des Baux €12.30, €8.60 concessions, under 7s free, free audioguide.

Seating close to 10,000 spectators, the Théâtre Antique d'Orange was built under Emperor Augustus during the first century AD, with the theatre's tiered bench seating (*cavea*) fitted snugly into the Colline St-Eutrope hill; over the centuries, this mode of construction has helped to shelter the theatre as a whole. Its massive stage wall, 103 m x 37 m, remains uniquely intact, allowing visitors a clear picture of the theatre's towering dimensions. Near the complex entrance are the remains of a Roman temple.

During July and August, **Les Chorégies d'Orange** (choregies.asso.fr) opera festival takes place in the theatre; quirkier annual events are also staged here, including June's Beach Concert, a beach volleyball competition followed by a concert, and September's Roman Festival.

Five of the best

Places to turn up and sip in Châteauneuf-du-Pape

❶ **Château Fortia** Route de Bédarrides, T04 90 83 72 25, chateau-fortia.com

❷ **Domaine Chante Cigale** Avenue Louis Pasteur, T04 90 83 70 57, chantecigale.com

❸ **Château Mont Redon** Route d'Orange, T04 90 83 72 75, chateaumontredon.fr

❹ **Vinadea Maison des Vins** 8 rue Maréchal Foch, T04 90 83 70 69, vinadea.com. Stocking wines from 90 nearby domaines.

❺ **Musée du Vin Père Anselme** Avenue Pierre de Luxembourg, T04 90 83 70 07, brotte.com. Daily Apr-Sep 0900-1300 & 1400-1900, Oct-Mar 0900-1200 & 1400-1800. Free. Owned by the Brotte family since 1931, this wine museum represents four local domains: Le Château de Bord, Le Domaine Barville, Le Domaine Grosset and Le Domaine de l'Aube. Exhibits include a 14th-century chestnut wine barrel and a 16th-century wine press, plus on-site cellars.

Ditch the car

The Châteauneuf-du-Pape Tourist Office produces various handouts charting hikes and cycling routes around the region. Two of the best are the bilingual 'From the vineyards of Châteauneuf-du-Pape to the Ouvèze plain', a 28.5-km bike trail that takes in Sorgues and Bédarrides, and 'A la découverte de Châteauneuf-du-Pape' (French only), a 1½-hour walk around Châteauneuf-du-Pape's Old Town. For local bike hire, see page 268.

Theatre Antique d'Orange and its unique, intact stage wall.

L'Isle-sur-la-Sorgue

Gushing forth at the pretty Provençal town of Fontaine de Vaucluse, the River Sorgue spills seven kilometres downstream to L'Isle-sur-la-Sorgue, a unique catchment of islands, waterways and picturesque bridges.

Originally a fishing village, during the Middle Ages the town morphed from a single island to a network of islets, as residents built canals, draining and firming the surrounding marshlands. L'Isle-sur-la-Sorgue gradually turned to larger-scale industry and giant waterwheels were installed on the canals. By the 19th century, an incredible 72 of these wheels served to power the local textile trade.

The very lucrative production of silk and wool paid off. Today, the town is still an affluent spot. Visit on a Sunday, when L'Isle-sur-la-Sorgue's **antique and brocante market** (from 0900, all day) fills the streets. Over 300 stalls join the village's many (permanent) antique stores, drawing thousands of visitors from the surrounding countryside.

Begin your walk at the **Jardin Public** on the corner of avenue des Quatres Otages and allée 18 Juin 1940. (If you've taken the bus from Avignon, you'll hop off just over the road.) It's here you'll catch your first glimpse of one of L'Isle-sur-la-Sorgue's nine remaining **waterwheels**, slowly spinning and draped in deep green moss.

Head into the Old Town, crossing over one of the Sorgue's streams, which edges the southern half of the town, and quai Jean Jaurès. Walk through **place Rose Goudard**; on a Sunday, this square will be packed with olive oil soaps, Provençal bedspreads and stacks of salami. Continue along rue Rose Goudard, bending left toward the town's **Eglise Notre-Dame-des-Anges**. Constructed in 1222, the church was almost entirely rebuilt during the mid-17th century; its stunning Baroque interior also houses a resplendent organ.

Essentials

Tourist information office Place de la Liberté, T04 90 38 04 78, oti-delasorgue.fr, Monday-Saturday 0900-1230 & 1430-1800, July-August Sunday 0930-1300, September-June Sunday 0900-1230.

Frequent **buses** and **trains** run between L'Isle sur la-Sorgue, Avignon and Marseille. Buses stop on avenue des Quatres Otages, while the train station is just off avenue de l'Egalité; both are an easy walk from the town centre.

Next door, the central Tourist Office is located in the town's former public granary, built in 1779. Poetry-lovers can dip down rue du Docteur Tallet to the **Maison René-Char** (Hôtel Donadeï de Campredon, 20 rue du Docteur Tallet, T04 90 38 17 41, maison-renechar.fr, Tue-Sun Jul-Aug 1000-1300 & 1500-1900, Sep-Jun 1000-1230 & 1400-1730, €6.30, €5.30 students, under 14s free). The museum has a permanent exhibition dedicated to the 20th-century poet, as well as contemporaneous temporary shows.

Alternatively, cross from the church to the opposite side of place de la Liberté, follow rue Danton to rue Jean Théophile and turn left. Half canal, half ambling alley, the street's left side is dotted with three waterwheels; wealthy old homes line the surrounding streets. Walk to rue Autheman, which marks the Old Town's former ramparts, and take another left. Look out for northbound rue Carnot, crowded with boutiques, bakeries and souvenir shops, while across place Char, avenue de l'Egalité is home to four large, permanent antique centres.

Continue straight along quai Rouget de Lisle to quai Jean Jaurès. Signposted on the left, antique shops selling 1920s posters, art deco garden furniture and old tin jugs cluster around La Cour, a small enclosed courtyard off the busy quay. Allée 18 Juin 1940 will take you back to your starting point near the public gardens.

To explore the River Sorgue and its crystal clear canals further, make your way along avenue des quatre Otages to avenue Charmasson. There's a **canoe and kayaking centre** on the canal (T04 90 38 33 22, mid Apr-mid Sep), or see page 268 for other kayaking options.

Market madness

There's a special **International Antiques Market** every April, and in August, sellers take to traditional, flat-bottomed *nego-chin* boats, during the town's annual **Marché Flottant**, or Floating Market.

Les Baux
& St-Rémy

Nestled within Les Alpilles mountain range south of Avignon, the towns of Les Baux-de-Provence and St-Rémy-de-Provence are postcard perfect, each in their own distinct way.

Below: Les Baux Chateau. Opposite page: Sculpture of Rieu at the Château des Baux.

Les Baux, a fortified village built of pale, golden stone, is laced with winding, medieval streets and skirted with heart-stopping vistas. Synonymous with Les Baux are the sprawling ruins of the **Château des Baux**, perched on the highest rocky tip of the town, overlooking olive groves and vineyards all the way to the sea. Within the village, the **Yves Brayer Museum** (T04 90 54 36 99, yvesbrayer.com, Apr-Sep daily 1000-1230 & 1400-1830, Oct-Mar Wed-Mon 1000-1230 & 1400-1700, closed Jan-mid Feb, €4, under 18s free), dedicated to the 20th-century painter, and the newly renovated **Musée des Santons** (T04 90 54 34 39, free), a display of nativity scene figurines ranging from 17th century Neapolitan to 19th century papier-mâché, are great freebies.

In contrast, St-Rémy is peppered with second homes, a wealthy bolthole overflowing with affluent French city-dwellers come the weekend. Head into its alluring Old Town and it's easy to see the appeal. St-Rémy was **Nostradamus's birthplace**: the signposted home (rue Hoche) is tucked down a tiny alley amongst the town's chicer shops. **Van Gogh** also lived here for an artistically prolific year, albeit at the psychiatric hospital of the **Monastère St-Paul de Mausole** just south of town.

Essentials

❶ Getting around Both the Les Baux and St-Rémy Old Towns can only be explored on foot. During high season, buses run between the two, though you'll need your own transport or a taxi to reach Les Baux from October to May. In St-Rémy, try Taxi Leinez (T06 09 52 71 54), in Les Baux Taxi Brunet (T06 80 27 60 92) or book through the Tourist Office.

❷ Bus station Buses to Avignon, Arles and Les Baux stop at place de la République in St-Rémy, on the avenue Durand Maillane corner.

❸ Pharmacy Maussane les Alpilles, Les Baux, T04 90 54 30 40; **Cendre**, cours Mirabeau, St-Rémy, T04 90 92 08 05.

❹ ATMs Plenty in St-Rémy, including on cours Mirabeau and boulevard Victor Hugo.

❺ Post office Rue Roger Salengro, St-Rémy, T04 90 92 78 70.

❻ Tourist information offices Maison du Roy, Les Baux, T04 90 54 34 39, lesbauxdeprovence.com, Saturday-Sunday & holidays 1000-1730, May-September Monday-Friday 0900-1800, October-April Monday-Friday 0930-1700; place Jean Jaurès, St-Rémy, T04 90 92 05 22, saintremy-de-provence.com, Easter-October Monday-Saturday 0900-1230 & 1400-1900, Sunday & holidays 1000-1200, November-Easter Monday-Saturday 0900-1200 & 1400-1800.

Château des Baux

T04 90 54 55 56, chateau-baux-provence.com. Summer 0900-2030, autumn 0930-1800, winter 0930-1700, spring 0900-1830. €7.70, €5.70 concessions, Château & Cathédrale d'Images €13, €7.50 students/child (7-17), under 7s free, free audioguide.

Les Baux's unique position, seemingly balanced atop an Alpilles mountain peak, makes the town an ideal military vantage point. Château des Baux, built during the 10th century by the Lords of Les Baux, was coveted from the moment it was constructed. During the 15th century, the castle was taken over by the Masons des Comtes de Provence barons. Successive French kings later

spent 200 years battling for its control, before ownership passed to Monaco's Grimaldis in 1643. The 7-ha Château and surrounding walled village eventually fell into disrepair, until its revival as a tourist attraction during the 20th century.

And what an attraction it is. From Easter until early autumn, expect to join hundreds of visitors exploring the Château, dungeon, Saracen and Paravelle towers, as well as the giant replica catapults and medieval siege weapons. The site also includes vestiges of daily life over the centuries, including townhouses, the Chapelle St-Blaise and a squat windmill. Walk out to the precipitous edge of the Château's southern plateau to admire breathtaking panoramas (all the way to the Camargue on a clear day). Note that during cooler weather, the *mistral* gusts across this area in particular.

Cathédrale d'Images

Route de Maillane, T04 90 54 38 65, cathedrale-images.com.
Daily Apr-Sep 1000-1800, Oct-Mar 1000-1700 (ticket desks close 1 hr earlier), closed Jan-mid Feb. €7.50, €3.50 child (7-17), Cathédrale & Château des Baux €13, €7.50 child (7-17), under 7s free.

Just outside Les Baux in the Val d'Enfer (Hell Valley), the Cathédrale d'Images is located within former quarries. It was here in 1959 that Jean Cocteau filmed his *Testament d'Orphée*, with Picasso's participation. Today, the space is used for annual exhibitions: the stone walls, ceilings and columns serve as natural screens on to which images of artworks are projected. Recent shows have been dedicated to Cézanne, Van Gogh and Picasso.

St-Rémy-de-Provence

Musée Estrine

8 rue Estrine, T04 90 92 34 72, ateliermuseal.net.
May-Sep Thu-Mon 1000-1230 & 1400-1900, Wed 1000-1800, mid Mar-Apr & Oct-Nov Wed-Mon 1030-1230 & 1400-1800. €3.20, St-Rémy Pass €2.30, €1.30 students.

Located within an 18th-century mansion, the Musée Estrine houses the *Centre d'Interprétation Van Gogh*, a permanent exhibition space that includes replicas of the artist's paintings, plus photos, letters and an annual selection of

Above: Vincent Van Gogh was a temporary resident at the Monastère Saint-Paul, St-Rémy.
Opposite page: Interior courtyard at the Monastère Saint-Paul de Mausole.

The remains of a windmill at Chateau Les Baux.

Tip...

Available at the tourist office and major sights, the St-Rémy Pass offers discounts on visits to the Musée Estrine, Musée des Alpilles, Monastère St-Paul de Mausole and Site Archéologique de Glanum. Pay full price for your first site's entrance, making sure your pass is stamped. You'll then receive around 30% off additional entry fees. The pass is valid for 15 days.

projected images. Also within the museum, 20 artworks by 20th-century cubist Albert Gleizes, who resided in St-Rémy from 1939 until his death in 1952, are displayed over two rooms. There are occasional temporary shows on site as well.

Monastère St-Paul de Mausole

Chemin de St-Paul, T04 90 92 77 00, cloitresaintpaul-valetudo.com. Daily Apr-Sep 0930-1900, Oct-Mar 1015-1700, closed Jan. €4, St-Rémy Pass €3, under 12s free.

A psychiatric centre since the 15th century, this monastery continues to serve as a retreat, providing therapy for the mentally ill. Its most famous patient was Van Gogh, who lived here from 1889-1890, creating 143 paintings (including his famous '*Starry Night*') and over 100 drawings during this brief but artistically intense period.

Visitors can take in the monastery's chapel, 11th- and 12th-century cloisters, the peaceful gardens and a re-creation of Van Gogh's bedroom. There's also a permanent exhibition of artworks for sale, created by current patients.

Site Archéologique de Glanum

Route des Baux-de-Provence, T04 90 92 23 79, glanum.monuments-nationaux.fr. Apr-Sep daily 0930-1830 (closed Mon in Sep), Oct-Mar Tue-Sun 1000-1700. €7, St-Rémy Pass €5.50, €4.50 18-25s, under 18s/EU citizens under 26 free.

Just around the corner from the Monastère St-Paul lie the ruins of Glanum, first a Celto-Ligurian, then Gallo-Greek and later Gallo-Roman, city. Excavations, which began in 1921, date finds from the sixth century BC to the third century AD, when the city was abandoned. The superb site's highlights include the sacred spring area, Roman temples and baths.

Over the route des Baux (also called avenue Vincent Van Gogh), **Les Antiques** – a well-preserved triumphal arch and mausoleum – have been attracting visitors since the 16th century.

Tip...

Pick up a 'Visiting St-Rémy-de-Provence' booklet from the Tourist Office for their mapped '**Follow the Footsteps of Van Gogh**' walking route. Looping from Glanum, past the Monastère St-Paul and into town, the trail is dotted with 21 reproductions of Van Gogh artworks, each one positioned where it's believed the artist set up his easel.

Arles

Capital of the Camargue, home to an impressive amphitheatre and the short-term residence for one of the world's most famous painters, the petite Provençal city of Arles has attractions to please any visitor. Aspiring artists will appreciate a wander through place du Forum, where Café Van Gogh still looks pretty similar to its portrayal in the artist's painting, *Café de Nuit*. Amateur archaeologists can delve into ruins that range from Roman baths to Gothic cloisters. And nature-lovers (particularly bird spotters) would do well to use the riverside city as a base, making daytime forays into the Parc Naturel Régional de Camargue to its south.

Arles' Amphitheatre, prepared for the summer's weekly bull races.

Amphithéâtre

Rond-point des Arènes, T08 91 70 03 70, arenes-arles.com. Daily May-Sep 0900-1900 (Wed Jul-Aug until 1500), Mar-Apr & Oct 0900-1800, Nov-Feb 1000-1700, ticket desk closes 30 mins earlier. €6, €4.50 students, ticket also allows entrance to the Théâtre Antique.

Built towards the end of the first century AD, Arles's amphitheatre was inspired by Rome's Coliseum, constructed around a decade earlier. Like the Roman theatre, large arches (two levels, 30 per level) ring the outer wall. Audiences of 20,000, seated along 34 tiers of internal benching, poured into the amphitheatre to watch re-enactments of famous battles, gladiators and humans pitted against beasts.

By the Middle Ages, the amphitheatre had slowly morphed into an actual town, as residents built hundreds of homes, businesses and two churches within the fortified walls. However the 1820s saw the structure cleared out; in 1830, the city held its first bullfight here, celebrating the French army's occupation of Algiers.

Today, visitors can wander the galleries and *cavea*, scaling the amphitheatre for towering views over the Old Town and the River Rhône. During July and August, Camargue bull races (Wed 1700, €9, €4 child (6-12), under 6s free) and gladiator combat shows (Tue & Thu 1600-1830, free with entrance ticket) are staged in the amphitheatre.

Palais de Luppé

24bis Rond-point des Arènes, T04 90 49 94 04, fondationvangogh-arles.org. Jul-Sep daily 1000-1900, Apr-Jun daily 1000-1800, Oct-Mar Tue-Sun 1100-1700. €6, €4 child (12-18)/students/over 60/under 12s free.

Across from the Amphithéâtre, this exhibition space houses a permanent display of Van Gogh-inspired artworks. The collection includes pieces by Fernando Botero, Cyril Christo, Francis Bacon, David Hockney and Robert Rauschenberg, among many others.

Tip...

Pick up one of the following passes for discounted entry to many of the city's sights. For further information regarding any of Arles's monuments, contact T04 90 49 59 05 or T04 90 49 38 20.

The **Passeport Avantage** (€13.50, €12 students, valid one year) allows access to all of Arles's monuments and museums.

The **Passeport Arelate** (€9, €7 students, valid one month) covers free entrance to the Amphithéâtre, Théâtre Antique, the Cryptoportiques, Thermes de Constantin and the Musée Départemental Arles Antique.

The **Passeport Liberté** (€9, €7 students, valid one month) allows the holder entry to five sights (at least one museum, and no more than four monuments).

Essentials

➊ Getting around Arles's Old Town is small and easy to walk around. The free Starlette shuttle bus runs from the train station to boulevard des Lices, near the Tourist Office. Taxis can be booked through Arles Taxi Services (T04 90 52 22 22, arles-taxis-services.fr).

➋ Train station Avenue Paulin Talabot, T36 35.

➌ Bus station Avenue Paulin Talabot, T04 90 49 38 01.

➍ Hospital Centre Hospitalier d'Arles, quart Haut de Fourchon, T04 90 49 29 29.

➎ Pharmacy Pharmacie St Julien, 25 rue Quatre Septembre, T04 90 96 00 04.

➏ ATMs Throughout the city, including ones around place de la République.

➐ Post office 5 boulevard des Lices, T04 90 18 41 15.

➑ Tourist information offices Boulevard des Lices, T04 90 18 41 20, arlestourisme.com, April-September daily 0900-1845, October-March Monday-Saturday 0900-1645.

Théâtre Antique

Rue de la Calade, T04 90 49 59 05 or T04 90 49 38 20.
Daily May-Sep 0900-1900, Mar-Apr & Oct
0900-1200 & 1400-1800, Nov-Feb 1000-1200 &
1400-1700, ticket desk closes 30 mins earlier. €6,
€4.50 students, ticket also allows entrance to the
Amphithéâtre.

Just south of the city's Amphithéâtre, the ruins of
Arles's first-century BC Théâtre Antique are tucked
into a residential Old Town neighbourhood. It was
here, in 1651, that the stunning two-metre *Venus*
sculpture (also dating from the first century BC, and
now in the Louvre) was discovered while labourers
were digging a well.

Seating 10,000 spectators in its heyday,
the theatre now hosts various performances
throughout the summer, including **Les Suds**
(suds-arles.com) and the **Fête du Costume**
(festivarles.com, both Jul).

Above: Sculpture detail on a column in the Cloître Saint-Trophime, Arles.
Opposite page: The flowering courtyard of Espace Van Gogh, Arles.

Cloître St-Trophime

*Place de la République, T04 90 49 59 05 or
T04 90 49 38 20.*
Daily May-Sep 0900-1900, Mar-Apr & Oct
0900-1800, Nov-Feb 1000-1700, ticket desk
closes 30 mins earlier. €3.50, €2.60 students.

The St-Trophime cloisters were constructed in
two distinct periods between the 12th and 14th
centuries, resulting in a mix of Romanesque and
Gothic architecture. Carved columns surround a
central courtyard; the complex also includes a
refectory, dormitory and the bishop's palace.
Rooms surrounding the cloisters are often used to
host contemporary art and photo exhibitions. Next
door, the façade of **Cathédrale St-Trophime** sports
an intricate, disturbing carved depiction of St
John's Last Judgment.

Espace Van Gogh

*Place Docteur Félix Rey, T04 90 49 39 39,
mediatheque.ville-arles.fr.*
Free access to the courtyard.

Formerly Hôtel-Dieu, the hospital where Van
Gogh was admitted after taking a razor to his ear,
Espace Van Gogh is a now a cheery cultural centre.
A *médiathèque*, temporary exhibition halls and
a gift shop surround the bright plant-filled
courtyard. The central gardens have been
recreated to emulate the flowerbeds as they
appeared during Van Gogh's stay.

Thermes de Constantin

*Rue Dominique Maisto, T04 90 49 59 05 or
T04 90 49 38 20.*
Daily May-Sep 0900-1200 & 1400-1900, Mar-Apr
& Oct 0900-1200 & 1400-1800, Nov-Feb
1000-1200 & 1400-1700, ticket desk closes 30
mins earlier. €3, €2.20 students.

Just a fraction of their sprawling fourth-century
size, Arles's Roman baths were constructed under
Emperor Constantine I. The public baths still
contain portions of the original frigidarium,

tepidarium and caldarium, the latter heated by roaring fires, funnelling hot air through brick piping in the walls. There's a unique rounded vault built of layers of limestone interspersed with brick, as well as the remains of a heated pool and a gymnasium.

Musée Réattu

10 rue du Grand Prieuré, T04 90 49 37 58, museereattu.arles.fr. Tue-Sun Mar-Sep 1000-1900, Oct-Mar 1000-1230 & 1400-1830, due to be closed for renovations until Jun 2010. €7, €5 students, under 18s free, free 1st Sun of month.

Partially renovated in 2009 and set for additional work at the time of writing, this small but densely packed museum is a delightful contrast to the city's largely ancient monuments. Modern and contemporary artworks are hung throughout the 15th-century building, formerly the Grand Priory of the Knights of Malta. Picasso is well represented, as are early 20th-century photographers, including Edward Weston.

South of Arles's Old Town

As well as the city's downtown historical highlights, it's worth venturing south of boulevard des Lices to explore a few other exceptional sites. **Les Alyscamps** (av des Alyscamps, daily May-Sep 0900-1200 & 1400-1900, Mar-Apr & Oct 0900-1200 & 1400-1800, Nov-Feb 1000-1200 & 1400-1700, €3.50, €2.60 students) is a Roman necropolis;

Day tripping

Pack a picnic lunch and head north to the **Abbaye de St-Roman** (Beaucaire, T04 66 59 19 72, abbaye-saint-roman.com, Jul-Aug daily 1000-1300 & 1400-1900, Apr-Jun & Sep Tue-Sun 1000-1300 & 1400-1800, Mar Tue-Sun 1400-1700, Nov-Feb Sun & hols 1400-1700, €5.50, under 18s free). Located between Arles and Avignon and overlooking the Rhône, the unique cavernous abbey was dug out by monks beginning in the fifth century.

Five of the best

Foodie souvenirs from Arles & the Camargue

You can pick up any of these treats at Arles's weekly Provençal market (bd Emile Comes, Sat 0730-1230), at shops in the Old Town or in Saintes-Maries-de-la-Mer.

❶ **Wild rice** grown in Camargue paddies.

❷ *Saucisson de taureau* (bull salami).

❸ **Absinthe** Van Gogh's tipple of choice.

❹ *Fleur de sel* harvested from the Camargue salt marshes.

❺ **Local olive oil** (see Fad'Oli & Fad'Ola page 267).

both Van Gogh and Paul Gauguin painted the burial ground here in 1888.

On the banks of the Rhône, the **Musée d'Arles Antique** (Museum of Ancient Arles, presqu'île du Cirque Romain, T04 90 18 88 88, arles-antique.cg13.fr, Wed-Mon 1000-1800, €7, €5.50 students, under 18s free) comprehensively covers Arles's history from prehistoric times through to the sixth century AD. The remains of a **Roman racetrack** are partially unearthed outside.

A pleasant half-hour's stroll south along the Canal d'Arles will bring you to **Pont de Langlois**, better known as Van Gogh's bridge. While not quite identical to the artist's *Le Pont de Langlois* (the bridge was originally positioned a few kilometres downstream), the current setting mirrors the 1888 painting.

The Camargue

Just north of Arles, the River Rhône splits into two branches – the Grand and Petit Rhônes – before tumbling on into the Mediterranean. The Camargue sweeps southwards: a triangular 930 sq km area of marshland contained between the river's two arms.

One of France's 44 national parks, the Parc Naturel Régional de Camargue is also Western Europe's largest river delta. It's home to vast *étangs* (shallow saline lakes), fresh water reed beds and salt marshes, as well as hundreds of bird species (including flamingos), indigenous bulls and whitish-grey Camargue horses. Dense with wildlife, the area is sparsely populated: Stes-Maries-de-la-Mer, counting less than 2500 permanent residents, is its largest town.

Below: Indigenous Camargue horses. Opposite page: A corrida-inspired mural, Stes-Maries-de-la-Mer.

Stes-Maries-de-la-Mer

Named for Ste Marie-Jacobé and Ste Marie-Salomé, who arrived here by boat along with Ste Sara during the first century AD, the tiny town of Stes-Maries-de-la-Mer swells to nearly twenty times its population during the summer months. Nature-lovers base themselves here, striking out on foot, bike and horseback to explore the Camargue's inland lagoons and protected shores.

In town, the prominent Eglise Forteresse pokes above the skyline. Constructed between the ninth and 12th centuries, it houses Ste Sara's statue and relic, surrounded by candles and ex-votos, in its subterranean crypt. Atop the church tower, there's a **terrace** (daily 1000-1200 & 1400-sunset, €2, €1.50 child (6-12), under 6s free) with panoramic views over the Camargue countryside.

Parc Ornithologique de Pont de Gau

RD 570, T04 90 97 82 62, parcornithologique.com. Daily Apr-Sep 0900-sunset, Oct-Mar 1000-sunset. €7, €4 child (4-10), under 4s free.

Set up in 1949 by naturalist André Lamouroux, 16 points of interest mark the 7-km loop around this

Essentials

❶ Getting around Buses run between Arles and Stes-Maries; walking is the best way to get around the latter. Stes-Maries' Allo Taxi can be reached on T04 90 97 94 49.

❸ ATMs Place Mireille, next to Tourist Office, and along avenue d'Arles, both Stes-Maries.

❓ Post office Avenue Gambetta, Stes-Maries, T04 90 97 96 00.

❹ Pharmacy 16 rue Victor Hugo, Stes-Maries, T04 90 97 83 02.

❶ Tourist information office 5 avenue Van Gogh, Stes-Maries, T04 90 97 82 55, saintesmaries.com, daily July-August 0900-2000, April-June & September 0900-1900, March & October 0900-1800, November-February 0900-1700.

Tip...

The terrain around Stes-Maries is flat, and well suited to exploration by bike. Rent your wheels at **Le Vélo Saintois** (19 av de la République, T04 90 97 74 56, levelosaintois.camargue.fr, from €15/day). They also hand out free flyers detailing five cycling circuits around the region.

Around the region

bird sanctuary; reed-flanked *étangs* and the two observation towers make good vantage points for spying flocks of pink flamingos, plus herons and egrets.

Musée de la Camargue

Mas du Pont de Rousty, T04 90 97 10 82, parc-camargue.fr.
Apr-Sep daily 0900-1800, Oct-Mar Wed-Mon 1000-1700. €4.50, €3 students/over 65, under 18s free.

On the site of a former sheep farm, the Camargue Museum charts the history of the region, with particular emphasis on local life and communities over the last two centuries. There's also a 3.5-km Discovery Trail traversing the Mas, taking in fields, crops, marshes and plenty of wildlife.

Salin de Giraud Saltworks

Place Péchiney, T04 42 86 70 20, salins.com.
Ecomuseum: Jul & Aug daily 0930-1230 & 1400-1900, Mar-Jun & Sep-Oct 1015-1215 & 1400-1800, Nov-Feb by appointment only. Free. Tours: Jul-Aug daily 1100, 1430, 1600 & 1730, Apr-Jun & Sep-Oct daily 1430 & 1530, Mar Sat & Sun 1430 & 1530, Nov-Feb by appointment only. €8.20, €6 child (4-13), under 4s free.

Learn about historical and contemporary salt production methods (it's more fun that it sounds), from the producer of popular French salts La Baleine and Le Saunier de Camargue. Or opt for a one-hour guided tour of the otherworldly salt marshes, dotted with clouds of pink flamingos.

Le Pèlerinage des Gitans

On 24-25 May, Romany gypsies flood into Stes-Maries-de-la-Mer for their patron saint Sara's (also called 'Sara the black') annual feast day. Festivities begin as the statue of Sara is paraded from the church to the sea. The lively procession is repeated on day two with statues of Marie-Jacobé and Marie-Salomé, finishing with a blessing, plus much singing, dancing and celebrations.

Pink flamingos in the Camargue.

Sleeping

Avignon

La Mirande €€€€
4 place de l'Amirande, T04 90 14 20 20, la-mirande.fr.
Map: Avignon, p244.
Stumble from the Palais des Papes over the road and into a palace of your own. Rooms are decked out with an eye for period detail: all sumptuous 18th-century, Provençal-inspired textiles and antiques. Foodies can book into one of Le Marmiton's (see page 269) on-site cooking lessons; a more sedate option is afternoon tea in the hotel garden.

Hôtel d'Europe €€€
12 place Crillon, T04 90 14 76 76, heurope.com.
Map: Avignon, p244.
With a roster of guests that reads like attendees of a wacky dinner party – Salvador Dali, Tennessee Williams, Charles Dickens and Napoleon, to name a few – it's surprising to find the Hôtel d'Europe so utterly unpretentious. Housed in a 16th-century mansion, 41 rooms and three spacious suites (the latter each with private balcony) cluster around a wisteria-draped courtyard.

Hôtel de Garlande €€-€€€
20 rue Galante, T04 90 80 08 85, hoteldegarlande.com.
Map: Avignon, p244.
Eleven simple rooms in a renovated city centre townhouse, under friendly new management since early 2009. With an unbeatable location just off place de l'Horloge, the Garlande is steps from a slew of lively bars and restaurants: light sleepers beware. A/C and free Wi-Fi; no lift.

Hôtel Mignon €€
12 rue Joseph-Vernet, T04 90 82 17 30, hotel-mignon.com.
Map: Avignon, p244.
Wedged in among rue Joseph-Vernet's back-to-back boutiques, Hôtel Mignon's 16 petite bedrooms couldn't be further from the neighbourhood's edgy trends. Simple bright walls complement Provençal-printed fabrics, as do exposed beams in some of the rooms. Unusually for these parts, breakfast is included, and there's a computer (free internet access for guests) in the foyer.

Hôtel Boquier €-€€
6 rue du Portail Boquier, T04 90 82 34 43, hotel-boquier.com.
Map: Avignon, p244.
This welcoming spot may be the city's best budget find: 12 airy rooms located just inside the Porte de la République. Friendly owners Sylvie and Pascal have renovated the 18th-century building, and many of the bedrooms now sport unfussy themed furnishings (e.g. Moroccan, Indian or Lavender). Book well in advance.

Châteauneuf-du-Pape

Hostellerie du Château des Fines Roches €€€-€€€€
Route de Sorgues, T04 90 83 70 23, chateaufinesroches.com.
Closed Sun-Mon Nov-Apr.
A 19th-century castle set among rambling vineyards and Tuscan cypress. Previously owned by the Marquis Falco de Baroncelli-Javon, the castle's 11 elegant rooms (rolltop bathtubs, canopied beds) have views over the Château des Papes and Mont Ventoux. There's also an outdoor pool and restaurant with panoramic terrace.

The Wine B&B €€
Bastide Chante Alouette, 20 av Général de Gaulle, T04 90 83 79 38, chateauneuf-wine-bb.com.
Oct-Apr open by advance reservation only.
Owned by expert sommelier Danièle Raulet-Reynaud, this cute B&B is located in the heart of Châteauneuf village. Three charming rooms, plus a 'cosy corner' common room, stocked with books on local wines, and a central garden, where breakfast is served during the summer.

L'Isle-sur-la-Sorgue

La Maison sur la Sorgue €€€€
6 rue Rose Goudard, T06 87 32 58 68, lamaisonsurlasorgue.com.
Four unique rooms as pampering as they are personal. La Maison is owned by Marie-Claude, a L'Isle native

brimming with undiscovered local tips, and the gregarious Frédéric, who mans their objets d'art-cum-furnishings shop, Retour de Voyage, next door. An ideal base, far from the region's tourist crowds; breakfast (included) is locally sourced.

Les Baux-de-Provence

Hostellerie de la Reine Jeanne €€
Rue Porte Mage, T04 90 54 32 06, la-reinejeanne.com.
Nine bargain doubles and one apartment for four (€100), in business since 1905 and just inside Les Baux's walled village. The terrace overlooks the valley below; the excellent on-site restaurant offers half-board options.

St-Rémy-de-Provence

Hôtel les Ateliers de l'Image €€€
36 bd Victor Hugo, T04 90 92 51 50, hotelphoto.com.
Closed Jan-Feb.
A verdant oasis on the edge of St-Rémy's old town, with 29 rooms and nine suites (including the charming Tree House Suite) spread over two wings – the Espace Atelier, previously a cinema and music hall, and the Espace Provence, the former Hôtel de Provence. There is a swimming pool and two restaurants on site, Origami Sushi and Restaurant Le Provence.

La Maison du Village €€€
10 rue du 8 Mai 1945, T04 32 60 68 20, lamaisonduvillage.com.
In an 18th-century townhouse, subtle Provençal hues deck the walls and decor of five sumptuous boudoirs. Downstairs, common areas are comprised of two drawing rooms and a dining room, a Diptyque sales corner (Parisian perfumes, bath products and candles) in the reception area and a walled garden with antique fountain out back. Ideal for a romantic weekend *à deux.*

Le Sommeil des Fées €-€€
4 rue du 8 Mai 1945, T04 90 92 17 66, Oct-Apr T06 98 01 98 98, angesetfees-stremy.com.
Five simple, friendly B&B rooms in the heart of St-Rémy; the abundant breakfast includes homemade bread, croissants and plenty of local fruit jams. On the ground floor, courtyard restaurant La Cuisine des Anges serves up simple Provençal fare.

Arles

Grand Hôtel Nord Pinus €€€-€€€€
Place du Forum, T04 90 93 44 44, nord-pinus.com.
The city's top historical hotel – both a favourite with visiting bullfighters (the designated room remains), as well as artists and authors, Picasso and Hemingway included. Decor in the bar and lounge evokes the hotel's 1950s

heyday. Well-positioned for visiting the city's central sights.

Le Calendal €€-€€€
5 rue Porte de Laure, T04 90 96 11 89, lecalendal.com.
A friendly hotel, complete with contemporary 'Roman' spa, located steps from Arles's amphitheatre. The on-site restaurant serves lunch in the leafy garden during summer, and Oli Pan, an organic gourmet deli, is just downstairs. Parking €8/day.

Hôtel du Forum €€-€€€
10 place du Forum, T04 90 93 48 95, hotelduforum.com.
Closed Nov-Mar.
Across from the buzzing square with Van Gogh's famed café, Hôtel du Forum boasts an outdoor pool (an essential delight during Arles's sweltering summers), stylish bar with billiard table and free Wi-Fi. Rooms are a little dated, but pleasantly quirky.

Stes-Maries-de-la-Mer

Le Pont des Bannes €€€
Route d'Arles, T04 90 97 80 81 09, pontdesbannes.com.
Between Stes-Maries-de-la-Mer and the Parc Ornithologique de Pont de Gau, these romantic country-style cottages are dotted over islands in the Etang des Massoucles. There's a tasty restaurant on site, as well as an outdoor pool. Breakfast included; discounts possible between October and March.

Eating & drinking

Avignon

**Restaurant Christian Etienne
€€€-€€€€**
*10 rue de Mons, T04 90 86 16 50,
christian-etienne.fr.*
Tue-Sat 1230-1400 & 1930-2200,
closed 2 weeks Nov.
Map: Avignon, p244.
With a terrace overlooking the
Palais des Papes, this Michelin-
starred restaurant is easily the
chicest spot in town. Go for
Etienne's summertime special,
the €65 Menu Tomate, featuring
heirloom tomato sorbet;
gourmets on a budget can opt
for the three-course €31 lunch
menu instead.

La Fourchette €€-€€€
17 bis rue Racine, T04 90 85 20 93.
Mon-Fri 1200-1400 & 1930-2130.
Map: Avignon, p244.
Informal, cosy and stylish,
La Fourchette's walls are
adorned with quirky cutlery.
In the evening, the three-
course menu (€30.50) may
include saffron salmon with leek
fondue, or *daube Avignonnaise*.
During summer months, the
bay windows are removed,
making both dining rooms
open and airy.

La Vache à Carreaux €€-€€€
*14 rue de la Peyrolerie,
T04 90 80 09 05.*
Daily 1930-2330.
Map: Avignon, p244.
A cheese-lover's paradise,
dishing up everything from

salmon with goat's cheese to
hot Camembert steeped in
garlic. Dip into their cellar for
local wines to match. Exposed
stone walls, low lighting and
excellent jazz make for a fun
and romantic ambience.

**La Compagnie des Comptoirs
€-€€€**
*83 rue Joseph Vernet, T04 90 85
99 04, lacompagnie
descomptoirs.com.*
Tue-Sat 1200-1430 & 1930-2300.
Map: Avignon, p244.
Located within a 14th-century
convent, and one of three
ultra-contemporary restaurants
set up by twin brothers, chefs
Jacques and Laurent Pourcel.
The €9 lunch *formules*, such as
gazpacho with cucumber sorbet,
are seasonal; clubby music and
designer-clad locals pick up the
pace early evening.

Le Verso €-€€
*3 place Nicolas Saboly,
T04 90 85 28 89.*
Daily 1200-1400, 1930-2230.
Map: Avignon, p244.
The place to go for Avignon's
finest, real Italian pizzas: thin,
crispy and generously laden with
toppings; wines by the *pichet*.

**Cafés & bars
Le Grand Café**
*4 rue des Escaliers Ste-Anne,
T04 90 86 86 77, legrandcafe-
avignon.com.*
Tue-Sat 1200-1430 & 1900-2300.
Map: Avignon, p244.

Artsy café and bar in a pretty
courtyard, next door to **Cinéma
Utopia** (see page 268).

Châteauneuf-du-Pape

La Mère Germaine €€-€€€€
*3 rue du Commandant Lemaitre,
T04 90 83 54 37,
lameregermaine.com.*
Daily 1200-1400 & 1930-2100.
A tasty, traditional restaurant and
wine bar, in business since
Germaine Vion flung open her
doors in 1922. Set menus start at
€19.50; opt for the seven-course
'pontifical' menu (€105, including
wine) and dine like a pope
instead. Specialities include pork
cheeks roasted in red wine.

Orange

Le Parvis €-€€€
*55 cours Pourtoules,
T04 90 34 82 00.*
Tue-Sat 1230-1400 & 1930-2130.
Chef Jean-Michel Bérengier
serves up outstanding value
plats du jour (€8 each) on a
terrace just around the corner
from the Théâtre Antique. His
pricier Menu Gourmand (€33.50)
may include aubergine
marmalade paired with tomato
coulis, or red mullet and shitake
mushrooms in a sesame crust.

L'Isle-sur-la-Sorgue

La Prévôté €€-€€€€
*4 rue Jean-Jacques Rousseau,
T04 90 38 57 29, la-prevote.fr.*

Thu-Mon 1230-1400, 1930-2130, closed Wed Sep-Jun.
In a former church sacristy, Jean-Marie Alloin's three-course lunch menu (€26, except Sun) gives you free rein over the seasonal menu: opt for courgette flowers with summer truffles, or the fig and rhubarb tart.

L'Islot Vert €-€€
52/54 rue Carnot, T04 90 24 86 62, islotvert.com.
Tue-Fri 1200-1415, Fri-Sat 1930-2130.
New all-organic spot in downtown L'Isle: go for chef Eric's cold melon soup (€5), south-east Asian curried chicken wings (€13) or a glass of freshly squeezed fruit juice. At lunchtime, a main course plus dessert weighs in at a bargain €13.50.

Café des Baux €€
Rue Trencat, T04 90 54 52 69.
Apr-Oct 1200-1430 & 1900-2200.
Perched at the top of the village, Café des Baux boasts a sunny, sheltered courtyard, much appreciated after exploring the exposed Château. Big seasonal salads are named after artists (the Picasso, or the Matisse), while divine desserts – try the caramel *pavé* with chocolate biscuits – are created by specialist chef Pierre Walter.

L'Aile ou la Cuisse €€-€€€
5 rue de la Commune, T04 32 62 00 25.
Tue-Sat boutique traiteur 1000-1900, restaurant Tue-Sat 1200-1430, 1930-2200.
Combination upscale deli and country cooking. At lunchtime, pick up a quick picnic; or book an evening table on the patio and order their signature dish *l'aile et la cuisse de coquelet* (cockerel wing and thigh), served with creamy morel mushrooms (€26).

Mistral Gourmand €€-€€€
12 av Durand Maillane, T04 90 92 14 65.
Jun-Aug Mon-Sat 1200-1430 & 1930-2200, Sep-May Tue-Sat 1200-1430 & 1930-2200.
Catering for locals rather than tourists in transit, this easy-to-miss restaurant dishes up exceptional Provençal cuisine. Try chanterelle mushrooms with *lardons* and egg, or the shrimp 'bouquet' served with homemade *aioli*. The top wine list has also been selected with care.

L'Atelier de Jean-Luc Rabanel €€€€
7 rue des Carmes, T04 90 91 07 69, rabanel.com.
Wed-Sun 1230-1400 & 1900-2300.
Exquisite double Michelin-starred cuisine, mostly centred around seasonal vegetables; no ordering à la carte allowed. The two daily set menus – seven (€45, €85 with wine) or 13 (€75, €150 with wine) small courses each – are pricey, but so totally unique they're worth it.

Le Galoubet €€-€€€
18 rue du Docteur Fanton, T04 90 93 18 11.
Daily 1200-1500 & 1900-2300.
Long a local favourite, this spot's new chef (Aug 2009) has freshened up the Mediterranean menu. Try grilled aubergine with Parmesan shavings, or *côte de bœuf* with chanterelle mushroom sauce. Two-course lunches are €18, and there's a shady summer terrace for dining out front.

Fad'Oli & Fad'Ola €€
44 bis/46 rue des Arènes, T04 90 49 70 73, fadoli.com.
Mon-Sat 1200-1430 & 1900-2200, closed Nov.
This Franco-Japanese eatery serves up unusual salads and light meals. Try Le Soleil Levant (€7), a mixture of wakame, radish and cucumber topped by the owner's grandmother's secret Zen sauce. Inside, there's a good range of local olive oils available to sample and purchase.

Cafés & bars
Comptoir du Sud
2 rue Jean Jaurès, T04 90 96 22 17.
Tue-Fri 1000-1800.
Gourmet sandwiches to eat at the high tables or take away. Try

the *sandwich du berger* (€3.50), goat's cheese and fig chutney squeezed between two slices of pistachio bread.

Stes-Maries-de-la-Mer

Le Bruleur de Loups €€-€€€
67 av Gilbert Leroy, T04 90 97 83 31, lebruleurdeloups.monsite. wanadoo.fr.
Tue 1200-1430, Thu-Mon 1200-1430 & 1930-2230, closed mid Nov-Christmas.
Traditional Camargue cuisine – including a plethora of dishes based around local bull (pavé, côte, filet, terrine and carpaccio) – served up with sea views. The lunch menu is a bargain (€19); evening set menus €25-40.

Entertainment

Cinema
Cinéma Utopia
4 rue des Escaliers Ste-Anne, Avignon, T04 90 82 65 36, cinemas-utopia.org/avignon.
Original language films, shown daily. Additional screening room at 5 rue Figuière.

Clubs
Le Privé
Lieu-dit Les Cavernes, Route de Tavel, Les Angles, Avignon, T06 17 76 42 14, leprive.tv.
Fri-Sat 2400-0600.
Historic mostly techno club in a former quarry, just outside the city.

Shopping

Books
Shakespeare
155 rue de la Carreterie, Avignon, T04 90 27 38 50.
Tue-Sat 0930-1200 & 1400-1800.
English-language books and DVDs, plus tearoom serving English cream tea with homemade scones.

Food & drink
Joël Durand
3 bd Victor Hugo, St-Rémy-de-Provence, T04 90 92 38 25, chocolat-durand.com.
Mon-Sat 0930-1230 & 1430-1930 (Mon until 1900), Sun & hols 1000-1300 & 1430-1900.
Heavenly chocolates, caramels and candied fruits from one of France's premier *chocolatiers*.

Moulin à Huile du Calanquet
Vieux chemin d'Arles, St-Rémy-de-Provence, moulinducalanquet.fr.
Mon-Sat 0900-1200 & 1400-1830, Sun 1000-1200 & 1500-1800.
Traditional olive oil mill, plus boutique selling Alpilles olive oil, olives, tapenade, jams and chutneys.

For Châteauneuf-du-Pape and other AOC wines, see Five of the best, page 248.

Activities & tours

Canoeing & kayaking
Kayak Vert
Fontaine de Vaucluse, T04 90 20 35 44, canoefrance.com.
Daily mid Apr-mid Oct, €34 canoe (max two adults & one child under 8), €17 kayak (one adult), students €14, prices include return to Fontaine de Vaucluse by bus. Canoe or kayak from Fontaine de Vaucluse 8 km down the River Sorgue to L'Isle-sur-la-Sorgue.

Bicycle hire
Giuliani Location Vélo
40 chemin St-Etienne, Bédarrides, T04 90 33 10 30, location-velo-vaucluse.com.
From €14/day; free delivery to your hotel. Cycle through the vineyards that surround Châteauneuf-du-Pape.

Cultural
Avignon Discovery
Office de Tourisme, 41 cours Jean Jaurès, Avignon, T04 32 74 32 74, ot-avignon.fr.
Historical walking tours of Avignon's city centre. 'When the Popes lived in Avignon': Monday, Tuesday & Thursday 1000 departing from the Tourist Office, Sunday 1000 departing from the Palais des Papes ticket office, €17, under 8s free; 'Avignon – A Fabulous Destiny': Wednesday, Friday & Saturday 1000, €11, €8 child (8-18), under 8s free.

Driving

Classic Bike Esprit

14 av Albin Gilles, St-Rémy-de-Provence, jurassicesprit.com.
Classic motorcycles and sidecars to rent, from €125/day.

Food & wine

Laboratoire d'œnologie Mouriesse

2 rue des Papes, Châteauneuf-du-Pape, T04 90 83 56 15, oenologie-mouriesse.com.
Wine-tasting school. Courses range from introductory (2 hrs, €40 per person) to professional (price varies).

La Mirande & Le Marmiton Cooking School

4 place de la Mirande, Avignon, T04 90 14 20 20, la-mirande.fr.
Twice a week chef Jean-Claude Altmayer puts together a historically accurate meal in the hotel's 19th-century kitchen (Tue-Wed 2000, max 14 guests, €85.60 per person including wine). Bilingual cooking classes also on site; instructors include Christian Etienne (see page 266) and Bruno d'Angelis, chef at the Hôtel d'Europe. Closed July and August, from €70.

Provence Panorama

37 av Pierre Sémard, Avignon, T04 90 29 76 05, provence-panorama.com.
Half-day vineyard tours to Châteauneuf-du-Pape and around. From €55 per person, including hotel pick-up.

Horse riding

Tamaris

Route d'Arles, Stes-Maries-de-la-Mer, T04 90 49 67 78, ballades-tamaris.camargue.fr.
Riding for all levels, through the Camargue and on the beach. From €15/hr.

Transport

The website vaucluse.fr gives timetables and prices for buses around Avignon and the Vaucluse.

Arles

Frequent trains to Avignon (20-25 mins) and Marseille (55 mins). Five to six buses daily to Stes-Maries-de-la-Mer (1 hr). Four buses daily (Jul-Aug only), Saturday-Sunday & hols only June & September to Les Baux and St-Rémy (35 mins & 50 mins; no buses Oct-May).

Avignon

Frequent trains to Arles (20-25 mins) and on to Marseille (1hr 10). One to three buses daily to Châteauneuf-du-Pape (45 mins-1 hr; no buses Sun). Four to eight buses daily to St-Rémy (45 mins).

Les Baux-de-Provence

Four buses daily (Jul-Aug only), Saturday-Sunday & hols only June & September to St-Rémy (15 mins; no buses Oct-May).

Châteauneuf-du-Pape

One to two buses daily to Avignon (45 mins-1 hr; no buses Sun).

L'Isle-sur-la-Sorgue

Seven to 12 daily trains to Avignon (25 mins); 5-8 daily trains to Marseille (1hr 20).

Orange

From Avignon, Orange is 12 minutes by train or 45 minutes by bus.

Stes-Maries-de-la-Mer

Five to six buses daily to Arles (1 hr).

St-Rémy-de-Provence

Four to eight buses daily to Avignon (45 mins). Four buses daily (Jul-Aug only), Saturday-Sunday & hols only June & September to Les Baux and Arles (15 mins & 50 mins; no buses Oct-May).

Contents

Practicalities

Getting there

Air

There are three airports serving Provence: **Nice Côte d'Azur** (nice.aeroport.fr, T08 20 42 33 33), France's second largest airport; **Marseille Provence Airport** (mrsairport.com, T04 42 14 14 14), midway between Marseille and Aix; and little **Toulon-Hyères** (toulon-hyeres.aeroport.fr, T08 25 01 83 87). Details of getting to and from each airport are listed in the transport section at the end of each chapter.

From UK and Ireland
Nice Côte d'Azur receives over 50 flights a day from nearly 20 airports in the UK and Ireland in summer, and around half that number in winter. **EasyJet** (easyjet.com) has services from Belfast, Bristol, Edinburgh, Liverpool, London Gatwick, London Luton, London Stansted and Newcastle. **BMIbaby** (bmibaby.com) has flights from Birmingham, East Midlands and London Stansted. **Jet2** (jet2.com) serves Nice from Manchester and Leeds Bradford. **British Airways** (ba.com) has services from London Heathrow and London City. **FlyBe** (flybe.com) has flights from Southampton and Exeter. From Ireland, **Aer Lingus** (aerlingus.com) has routes from Dublin and Cork, while **Ryanair** (ryanair.com) flies in from Dublin. **Marseille Provence Airport**'s hanger-type budget airline terminal, MP2, is linked to Dublin and Edinburgh on **Ryanair**. **EasyJet** flies in from London Gatwick and Bristol. **BA** flies to Marseille's main terminal from London Gatwick. **Toulon-Hyères** receives flights from London Stansted and Bristol on **Ryanair**.

From North America
Delta (delta.com) flies daily from Nice direct to New York.

From rest of Europe
There are direct flights from Nice and Marseille to almost every country in Europe and north Africa.

Rail

Rail travel from London St Pancras to any major city in Provence on the high speed **TGV** (see page 274) is a delight. The journey runs under the channel to Paris or Lille on **Eurostar** (eurostar.com, T08705 186 186), then rushes on to Aix-en-Provence, Avignon, Marseille or Nice at speeds of up to 300 km/hr. A summer service also runs directly from London to Avignon (journey time six hours). Fares are much cheaper if booked in advance on the Eurostar website all the way through to your local destination in Provence, such as Antibes or Arles. Prices start from around £120 return if booked in advance. Single journeys are sadly not much cheaper.

If you are planning a cycling holiday and wish to take your own transport there are several ways to carry bikes on Eurostar. They can be folded down and carried in a bike bag free of charge, as luggage. Alternatively, for a £20 fee your bike can be sent as is from London to Paris using Eurostar's registered baggage service, or it can be booked on to the same train on which you're travelling, subject to space.

Road

London to Aix-en-Provence is a 750-km journey, with a drive-time of around 10 hours via Rheims. The motorways are excellent, but drivers will clock up around €80 of tolls on the way. Allow another two hours and another €20 to get to Nice.

If you're planning a city break, especially along the coast where public transport is world class, then a car will be an unnecessary encumbrance. Direct flights from the UK and Ireland, or train services from London, are normally quicker than driving. Don't forget, you can rent a car in any town in Provence for a few days if necessary.

The National Centre for Traffic Information 'Bison Futé' (bison-fute.equipement.gouv.fr) website offers drivers current information on all major routes in France in English and in French, including roadworks, accidents and hazardous weather conditions.

Bus/coach

Given the speed and affordability of air and rail links, there's really no reason to resort to coach travel. Eurolines (T08717 818 181, eurolines.co.uk) does run from London to Marseille and Nice; their schedule is fairly inconvenient.

Going green

Weigh up the pros and cons of train vs plane

Budget flights from the UK to Nice, Marseille and Toulon can appear attractive because of the low price, but their drawbacks need to be taken into consideration. Clocking up air-miles is generally accepted as being one of the most environmentally unsound ways of travelling. Factor in journey times to and from the airport, check-in time and the inconvenience of restricted baggage allowances and you can't help but conclude there must be a better way to travel. Trains to Aix-en-Provence, Nice and a score of stations in between can take a little longer but are environmentally much less damaging, and you'll travel more calmly with plenty of leg room and as much baggage as you can manage. Booked in advance, trains are as competitively priced as any of the airlines. And you can gaze at the varying scenery out of the window, stroll around, grab lunch, or watch a rented DVD from the snack bar.

Getting around

Rail

The rail network in Provence is extensive and efficient. High-speed TGV (*Train à Grande Vitesse*) services link Nice, Marseille, Avignon and Aix-en-Provence both with each other and all major points north. St-Raphaël, Cannes, Antibes and Toulon are also frequent stops for these speedy intercity services. Tickets must be reserved in advance from the station, at an SNCF boutique or online (voyages-sncf.com). Standard prices from Nice to Marseille or Aix, for example, are around €25, with journeys taking approximately 2 hours and 30 minutes.

Most local rail journeys are made on comfortable and affordable TER (ter-sncf.fr) regional trains. No reservation is necessary: just buy a ticket at the station and get on any TER train. A standard journey from Avignon to Arles costs around €7 and takes 50 minutes. Remember, all train passengers on a TER or TGV service must *composter* (validate) their tickets in the yellow machines on the platform before boarding a train. Most journeys are incredibly scenic, especially the private Train des Pignes (see page 165) route from Digne to Nice and the Tende line (see page 167) up the Roya valley.

Bikes travel free on TER services but there are restrictions during rush hours and on some TGV services. Disabled passengers will find wheelchair spaces on most trains (clearly marked on the carriage) – look for the wheelchair symbol on the timetable.

Boat

Many locals rely on ferry transportation, especially around the St-Tropez peninsula, where parking and traffic jams can be a nightmare. To visit the many islands of the coast – one of Provence's great highlights – just grab a ticket from the booth and jump on board. In summer, frequencies are so intense that one could be based in Cannes, Nice or St-Tropez and visit much of the surrounding coast by ferry. **Corsica Ferries** (Quai Lunel, Nice, T04 95 32 95 95, corsicaferries.com) run daily year-round ferries to Calvi, Ajaccio, Ile Rousse and Bastia from Nice port.

Road

Bicycle
The weather makes cycling in and around the towns of Provence a cinch, particularly along the coast or in rural areas. Bike shops are common, as are rental stations. The going rental rate is around €15 per day. The Camargue is flat and great for cycling, as is the car-free Ile de Porquerolles and the

fragrant hills of Haute Provence, some of which form the backdrop for several Tour de France stages. Aix, Avignon and Nice have electronic bike rental stands, and city cycle routes spread around the surrounding regions, especially along the Riviera. Marseille, hilly and congested, is not a fun city to bike around. See listings at the end of each chapter for bike hire details and cycle websites.

Bus
The train's cheaper, yet less comfortable, cousin. The frequency of buses in Provence is normally excellent, with a few exceptions in the Haute Provence region. For trips to outlying towns, or along the Hyères to St-Tropez coast, they are a necessity.

Car
Speed limits on French roads are 130 kph (*autoroutes*), 110 kph (dual carriageways and urban *autoroutes*), 90 kph (single carriageways) and 50 kph (villages and towns) unless stated otherwise. Speed limits drop by 20 kph on motorways and dual carriageways when it's raining. *Péage* motorways are toll routes. Take a ticket on entry and pay by cash or card when you exit a *péage* section. Do not enter the toll lane marked with an orange 't' as these are reserved exclusively for automatic payments under the *télépéage* scheme.

Tip...
Unleaded (*sans plomb*) petrol (95 & 98 octane), diesel (sometimes labelled *gasoil* or *gazole*) and LPG are available. The SP95-E10 (unleaded 95 octane containing 10% ethanol) is now being sold throughout France. This fuel is not compatible with all vehicles, so check with the manufacturer before use. *Autoroute* service areas charge much more for fuel than French supermarkets. The self-service 24-hr pumps are popular in Provence and accept Visa and Mastercard.

Since October 2008 it has been compulsory to carry one warning triangle and one reflective jacket when driving in France – the jacket must be in the car, not in the boot. The regulations also apply to hire cars, so check that they are present when you collect your car. The regulation is enforced by on-the-spot fines of between €90 and €135. For regulations and advice on driving in France, visit theaa.com

It's generally easy to find parking in smaller towns (except on market days) or along the beach, often for free. In larger towns and cities, street parking is often charged (*payant*) with ticket machines (*horodateurs*) nearby. Expect to pay around €1/hour, and be sure to read the details on the machine, as parking is usually free at lunchtimes and after 1830. The multi-storey car parks in cities issue a ticket on entry. Expect to pay €2-3/hour, depending on the location.

Roads in much of Provence are relatively quiet, and touring on empty countryside lanes is a pleasure. Some routes can get busy however, especially in July and August and particularly along the coast, so set off early or leave the car at home (get the train in and out of Monaco, for example) where appropriate.

Most French drivers are impatient with dawdlers of any nationality, including other French drivers, so don't take it personally. Town centre traffic systems can be confusing but if in doubt just follow Centre Ville or Office de Tourisme signs.

Car hire
There are heaps of car hire places dotted around Provence renting everything from a Ferrari to a 50cc scooter. By far the cheapest method is to book a vehicle online before you go (try holidayautos.co.uk, hertz.co.uk or easycar.com) and pick it up at the airport or train station upon arrival. In Nice, try **Sixt** (Le Méridien hôtel, 1 promenade des Anglais, T04 93 16 89 51, sixt.com).

Directory

Customs & immigration

UK and EU citizens do not require a visa, but will need a valid passport to enter France. You are required to carry a form of identification with you at all times in France, although a photocopy will often suffice. Travellers from outside the EU may need to obtain a standard tourist visa valid for up to 90 days. Apply to the French consulate in your country, addresses on the French Ministry of Foreign Affairs website mfe.org.

Disabled travellers

Tourism sites have improved facilities for disabled visitors over recent years with the installation of ramps, dedicated car parking and toilets with wheelchair access. However, many historic buildings and town centres have uneven surfaces underfoot, lots of gravel and an array of street furniture which can pose difficulties for wheelchair users and partially sighted and blind visitors. Often people with physical disabilities may be disappointed in gaining access to the ground floors and gardens only. Look at the tourist office listings for an indication of accessibility and disabled facilities at individual sites.

Since 2001 the Ministry of Tourism has been working with the industry to develop the *Tourisme & Handicap* label to communicate reliable, consistent and objective information regarding accessibility to tourist sites and facilities for people with any kind of disability. Look out for the blue and white logo depicting four specific types of disability. The symbols are displayed in airports, other public places and guidebooks to indicate where help is available. Visit tourisme-handicaps.org (in French only) for links to departmental tourism websites and detailed listings of attractions and accommodation that have earned the Tourisme & Handicap label.

Accommodation lists obtainable from the tourist offices (usually available online) indicate which have facilities for the disabled. However, note that this does not indicate a uniform standard of accessibility, and if your requirements are specific, it is important that you check directly with the accommodation provider.

Ticket concessions are often available to disabled visitors and sometimes to their companion, on entry to historic sites. Proof of your entitlement may be required. With regard to parking your vehicle, if you use a disabled parking space, the international blue badge scheme applies. Always display documentation in your vehicle and have proof of entitlement with you if you encounter any problems.

If you intend to travel to Provence by train, Eurostar and SNCF welcome customers with specific needs or who require extra assistance. Raileurope (raileurope.co.uk) strongly recommends that all bookings for access with wheelchairs or assisted access are made through their Customer Call Centre (T08448-484064, Mon to Fri 0800-2100, Sat 0900-1800) where you can get help with rail information, request mobility assistance, and reserve seats and wheelchair spaces. SNCF has an AccessPlus service to help plan your train journey whatever your disability, though it's only in French (T08 90 64 06 50, accessibilite.sncf.com). The regional TER trains have wheelchair spaces on some trains, indicated by a wheelchair symbol on the timetable and again on the relevant carriage.

Emergencies

Ambulance T15, Police T17, Fire Service T18 if calling from a landline. The European emergency number 112 can be dialled free from any phone, including mobiles and call boxes.

Etiquette

The French are a formal and very courteous society and it is normal to greet everyone you meet. *Bonjour* (*bonsoir* during the evening), followed by *Monsieur, Madame*, or for a young single woman, *Mademoiselle* (pronounced '*mam'selle*') will start you off on the right foot. At what time *Bonjour* changes to *Bonsoir* is never clear, so you'll occasionally be dismayed to hear a *Bonjour* in response to your cheery *Bonsoir* – and vice-versa. You will usually hear *Bonne journée* or *Bonne soirée* as you leave somewhere. A simple reply would be: *A vous, aussi!* (To you, too!). When meeting someone for the first time people always shake hands, although women often leave this to the men. Even with people you know, such as a waiter at your favourite restaurant, a greeting will start with a crisp handshake.

A *bisou* (a kiss on the cheek) is for good friends and family. It would be highly embarrassing if you initiated kissing someone you had just met, but don't be surprised if this occasionally does occur. The number of *bisous* is normally two, although it varies from region to region and can be as many as four.

Always use the formal "*vous*" to say "you" in French rather than the more intimate form "*tu*" which is normally reserved for friends and family. It is best to let the French decide, then you can return the compliment.

Since smoking has been banned in restaurants and cafés, smokers must go outside if they want to light up. Asking people if they wouldn't smoke while you're enjoying your meal *en terrasse* would most likely be ignored. Smoking is not allowed in any public places such as historic sites and tourist attractions. Increasingly, hotels and *chambres d'hôtes* are also making their establishments non-smoking.

You rarely see drunken behaviour in public. Social drinking is generally limited to one or two small beers or an aperitif. When drinking wine with a meal, glasses are never filled to the brim and if you order a bottle, check that the waiter has brought the correct wine before accepting a drop to taste, confirming whether or not it is corked.

Families

Provence, like most regions of France, is extremely family-friendly. Children are welcomed in restaurants with their own menu and, in larger establishments, an outdoor play area. Hotels often have family rooms, or can wheel in an extra cot or bed for a few euros extra. Trains, bus rides, boat trips and sights have reduced fares for under 25s or under 18s, and are normally free for those still of primary school age. While most kids will love to scramble around Roman ruins, National Parks and fairytale hill villages, a major children's activity, be it Aquasplash or an adventure theme park, is never far away from any of the towns listed in this book. Better still, the countless beaches of Provence are clean, fun and mostly long and sandy.

Health

Comprehensive travel and medical insurance is recommended. EU citizens should apply for a free European Health Insurance Card or EHIC (ehic.org), which entitles you to emergency medical treatment on the same terms as French nationals. Note that you will have to pay all charges and prescriptions up front and be reimbursed once you return home. If you develop a minor ailment while on holiday a visit to any pharmacy will allow you to discuss your concerns with highly qualified staff, who can give medical advice and recommend treatment. Outside normal opening hours, the address of the nearest duty pharmacy (*pharmacie de garde*) is displayed in the pharmacy window. The out-of-hours number for a local doctor (*médecin généraliste*) may also be listed.

In a serious emergency, go to the accident and emergency department (*urgences*) at the nearest Centre Hospitalier (numbers listed in the Essentials section at the beginning of each chapter) or call an ambulance (SAMU) by dialling T15.

Insurance

Comprehensive travel and medical insurance is strongly recommended, as the European Health Insurance Card (EHIC) does not cover medical repatriation, ongoing medical treatment or treatment considered to be non-urgent. You should check any exclusions, and ensure that your policy includes cover for any specific activities you wish to undertake. Remember to take your insurance documents with you on holiday – emailing all the details to yourself is a good way to keep the information accessible. Ensure you have adequate insurance when hiring a car and always ask how much excess you are liable for if the vehicle is returned with any damage. It is generally worth paying a little more for collision damage waiver. If driving your own vehicle, contact your insurers before you travel to ensure you are adequately covered, and keep the documents in your vehicle in case you need to prove it.

Money

The French unit of currency is the Euro. ATMs throughout France accept major credit and debit cards. Most ATMs have an English language option or will automatically recognise the country of issue and display instructions in the appropriate language. ATMs inside shops usually levy a charge for cash withdrawals, and will state the amount before you confirm the transaction. Currency exchange is available in some banks, and at airports, train stations and *bureaux de change*. An exchange fee is discretionary. Most restaurants, shops, and tourist attractions accept major credit cards, although restaurants in smaller towns may refuse to take cards and only accept cash. Normally, this will be clearly displayed in the restaurant or on the menu. Toll routes (*péage*) accept Visa, Mastercard and American Express cards but not Maestro or Visa Electron. On remote or minor autoroute exits there are often unmanned toll points which only accept payment by card. Throughout France personal cheques are becoming less welcome as a means of payment. If you require a receipt, ask for *un ticket* (the last 't' is silent).

Police

There are three national police forces in France. The *Police nationale* operate mainly in urban areas and are distinguished by silver buttons on their uniforms. The *Gendarmerie nationale* are under the control of the Ministry of Defence and wear blue uniforms with gold buttons. The *Gendarmes* deal with serious crime on a national level, although tourists most often see them on autoroute patrol, usually riding in pairs on motorcycles. The *Douane* is a civilian customs service whose officers are often seen searching vehicles at autoroute toll booths. It is only these three services who legally have the power of arrest or can issue search warrants. French municipalities may also maintain a *Police municipale*, who have limited powers but deal with traffic issues and enforce by-laws. You may also come across a *garde champêtre* or the *Police rurale* who patrol rural areas and protect the environment. All police in France are armed.

In case of an emergency requiring police attention dial 17, approach any member of the police or visit a police station. If you need to report a theft go to the nearest Gendarmerie who will give you a copy of the resulting report for insurance purposes. Take care of this document, as further copies will not be issued.

Police Nationale offices:
Aix-en-Provence 10 av de l'Europe, T04 42 93 97 00.
Avignon bd St Roch, T04 90 16 81 00
Marseille La Canebière, T04 88 77 58 00.
Nice 1 av Maréchal Foch, T04 92 17 22 22.
St-Tropez rue Francois Sibilli, T04 94 56 60 30.

Post

You can buy stamps (*timbres*) in post offices or over the counter in *tabacs*. A stamp for a postcard will cost a minimum of €0.60. Many post offices now have self-service stamp machines with instructions in several languages, including English.

278 Provence & Côte d'Azur

Safety

Away from very large cities the crime rate in France is generally low. Think carefully, though, about where you park your car at night – and never leave valuables in your car, even for a short time. In provincial towns and cities it is generally safe to walk where you please, although at night avoid wandering into unlit areas. Only carry small amounts of cash, and keep passport, credit cards and cash separate. In restaurants waiters will normally take your card payment at the table, so be suspicious if they take your card elsewhere to process the payment.

Travelling on public transport in Provence is generally very safe. Never leave your luggage unattended at bus or railway stations and always be alert to risk, especially late at night. If you are a victim of theft, report the crime to the police (*Gendarmerie*) immediately as you will need the report (*constat de vol*) to claim on your insurance.

Telephone

French telephone numbers consist of 10 digits and always start with a zero. The area codes are incorporated into the number so the first two digits denote the region (04 in Provence), the second pair is the town, the third pair the district. To call France from abroad dial the international prefix 00 plus 33 (the country code) followed by the phone number required (drop the first 0). Search online for phone numbers using pagesblanches.fr (private numbers) or pagesjaunes.fr (business numbers). For France Télécom directory enquiries dial 118 712 (calls cost a min €1.12) or visit 118712.fr.

Time difference

France uses Central European Time, GMT+1.

Tipping

Many restaurants include service in their prices (*servis inclus* or *compris* is usually stated at the foot of the menu), so leaving extra for a tip is not necessary. In pre-euro years it was the practice to leave about 10-15% as a tip, but in recent years this has declined among French nationals and now it's mostly foreign visitors who tend to leave tips; be aware as a foreigner, this means a tip is often expected. Where service is not included, or where you are happy to leave a little extra for excellent service, there are no hard and fast rules: 10% is usually appropriate.

Voltage

France functions on a 230V mains supply. Plugs are the standard European two-pin variety, so carry an adaptor if you need to connect your non-French phone-charger or other items.

Regional tourist information offices

Comité Régional du Tourisme Riviera Côte d'Azur
400 promenade des Anglais, Nice, T04 93 37 78 78, cotedazur-tourisme.com.
Comité Départemental du Tourisme des Bouches du Rhône
13 rue Roux de Brignoles, Marseille, T04 91 13 84 13, visitprovence.com.
Comité Départemental du Tourisme de Vaucluse
Rue Viala, Avignon, T04 90 16 15 00, provenceguide.com.
Agence de Développement Touristique des Alpes de Haute Provence
Immeuble François Mitterrand, Digne-les-Bains, T04 92 31 57 29, alpes-haute-provence.com.

Language

Basics

hello *bonjour*
good evening *bonsoir*
goodbye *au revoir/salut* (polite/informal)
please *s'il vous plaît*
thank you *merci*
I'm sorry, excuse me *pardon, excusez-moi*
yes *oui*
no *non*
how are you?
  comment allez-vous?/ça va? (polite/informal)
fine, thank you *bien, merci*
one moment *un instant*
how? *comment?*
how much? *c'est combien?*
when? *quand?*
where is …? *où est …?*
why? *pourquoi?*
what? *quoi?*
what's that? *qu'est-ce que c'est?*
I don't understand *je ne comprends pas*
I don't know *je ne sais pas*
I don't speak French *je ne parle pas français*
how do you say … (in French)?
  comment on dit … (en français)?
do you speak English? *est-ce que vous parlez anglais? / Parlez-vous anglais?*
help! *au secours!*
wait! *attendez!*
stop! *arrêtez!*

Local tongues

The Provençal language is derived from a wider group of southern European Romance languages spoken in parts of Catalonia, Italy and Monaco and known as Occitan. It's most commonly come across by visitors in the names of local restaurants, such as *Lou Pescadou* (Le Pêcheur, The Fisherman), *Lou Prouvençau* (Le Provençal, The Provençale) and similar, no doubt to lend a sense of tradition to the establishment.

While half a million Provençal locals are said to understand the dialect, it is spoken on a daily basis by a dwindling number, to whom French, or even Italian, English or Maghreb Arabic, may be the language of the home. Nevertheless, a recent resurgence of interest has led to a raft of French-Provençal (and English-Provençal) dictionaries. It is also now taught in some primary schools. Niçois, or Nissart as it's known locally, is a subdialect of Provençal, spoken by many a market-trading local in Nice. Easily translated Niçois graffiti ('*Libera Nissa*' et al) appears all over town.

Numbers

one	*un*	nine	*neuf*	17	*dix-sept*
two	*deux*	10	*dix*	18	*dix-huit*
three	*trois*	11	*onze*	19	*dix-neuf*
four	*quatre*	12	*douze*	20	*vingt*
five	*cinq*	13	*treize*	21	*vingt-et-un*
six	*six*	14	*quatorze*	22	*vingt-deux*
seven	*sept*	15	*quinze*	30	*trente*
eight	*huit*	16	*seize*	40	*quarante*
				50	*cinquante*
				60	*soixante*
				70	*soixante-dix*
				80	*quatre-vingts*
				90	*quatre-vingt-dix*
				100	*cent*
				200	*deux cents*
				1000	*mille*

Shopping

this one/that one   *celui-ci/celui-là*
less   *moins*
more   *plus*
expensive   *cher*
cheap   *pas cher/bon marché*
how much is it?
   c'est combien? / combien est-ce que ça coûte?
can I have ...? (literally 'I would like')   *je voudrais...*

Travelling

one ticket for...   *un billet pour...*
single   *un aller-simple*
return   *un aller-retour*
airport   *l'aéroport*
bus stop   *l'arrêt de bus*
train   *le train*
car   *la voiture*
taxi   *le taxi*
is it far?   *c'est loin?*

Hotels

a single/double room
   une chambre à une personne/deux personnes
a double bed   *un lit double/un grand lit*
bathroom   *la salle de bain*
shower   *la douche*
is there a (good) view?
   est-ce qu'il y a une (belle) vue?
can I see the room?
   est-ce que je peux voir la chambre?
when is breakfast?
   le petit dejeuner est à quelle heure?
can I have the key?
   est-ce que je peux avoir la clef?/La clef, s'il vous plaît

Time

morning   *le matin*
afternoon   *l'après-midi*
evening   *le soir*
night   *la nuit*
a day   *un jour*
a week   *une semaine*
a month   *un mois*
soon   *bientôt*
later   *plus tard*
what time is it?   *quelle heure est-il?*
today/tomorrow/yesterday
   aujourd'hui/demain/hier

Days

Monday	*lundi*	Tuesday	*mardi*
Wednesday	*mercredi*	Thursday	*jeudi*
Friday	*vendredi*	Saturday	*samedi*
Sunday	*dimanche*		

Months

January	*janvier*	February	*février*
March	*mars*	April	*avril*
May	*mai*	June	*juin*
July	*juillet*	August	*août*
September	*septembre*	October	*octobre*
November	*novembre*	December	*décembre*

Index

Index

credits

Footprint credits

Project editor: Alan Murphy
Text editor: Tamsin Stirk
Picture editors: Angus Dawson, Rob Lunn
Layout & production: Angus Dawson
Maps: Kevin Feeney
Proofreader: Carol Maxwell
Series design: Mytton Williams

Managing Director: Andy Riddle
Commercial Director: Patrick Dawson
Publisher: Alan Murphy
Publishing managers:
Felicity Laughton, Jo Williams
Digital Editor: Alice Jell
Design: Rob Lunn
Picture research: Kassia Gawronski
Marketing: Liz Harper,
Hannah Bonnell
Sales: Jeremy Parr
Advertising: Renu Sibal
Finance & administration:
Elizabeth Taylor

Print

Manufactured in India by Nutech
Pulp from sustainable forests

Every effort has been made to ensure
that the facts in this guidebook are
accurate. However, travellers should still
obtain advice from consulates, airlines etc
about travel and visa requirements before
travelling. The authors and publishers
cannot accept responsibility for any loss,
injury or inconvenience however caused.

Publishing information

FootprintFrance
Provence & Côte d'Azur
1st edition
© Footprint Handbooks Ltd
May 2010

ISBN 978-1-906098-91-9
CIP DATA: A catalogue record for this
book is available from the British Library

® Footprint Handbooks and the Footprint
mark are a registered trademark of
Footprint Handbooks Ltd

Published by Footprint
6 Riverside Court
Lower Bristol Road
Bath BA2 3DZ, UK
T +44 (0)1225 469141
F +44 (0)1225 469461
footprinttravelguides.com

Distributed in North America by
Globe Pequot Press